3D MODELING
ANIMATION
AND
RENDERING

An Illustrated Lexicon

Black and White Edition

Michael E. Mortenson

LEXICON

A wordbook or dictionary

The vocabulary of a particular field of study

VOCABULARY

A list or collection of the words or phrases of a language,
branch of science, occupation or profession

PREFACE

3D Modeling, Animation, and Rendering: An Illustrated Lexicon presents definitions for over 1200 terms, with hundreds of illustrations, in both black and white and color (color edition only). The lexicon includes terms from many related subjects, such as CAD, CAD/CAM, cinematography, light, physics, natural behaviors, and atmospheric phenomena. It was written for students, teachers, and professionals, as well as for lay readers who want a broader understanding of the tools and concepts involved.

Terms related to 3D modeling include **bicubic surface**, **constructive solid geometry**, **intersection**, **mesh optimization**, **polygonization**, **ruled surface**, and **spline**. Terms related to animation include **character rigging**, **flash animation**, **keyframing**, **lattice animation**, **light animation**, **motion capture**, **onion skinning**, **skeletal animation**, **storyboard**, and **velocity curve**. Animation and rendering often encompass techniques from cinematography, including lighting, camera work, and mood-setting atmospherics. Terms related to these major subjects and rendering itself include **ambient light**, **beauty pass**, **caustics**, **color models**, **crane shot**, **Dutch angle**, **Gouraud shading model**, **graphics pipeline**, **lead room**, **matting**, **montage**, **photon mapping**, **ray casting**, **ray tracing**, **reflection pass**, **shutter angle**, and **wipe**. Some of the key terms refer to other sources for more in-depth coverage of the topic.

Any new terms, illustrations, and corrections to existing terms are welcome to be submitted for inclusion in this lexicon. The creator or source of an illustration used in the lexicon will be cited. By submitting an illustration you are granting a nonexclusive right to its use in the lexicon, in either electronic or print form, without cost or restriction. Please submit new terms, corrections, and illustrations to the author at 3dmodeling@olympus.net.

REFERENCES

Barnsley, Michael, *Fractals Everywhere*, Morgan Kaufmann, 2nd Ed., 2000

Birn, Jeremy, [digital] *Lighting & Rendering*, 2nd Ed., New Riders Publishing, 2006

Demers, Owen, [digital] *Texture & Painting*, New Riders Publishing, 2001

Giambruno, Mark, *3D Graphics and Animation*, 2nd E., New Riders Publishing, 2002

Grünbaum, B., and G. C. Shephard, *Tilings and Patterns*, Dover, 2010

Mandelbrot, Benoit B., *The Fractal Geometry of Nature*, W. H. Freeman, 1983

Mortenson, Michael. E., *3D Modeling, Animation, and Rendering*, Available 2011.

_____, *Geometric Modeling*, 3rd Ed., Industrial Press, 2006

_____, *Geometric Transformations for 3D Modeling*, 2nd Ed., Industrial Press, 2007

_____, *Mathematics for Computer Graphics Applications*, 2nd Ed., Industrial Press, 1999

Naylor, John, *Out of the Blue*, Cambridge University Press, 2002

O'Rourke, Michael, *Principles of Three-Dimensional Computer Animation*, 3rd Ed., W. W. Norton, 2003

Ratner, Peter, *3-D Human Modeling and Animation*, 2nd E., John Wiley & Sons, 2003

Watt, A. and M. Watt, *Advanced Animation and Rendering Techniques*, Addison-Wesley, 1992

2D ANIMATION The computer graphics and computational processes that create and edit frame-by-frame moving two-dimensional images by the interactive manipulation of (usually) a two-dimensional model, including interactive and automated versions of traditional animation techniques such as 'tweening, morphing, onion skinning, stop motion of physical models, and interpolated rotoscoping. For 2D vector animation, the rendering process is the keyframe illustration process, with 'tweened frames rendered as needed.

3D ANIMATION The computer graphics and computational processes that create and edit moving two- or three-dimensional images based on 3D models. All of the techniques of 2D animation may be used as well as mesh manipulation, rigging, natural force behaviors, and simulation of natural phenomena such as water, fire, clouds, and fur. For 3D animations, all frames are rendered after completion of the modeling process.

Animation is done in three parts, the modeling, the actual animation and the rendering. The actual animation can be:

1. Keyframe animation, where each movement is entered into the computer by describing the position of objects at specific frames or points in time. The animation program, using rules set up by the animator, calculates the movement between these key points.

2. Programmed animation: where, for example, to animate the motions of a flock of birds, rather than define the position and movement of each bird, a computer program calculates where all the birds go and how they move.

3D MODELING Creating a digital representation of the surface of a solid object using computer graphics and the mathematics of geometric modeling. A model is designed so that it can be animated and rendered.

3D RENDERING The computational process that creates a 2D or 3D image based on a three-dimensional mathematical model stored in a computer. For a full 3D effect, the image is projected and viewed with special equipment, giving a viewer the illusion of depth. The software may include render-ing a scene from two slightly different points of view, in affect using a virtual stereoscopic camera.

A

ABLATION The slow loss of material by erosion of an object's surface, through melting, vaporizing, chipping or weathering, as can been seen in ancient statues, glaciers, or rock formations. Incorporating the visual effects of this process into scenes is a way to depict the passage of time, either through time-lapse sequences of scenes or abruptly moving ahead in time.

ABSOLUTE POINTS One of two kinds of points used in geometric modeling or in a computer-graphics display: *absolute points* and *relative points*. The distinction between them arises because of the way coordinates are computed and the way they are plotted and displayed. An absolute point is defined directly by its coordinates in a specific coordinate system. A relative point is defined relative to its preceding point. For example, a set of absolute points is $\mathbf{p}_i = \left(x_i, y_i \right)$, for $i = 1, \ldots, n$

ABSORPTION The reduction of light intensity by a transmitting medium or reflecting surface. The apparent color of light changes when some parts of its spectrum are more readily absorbed than others in a process called *selective absorption*. During the process of absorption, matter takes up a photon, usually by the electrons of an atom. The *absorbance* of an object quantifies how much of the incident light is absorbed by it. Some photons are absorbed and some are reflected or refracted. Physics textbooks describe light absorption quantitatively as the reduction of energy in the form of electromagnetic radiation by a transmitting medium or reflecting surface, where the energy loss is balanced by heat gained in the transmitting medium or the reflecting surface.

Shows best in color edition.

This is easily demonstrated: Sit on a sunny park bench on a cool, still spring morning. Reflected sunlight makes your hands visible, while the sunlight absorbed by your skin makes your hands feel warmer than the surrounding air.

When an atom absorbs a photon of light of a specific wavelength, the atom's energy increases and the photon ceases to exist. Depending on the kind and state of the atoms of a light-absorbing object, the energy of the absorbed photon may increase the object's temperature, promote a chemical reaction, or be emitted as photons of a different wavelength. The light (photons) that is not absorbed produces the color of the absorbing material; for example, leaves and grass appear green to us because they contain chlorophyll molecules whose atoms absorb light from the red end of the spectrum, leaving the greenish part of the light spectrum to be reflected into your eyes. See *light* for a brief discussion of photons.

Other physics-based interactions between light and a transmitting medium or a reflecting surface include reflection, transmission, diffraction, refraction, and interference.

Read more about this:
Naylor, John, *Out of the Blue*

ACADEMY RATIO A standard aspect ratio for a film frame, established by the Academy of Motion Picture Arts and Sciences. For 35 mm film this ratio is 1.33:1, for widescreen the ratio is 1.85:1, and for anamorphic widescreen the ratio is 2.35:1.

ACCELERATION A physics-based natural force behavior of an object. When the velocity of an object in motion increases or decreases, it is undergoing acceleration or deceleration, respectively, both of which produce deforming forces and effects. If the path is a straight line, the forces act along the line of motion. An object moving with a constant speed along a curved path experiences a force perpendicular to the path. An object accelerating along a curved path experiences both a force tangent to the path and a force perpendicular to it. Gravity produces acceleration and consequent forces along a line through the centers of mass of two attracting bodies. In mathematics and physics acceleration is a vector quantity.

Animators often exaggerate the deformations caused by acceleration or deceleration, particularly in computer graphics animation and special effects in cinematography; otherwise, the deformations may be imperceptible. Keyframes may be set at nonlinear times (for example, using trigonometric functions).

Read more about this:
O'Rourke, Michael, *Principles of Three-Dimensional Computer Animation*

ACHROMATIC Without color, only shades of gray; having little or no hue because almost all incident light is absorbed rather than being reflected by a surface; zero saturation. Thus, achromatic colors are grays or neutral colors; an achromatic lens is one designed to minimize chromatic aberration; and achromatic vision indicates color blindness. The achromatic image shows ammonite fossils in a stone wall.

Wikipedia, Immanuel Giel (date unknown)

ACHROMATIC LENS A lens designed to bring two distinct and separate wavelengths into focus at the same point, correcting a phenomenon of optics called *chromatic aberration*, where different wavelengths (i.e., colors) have different focal points.

ACTION Changes and movements that occur in a scene, usually consisting of an anticipation phase or beginning, the middle or main action, and the follow through or end. Actions overlapping several scenes or an entire animation production contribute to a work's continuity.

ACTION! As in "Lights, camera, action!," the traditional cue shouted to the filming crew on a set or location at the beginning of a *take*; a directorial command initiating motion and effects in animation, scene composition, and rendering, including such things as choreography, lighting effects, timeline, cross dissolve, and camera position and camera movement.

ACTIVE BODY An object that reacts when colliding with another object in an animation sequence, simulating natural force behavior. See also **COLLISION, PASSIVE BODY,** and **SOFT BODY**.

ACTIVE LAYER The currently active construction plane or level in a 2D or 3D modeling space that is organized into one or more superimposed layers. See **ACTIVE PLANE**.

ACTIVE PLANE Any one of the three principal planes of the current working box may be selected as the active plane; a plane in which model geometric elements are being created or modified (often displayed with a superimposed reference grid). It is the plane on which objects are moved when dragged with a mouse or trackball. See also **CONSTRUCTION PLANE**.

ACTOR A character participating in an animated scene.

ADAPTATION A film based on a pre-existing work; for example, an earlier film or novel.

ADAPTIVE MESH REFINEMENT Also called *adaptive subdivision*; a dynamic technique for dividing a surface into a triangular mesh, which may vary from point to point on the surface and over time if the surfaces shape changes. It gives local and temporal control over grid resolution, minimizing the number of triangles required to cover the surface by adjusting their size according to the local curvature of the surface, making rendering faster and more efficient. See also **POLYGON COUNT, SUBDIVISION SURFACE,** and **TRIANGULATION**.

ADAPTIVE SUBDIVISION A technique for dividing a surface into triangles (adaptive mesh refinement, subdivision surface, triangulation) in a way that minimizes the number required to cover the surface (see also polygon count) by adjusting their size according to the local curvature of the surface, making rendering faster and more efficient.

Read more about this:
O'Rourke, Michael, *Principles of* Three-*Dimensional Computer Animation*

ADDITIVE COLOR MODEL The color model that creates colors with light, as opposed to pigment. In the additive color model, red, green, and blue (RGB) are the primary colors, and mixing them together in equal parts creates white.

Shows best in color edition.

Computer displays and television screens use optical mixing and are not additive light display devices because the colors do not overlap. The red, green and blue pixels are side-by-side. If only the green pixel is on we perceive green. We perceive a cyan color when both green and blue pixels are on, and white when all the pixels are on. The pixels are very small and close together so that the human visual system blends them together, producing an effect similar to that of additive light. See also **SUBTRACTIVE COLOR MODEL**

Read more about this:
Birn, Jeremy, [digital] *Lighting & Rendering*
Demers, Owen, [digital] *Texture & Painting*
Giambruno, Mark, *3D Graphics and Animation*

ADDITIVE LAYERING Adding the color values of two or more images to produce a new, brighter image.

AEC CAD The acronym for Architecture, Engineering, and Construction CAD. AEC CAD is the CAD technology that encompasses architecture, construction, structural and civil engineering, mapping, and geographic information systems (GIS), all of which use 3D modeling and computer graphics.

AERIAL PERSPECTIVE A technique of rendering depth or distance by modifying the tone or hue of objects so that they are perceived as receding from the picture plane, often by reducing distinctive local colors and contrasts of light and dark to a uniform light, bluish-gray color; also called atmospheric perspective. It is part of a painting technique called *chiaroscuro*.

In the real world aerial perspective is produced by the scattering of light between a viewer and the scene. If the atmosphere is clear, there is little scattering and the effect is minimal. Otherwise sunlight reflects off a distant object and is scattered by molecules and particles in the atmosphere. Some light is scattered toward the viewer: this is airlight. Some is scattered away from the viewer's line of sight, reducing the object's apparent brightness. Both effects acting together reduce the contrast between the object and its background and produce a more uniform brightness over the scene, reducing apparent detail. The murkier the atmosphere, the more distant an object appears to be.

The contrast between an object and its background decreases as the distance between an object and a viewer increases, and its colors appear less saturated, shifting towards the background color. In the photo, this effect is demonstrated by a group of mountains lying one behind the other at different distances from the viewer.

Serra da Estrela, Portugal, Joaquin Alves Gaspar (2007)

AERODYNAMIC ANALYSIS Uses the surface properties and geometry of an object, as well as its mass properties, to determine the effects on its motion through a gaseous medium and the resulting forces acting on it. These effects are often animated and graphically represented and displayed, superimposed on the 3D geometric model of the object, to help an analyst visualize the interplay of geometry and aerodynamic forces. Automotive and aerospace designers and engineers use aerodynamic analysis extensively to develop efficient body and wing shapes.

AEROSOL Small particles dispersed in the atmosphere or in a gas, smoke, or fog; drops of water or other liquid, or solid particles ranging in size from 5 to 50 microns (1 micron = 1 millionth of a meter), small enough to remain suspended for long periods of time in the atmosphere. Aerosols may consist of mixtures of dust particles, water vapor, hydrocarbons or other smog components suspended in the atmosphere, either in layers or uniformly dispersed, depending on atmospheric conditions. They affect the way light is transmitted through the atmosphere and its color.

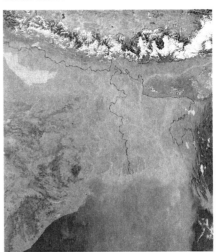

NASA (2001). Shows best in color edition.

The figure shows aerosol pollution over northeast India. The east coast of the Indian subcontinent runs from the lower left corner toward the upper right.

AFFINE TRANSFORMATIONS Also *affine geometry*; a geometry where distances are only preserved between points on the same or parallel lines, and angles are not preserved at all. Parallelism and collinearity are important invariants of affine transformations. Distances are comparable only on the same line or on parallel lines, and affine geometry becomes Euclidean geometry only when perpendicularity is introduced. Such transformations are employed in scene and object deformations.

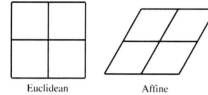

Euclidean   Affine

AIM POINT Directs a camera where to point. A vector from the camera location to the aim point defines the direction in which the camera is looking.

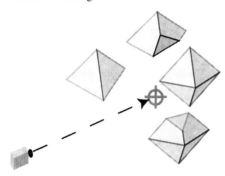

AIRBRUSH A technique used by an artist to create a smooth gradation of color, sometimes used to cover imperfections in a photograph (e.g., in a model's skin). The artist uses a pen-shaped tool supplied with compressed air to dispense a fine mist of paint or ink onto a photograph, illustration, or artwork.

AIRBRUSH COLORING A technique often used in animé to give images a soft look because of indistinct separation between colors; digital airbrush.

AIR LIGHT Light scattered or diffused by dust or water vapor in the atmosphere limiting the visibility of distant objects by causing them to blend with the background sky. See also **RAYLEIGH SCATTERING**.

Read more about this:
Naylor, John, *Out of the Blue*

ALBEDO The ratio of the light reflected by an object to that received by it; a measure of the reflectivity of a surface expressed as the fraction of incident light that is reflected by the surface; alternatively, the ratio of total

brightness of an object or region to the known intensity of incident radiation. For example, the albedo of fresh snow is very close to 1, while that of lampblack is almost zero.

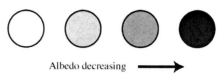

Albedo decreasing ⟶

The albedo of an object is the extent to which it diffusely reflects light from the Sun. It is therefore a more specific form of the term *reflectivity*. Albedo is defined as the ratio of diffusely reflected to incident electromagnetic radiation. It is a unitless measure, indicating a surface's or a body's diffuse reflectivity. The word is derived from Latin *albedo* meaning "whiteness."

Read more about this:
Naylor, John, *Out of the Blue*

ALIASING An undesirable effect sometimes present in a computer graphics image, caused by high-resolution image data approximated by low-resolution display data. The most common undesirable artifact is the so-called staircase effect, or jaggies, instead of an intended straight line or smooth curve. Although the staircase effect does not strictly conform to the formal technical definition of aliasing, it is nonetheless commonly classified as an aliasing problem.

Aliasing is also evident in film and animation sequences that display spoked wheels turning in a direction just the reverse of what is expected. This is a result of frame under sampling: too few frames to capture the proper effect of the wheel's rotation. Anti-aliasing techniques are a major subdiscipline of computer graphics and an important subject for study by the animator, for film, video, or the Web.

Here is an example using the letter "A" in Times New Roman. The aliased image is on the left; the antialiased image is on the right (Mwyann 2009, and others).

Aliased   Antialiased

ALIGN A 3D modeling command that brings two objects into a specific spatial relationship with each other. A designer may align a geometric feature of one object with a similar geometric feature of another object. For example, the axes of two cylindrical shapes may be brought into alignment, or two or more objects may be aligned in a common plane, such as a construction plane. See also **COAXIAL**

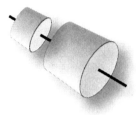

ALPHA COMPOSITING The process of combining a primary image with a background to create the appearance of partial transparency; an optional layer of image data, providing information about pixel transparency, which can be used to define a mask for compositing one image over another; also called *alpha channel*. Adding an 8-bit alpha channel to 24-bit color produces 32-bit color.

Read more about this:
Birn, Jeremy, [digital] *Lighting & Rendering*
Giambruno, Mark, *3D Graphics and Animation*
O'Rourke, Michael, *Principles of Three-Dimensional Computer Animation*

AMBIENCE MAPPING See **LUMINOSITY MAPPING**.

AMBIENT COLOR The hue an object reflects if it is not directly lit by a light source; the color of light reflecting off objects in a scene. *Radiosity rendering* is required to account for and achieve a realistic effect. The diffuse inter-reflection components of global illumination can be approximated by an ambient term in the lighting equation, called ambient lighting or ambient color in rendering programs. Used alone this method does not produce a fully realistic effect.

In real-time 3D graphics, the diffuse inter-reflection component of global illumination is sometimes approximated by an ambient term in the lighting equation, which is also called *ambient lighting* or ambient color in 3D software packages.

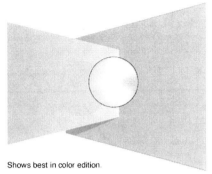

Shows best in color edition.

Though this method of approximation (also known as a *cheat* because it's not really a global illumination method) is easy to perform computationally, when used alone it does not provide an adequately realistic effect. Ambient lighting may flatten shadows in 3D scenes, making the overall visual effect blander. See also **AMBIENT LIGHT**.

Read more about this:
Giambruno, Mark, *3D Graphics and Animation*

AMBIENT LIGHT The illumination surrounding a subject or scene, not provided by the cinematographer or photographer; the cumulative effect of all the light bouncing off all objects in a scene; global illumination lighting all objects in a rendered scene equally, and therefore producing no shadows or surface shading. It has no distinct source. In the absence of any other type of lighting, objects in a scene lighted only by ambient light appear flat or two-dimensional. Ambient light is used with great care, and rarely as the only source of light. Ambient light is also called *ambience* and *global lighting*.

If only direct lighting is used, then the parts of a scene in complete shadow are pitch-black, and many details are not seen. In the real world at least a small amount of light reaches every point in a scene, and completely dark shadows are rare. This happens because of multiple reflections. One way to model this effect in computer-generated scenes is to assign a small constant light intensity to every surface, ensuring that no surface is rendered as completely dark. It is this light that is known as ambient light. A more advanced model uses a radiosity algorithm, which follows the diffuse reflections throughout a scene, and produces a more realistic ambient term.

The first image is rendered without global illumination. Areas that lie outside of the ceiling lamp's direct light lack definition. For example, the lamp's housing appears completely uniform. Without the ambient light added into the render, it would appear uniformly black. The second image is rendered with global illumination. Here light is reflected by surfaces, and colored light transfers from one surface to another. Notice how color from the red wall and green wall (not visible in the image) reflects onto other surfaces in the scene. Also notable is the caustic projected onto the red wall from light passing through the glass sphere.

Public domain images , Grzegorz Tanski with Kray renderer. Shows best in color edition.

Read more about this:
Giambruno, Mark, *3D Graphics and Animation*
O'Rourke, Michael, *Principles of Three-Dimensional Computer Animation*

AMBIENT OCCLUSION A shading method used in rendering a computer graphics scene that enhances the realism of local reflections. It adjusts for the attenuation of ambient light that is blocked by objects in a scene.

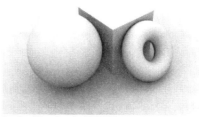

{renderwiki} and render3d (2010)

ANALYTIC MODELS 3D models capable of being quantitatively analyzed and graphically interpreted; for example, spatial analysis, volumetric analysis, structural analysis, aerodynamic and hydrodynamic analysis, thermodynamic analysis, transmissivity, molecular modeling (molecular graphics). Other examples of analytic models that depend on natural forces include cloth models, water, and wave models, all of which may be animated to reveal the dynamic side of their character.

ANAMORPHIC FORMAT A technique that alters the scale and geometric proportions of images created in a wide panoramic mode (aspect ratio = 2.35) to fit a 35 mm format; and conversely an optical subsystem of a film projector for converting standard 35mm film images into wide-screen format. The word anamorphic is from the Greek meaning "formed again."

The first image shows the effect of shooting in widescreen picture format. Without an anamorphic lens, the available film area is not completely used.

Eric Pierce (2005)

The second image of the same scene is shot with an anamorphic lens; the image is optically squeezed in the horizontal dimension to cover the entire film frame, resulting in a better picture quality. A projector lens of the same anamorphic power is required to stretch the image horizontally back to its original proportions.

Eric Pierce (2005)

Read more about this:
Birn, Jeremy, [digital] *Lighting & Rendering*

ANCHOR A control used in page layout and illustration to fix the location of a graphic element with respect to a section or paragraph of text. An anchor makes these features move together as a unit when changes are made to the work in which they are both embedded.

ANCHOR POINT A point that defines one end of a curve or straight line and that can be moved to alter the shape of the curve or direction and length of the line; used with control handles that may also be moved to alter the shape of the curve.

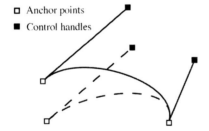

□ Anchor points
■ Control handles

ANGLE OF INCIDENCE The angle at which a light ray strikes a surface and is reflected into the viewer's eyes. For a mirror-like surface, the angle of incidence equals the angle of reflection, where the angles are measured from the normal to the reflecting surface to the tangent plane at the point being investigated.

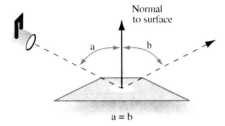

ANGULAR DIAMETER The angle an object subtends at the eye. The angle is the vertex of a triangle whose base is the width or height of the object.

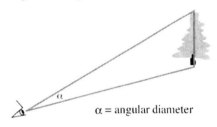

α = angular diameter

ANGULAR FALLOFF The rate at which the intensity of light decreases as an object moves away from direct alignment with a spotlight.

ANIMAL MODELING 3D modeling, animation and rendering techniques used to model the external shape, appearance, and motions of real or imaginary creatures. For example, to realistically animate the motion of a legged animal, a modeler must consider the dynamics of gait, which consists of a sequence of step and stance phases. The stepping phase brings a leg up and forward, and the stance supports the body and drives it forward.

Read more about this:
Ratner, Peter, *3-D Human Modeling and Animation*
Watt, A. and M. Watt, *Advanced Animation and Rendering Techniques*

ANIMATE An object that lives or moves, as opposed to inanimate, that doesn't live or move. Animation creates images that move or appear lifelike.

ANIMATED GIF An animated image that is created by cycling through a series of GIF images.

ANIMATED LIGHT Moving light sources that add drama and realism to a scene; for example, a rotating lighthouse beam sweeping across rocks and ocean, or a car's headlights sweeping along an urban scene as the car moves along a street.

ANIMATED TEXTURE A texture mapped onto the surface of an object, where the texture changes over time; for example, the shadows of clouds moving over a landscape, or the tremulous motion of shadows of wind-blown leaves on a rock.

Read more about this:
Giambruno, Mark, *3D Graphics and Animation*

ANIMATIC A sequence of storyboard frames or preliminary scene renderings recorded and played back for evaluation and planning in an animation project; a preliminary version of a movie, including a sequence of drawings and a soundtrack. At its simplest, an animatic is a series of still images edited together and displayed in a sequence.

This allows the animator and director to develop and resolve screenplay, camera positioning, shot list and timing problems with the current storyboard. The storyboard and soundtrack are then changed, if necessary, and a new animatic created and reviewed until the storyboard is accepted and approved. Editing the film at the animatic stage can help avoid the time and expense of animating scenes that might later be cut.

Storyboards can be animated with simple zooms and pans to simulate camera movement. These animations can be combined with animatics, sound effects and dialog to create a presentation draft of how a film could be shot and cut together.

Read more about this:
Giambruno, Mark, *3D Graphics and Animation*

ANIMATION A motion-picture technique that creates the illusion of motion by filming a sequence of still images instead of filming a live action; the simulation of motion and change in a computer graphics scene; rendering consecutive images (frames) of a computer graphics scene to capture rigid-body movement or other time-dependent changes of objects (including shape transformations), scene lighting, camera position, and many other visible characteristics of a composition. Consider, for example, a slowly morphing object or lively bouncing balls as components of a computer graphics game sequence.

The methods and terminology of computer graphics animation are closely related to traditional cel-based animation developed for film, where the principal animator draws the most important (or "key") parts of the animation, producing the keyframes. These were then passed on to dozens of supporting artists, or apprentices, who completed all the frames between the keyframes. The use of keyframes and storyboarding today are two important examples of this historical relationship. Animation and special effects in both film and computer graphics rely on the number-crunching power of a computer to accurately simulate the effects of physical forces and phenomena and to place a virtual camera where no real camera can go.

Other types of animation include puppet animation and clay animation, which are used to support computer-graphic animation. See also **FORWARD** and **INVERSE KINEMATICS**, **KEYFRAMES**, **COLLISION**, and **NATURAL FORCE BEHAVIOR**.

Read more about this:
Giambruno, Mark, *3D Graphics and Animation*
O'Rourke, Michael, *Principles of Three-Dimensional Computer Animation*
Watt, A. and M. Watt, *Advanced Animation and Rendering Techniques*

ANIMATION CONTROLLER Software that allows a user to create or modify keyframes. See also **SKELETAL ANIMATION**.

ANIME' Highly stylized Japanese animation, in a cartoon form, using strongly outlined images, often in high detail, with simple motions and depth; an abbreviated Japanese pronunciation of "animation", pronounced "ah ni may". The rest of the world regards anime' as Japanese animation.

http://www.centralparkmedia.com/catsoup/images.html.
Shows best in color edition.

The images above are screenshots from movies and the television series *Dead Leaves*, *FLAG*, *Gurren Lagann*, *Serial Experiments Lain*, *Monster*, *Lucky Star* and *Mind Game*, and *Cat Soup* from www.centralparkmedia.com

ANISOTROPIC FILTERING A method of enhancing the image quality of textures on surfaces that are at oblique viewing angles with respect to the camera, where the projection of the texture (not the polygon or other primitive on which it is rendered) appears to be non-orthogonal. Like bilinear and trilinear filtering it eliminates aliasing effects but improves on these other techniques by reducing blur and preserving detail at extreme viewing angles.

ANISOTROPIC SHADING A lighting effect produced by hair, grooved surfaces, or surfaces with a grain, such as brushed metal or wood , visible as elongated and striated patterns in highlights and reflections; concentrating reflections and highlights in a direction perpendicular to the grain or groves. In this shading model, specular highlights are not uniform in all directions, but depend on the orientation of surface irregularities. The rendered image below exhibits anisotropic shading caused by a modeled brushed metal surface.

ucbugg.berkeley.edu. Shows best in color edition.

Read more about this:
Birn, Jeremy, [digital] *Lighting & Rendering*

ANTI-ALIASING A technique used to smooth out jagged lines on a computer graphics display or to remove other unwanted artifacts caused by aliasing. An anti-aliasing application fills in the stair-step angles with intermediate shades of color. However, this may make the affected lines and curves look a little fuzzy. Increasing the resolution of the graphics monitor also reduces the effects of aliasing. Many printers are capable of smoothing out jaggies by changing the size and horizontal alignment of the printing dots to make lines and curves look smoother. See also **ALIASING**.

The image on the left shows the problem that occurs when anti-aliasing is not used. Near the top, the checkered pattern becomes distorted and is not aesthetically pleasing. The image on the right is anti-aliased, and the checkerboard pattern near the top blends into gray, even though the resolution is too low to show any detail. The edges appear much smoother in all areas of the anti-aliased image.

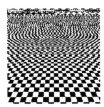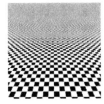

Read more about this:
Giambruno, Mark, *3D Graphics and Animation*
O'Rourke, Michael, *Principles of Three-Dimensional Computer Animation*
Watt, A. and M. Watt, *Advanced Animation and Rendering Techniques*

ANTICIPATORY SHOT Also *anticipatory camera* or *anticipation*; the preparation for an action; a technique that directs the camera to an aim point within the scene where some action is about to occur just before it does occur. Although there is great overlap in their meaning, *anticipation* and *anticipatory shot*, some examples may clarify their difference. Thus, when a character that is golfing is first shown swinging a club backwards, the viewer anticipates the forward stroke. If the camera then switches to a close-up of a golf ball on a tee, this is an anticipatory shot, where again the viewer expects the club head to enter the scene and strike the ball. The specific subject matter of an action determines the timing of both anticipation and follow through.

ANTISOLAR POINT The point in the opposite direction of the sky from the sun relative to an observer or camera. A line joining the antisolar point to the sun passes through the eye of the observer. A consequence of this is that the shadow of an observer's head always falls on the antisolar point.

APERTURE The opening in a camera through which light passes to expose the film. The aperture size is variable and measured in f-stops: the higher the f-stop, the smaller the aperture, reducing the amount of light reaching the film. The aperture size, or f-stop setting, also effects the depth-of-field. Rendering programs simulate the effects of these variables.

APPROXIMATING SPLINE A spline curve that passes near, but not necessarily through, its control points. It is less sensitive to abrupt changes in curvature and tends to produce a smoother curve than the interpolating spline.

Read more about this:
Mortenson, Michael E., *Geometric Modeling*
O'Rourke, Michael, *Principles of Three-Dimensional Computer Animation*

ARC The visual path following an action from start to finish. In animation, the path of action may follow a spline curve that also controls, or at least closely matches, the timing curves for other elements of a scene.

In geometry, an arc is a segment of the circumference of a circle or ellipse; a segment of any curve.

Read more about this:
Mortenson, Michael E., *Geometric Modeling*

AREA LIGHT A light source whose shape is geometrically defined by the modeler, such as a rectangle, and which radiates a light beam whose cross section is also rectangular, and similarly for a circle, sphere or other shapes. A point light is not an area light, because it radiates from a point.

Read more about this:
Birn, Jeremy, [digital] *Lighting & Rendering*
O'Rourke, Michael, *Principles of Three-Dimensional Computer Animation*

ARMATURE The kinematic chain of links and joints used in computer animation to describe and define the motions of human and animal characters. Inverse kinematics is used to propagate the appropriate motions throughout the armature. See also **RIGGING** and **SKELETAL ANIMATION**.

ARRAY A linear or rectangular arrangement of mathematical elements or geometric shapes; for example, the vertices of a polyhedron may be organized into a rectangular array that describes how they are connected to form the polyhedron's edges, which is called a *connectivity matrix*. The following example of an array is the matrix of vectors defining a Hermitian bicubic surface:

$$\begin{bmatrix} P_{00} & P_{01} & P_{00}^{w} & P_{01}^{w} \\ P_{10} & P_{11} & P_{10}^{w} & P_{11}^{w} \\ P_{00}^{u} & P_{01}^{u} & P_{00}^{uw} & P_{01}^{uw} \\ P_{10}^{u} & P_{11}^{u} & P_{10}^{uw} & P_{11}^{uw} \end{bmatrix}$$

An array in a computer graphics scene may consist of an alignment of identical objects such as furniture, landscape elements, or mechanical parts; or an array may be in the form of a repetitive pattern of shapes, such as in a frieze or wallpaper group.

Read more about this:
Mortenson, Michael E., *Mathematics for Computer Graphic Applications*

ARTBOARD The printable area of an artwork in illustration applications.

ARTICULATED MOTION The motion of an articulated object subject to the kinematic constraints of a system of links and joints defining the object. Kinematics is the physics of moving mechanical systems without regard to forces causing the motion or to forces dampening it. In kinematics, attention is focused on the position, velocity, and acceleration of the various joints and links of a mechanical system. It describes the geometric and time-dependent properties of motion, including determining the paths of joints, the geometric envelopes swept out by combinations of joint and link motions, and interference studies.

ARTICULATED OBJECT A structure or mechanical system composed of links and joints; an idealized model aiding the design, analysis and control of computer animation and robotics.

Read more about this:
Watt, A. and M. Watt, *Advanced Animation and Rendering Techniques*

ARTIFACT A discontinuity or imperfection in the output of a renderer. Computational or numerical approximations are common sources of artifacts.

ASPECT RATIO The ratio of the width to height of the frame of an image; image width divided by height; for example, an image 24 cm wide and 18 cm high has an aspect ratio of 4 to 3 or 1.333. The convention is to assign a value of 1 to the image height.

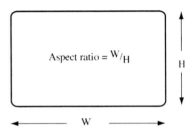

The aspect ratio of a graphics image or monitor is measured in pixels; for example, 1024×648. It may also describe the shape of a pixel in a digitized image. Some common aspect ratios for film are 1.85 (Academy Aperture), 2.35 (Cinemascope, Panavision), 1.66 (film more compatible with television format), 1.78 (HDTV), and 1.33 (standard television).

Read more about this:
Giambruno, Mark, *3D Graphics and Animation*
O'Rourke, Michael, *Principles of Three-Dimensional Computer Animation*

ASSEMBLY CONSTRAINTS Physical and functional limits governing how an object fits into an assembly of objects. Object size, shape, and spatial relationships to other objects determine some limits, and accessibility and freedom of movement (or mechanical motion envelopes) determine others. 3D modeling is an effective way to study assembly constraints.

ASSEMBLY LAYOUT The overall plan and organization of individual mechanical parts comprising a larger structure or mechanism, including spatial relationships and constraints, methods of attachment, assembly procedures, tool access, and tolerances.

ASSEMBLY MODEL The geometric model of a set of parts, showing them in their assembled positions. An assembly model may include assembly layout, constraints, component-part placement, hierarchical assembly procedures, tool access, and tolerance information. In a 3D assembly-modeling program, a designer defines assembly constraints between parts, constraints such as contacts, offsets, and alignments (for example, coaxial or coplanar alignment). Some systems automatically place and orient a part within the assembly.

ASSOCIATIVITY Establishing links between objects, functions, or modules in a CAD system, so that when a change is made to one element, associated elements are automatically changed accordingly. For instance, if a designer associates elements in an engineering drawing with its precursor 3D model, then any change in the model automatically updates the drawings. Bi-directional associativity means that the updates happen both ways no matter where the change was made.

ATLAS A kind of data map showing the connectivity of a piecewise-flat surface. The most straightforward representation is simply to describe each face separately and keep track of which edges are adjoining.

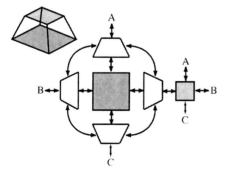

The figure above shows the atlas of a truncated pyramid. This topological atlas is similar to an ordinary road atlas, which is a collection of separate maps, each containing information directing the user to the next map.

Read more about this:
Mortenson, Michael E., *Geometric Modeling*

ATMOSPHERIC OPTICS The study and application of the physical behavior of light passing through the atmosphere; for example, the interaction between sunlight, air and water in the form of drops or ice crystals. Accounting for this behavior improves the realistic look of a rendered scene when set outdoors. Furthermore, some behaviors can be exaggerated to produce special effects in a rendered scene.

Read more about this:
Naylor, John, *Out of the Blue*
O'Rourke, Michael, *Principles of Three-Dimensional Computer Animation*

ATMOSPHERIC REFRACTION As light rays travel through the atmosphere they are bent toward the ground. This is particularly pronounced when the air close to the ground is colder than that just above it. Light travels slower in the colder thus denser air, enhancing the refraction effect. This allows an observer to see ground-level objects that are beyond the true horizon. The figure below shows how atmospheric refraction raises the sun's image above the horizon either before actual sunrise or after sunset.

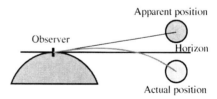

Read more about this:
Naylor, John, *Out of the Blue*

ATMOSPHERICS Special background effects, such as fog or haze, rain or snow, applied to a scene to create the effect of objects seen through a mist, or seen from great distances when the scene is rendered. These effects vary with distance, the farther an object is from the camera or viewer the greater the atmospheric effect in diminishing its visibility.

A variety of other atmospheric effects can be used to produce a scene background that supports dramatic intent, for example, dark storm clouds or puffy white clouds in a bright blue sky. Another meaning of *atmospherics* refers to mood-evoking dark lighting, suggestive of a coming storm, and another to a character's behavior, as in *storming out of a room.*

NOAA Photo Library; OAR/ERL/NSSL

Read more about this:
Giambruno, Mark, *3D Graphics and Animation*
Mortenson, Michael E., *3D Modeling, Animation, and Rendering*

ATTACH A 3D modeling procedure that combines the geometric models of two separate objects into one object, where only contact without intersection or interpenetration is allowed. It is a variation of the union operation of constructive solid geometry.

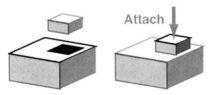

Attach

ATTACHED SHADOW See **SELF-SHADOWING**.

ATTENUATION Reduction of light intensity with increasing distance from the source. As light spreads out through the atmosphere or other transmitting medium, it is occluded, scattered, and absorbed. The inverse-square law determines the intensity of light at a distance r_1 from a point-like source. It is the total light energy, E, emitted by the source divided by the area of a sphere with radius r_1, or $I_1 = E / 4\pi r_1^2$. The intensity of the same light at another point at a distance r_2

is $I_2 = E / 4\pi r_2^2$. The two intensities are related by $I_2 = (r_1^2 / r_2^2)I_1$. In 3D modeling and rendering programs, attenuation is a light-source option controlled by range settings.

The inverse-square law of light attenuation is not always the best way to light a scene. Hot spots can occur near a light source if its intensity is high enough to sufficiently light distant objects in a scene. Other options are linear attenuation, or no attenuation. For linear attenuation, a distance from a light is specified at which the intensity is set to zero. The intensity at some intermediate distance is computed by a straight-line interpolation.

Read more about this:
Giambruno, Mark, *3D Graphics and Animation*

AUGMENTED REALITY (AR) Scenes or animation sequences comprised mostly of real-world content enhanced with computer graphics elements.

AUGMENTED VIRTUALITY (AV) Scenes or animation sequences comprised mostly of a virtual environment enhanced with real-world elements; also called *mixed reality.*

AUREOLE A bright, colorless glow often seen around an object that is directly between an observer and the sun or bright light. It is due to forward scattering by aerosols in the atmosphere. See also **CORONAE**.

Photographer unknown. Shows best in color edition.

Read more about this:
Naylor, John, *Out of the Blue*

AUTOTRACING A technique used to convert a bitmapped image into a vector image; a graphics tool used to automatically trace the outline of an imported image.

AUXILIARY PLANE See **CONSTRUCTION PLANE**.

AVAILABLE LIGHTING Natural lighting of a scene, without artificial light.

AXIS A straight line in space, representing a coordinate axis, an axis of rotation, or an alignment axis. Two or three mutually orthogonal axes are arranged at a common point, the origin, to form a coordinate system. The figure shows left-hand and right-hand sets of coordinate system axes (CS).

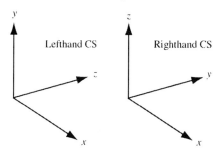

AXIS-ALIGNED BOUNDING BOX The minimum or smallest bounding box, whose sides are parallel to the coordinate system, for a point set in two or three dimensions (or *n* dimensions, for that matter) It is the box with the smallest area or volume that just contains all the points. In the two-dimensional case it is called the **MINIMUM-BOUNDING RECTANGLE**.

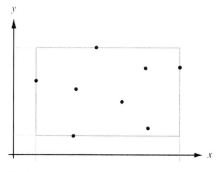

AXIS DEFORMATION A technique that produces shaping operations, such as scaling, bending, twisting, and stretching, by reference to a coordinate system whose geometry is deformed and thus passed on to an em-bedded 3D model. If the model itself is represented by a set of control points, as is the case for Bézier and B-spline curves and surfaces, then axis deformations are simply passed on to these points. Each control point is "attached" to a point on the axis and located within a local coordinate system defined at that point. Next, the axis is deformed to achieve the desired results in the 3D model. If control points define the axis itself, then the points may be moved to produce the axis deformation. Finally, the transformed model control points are computed and now represent the deformed model.

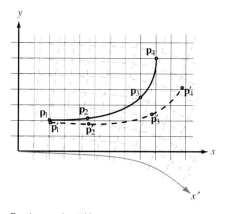

Read more about this:
Mortenson, Michael E., *Geometric Modeling*
_____, *Geometric Transformations for 3D Modeling*

AXIS-OF-ACTION An imaginary line in a scene that passes through the main actor(s), defining the spatial relationships of all the major elements of the scene

AXONOMETRIC PROJECTION Produces an image of an object viewed from a skew direction, so that more than one side can be seen in the same image. The term *axonometric* means to measure along axes. The term *orthographic* applies to images of objects where the axes or planes of major geometric elements of the object are parallel to or perpendicular to the projection plane. In axonometric projection the major planes or axes of an object are constructed so that they are neither parallel nor perpendicular to the projection plane.

The three most-used types of axonometric projection are isometric projection, dimetric projection, and trimetric projection. Typically in an axonometric drawing, one axis of space is shown as the vertical.

In isometric projection the direction of viewing is such that the three axes of space appear equally foreshortened.

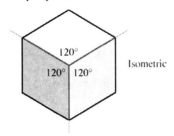

Isometric

In dimetric projection, the direction of viewing is such that two of the three axes of space appear equally foreshortened.

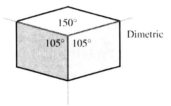

Dimetric

In trimetric projection, the direction of viewing is such that all of the three axes of space appear unequally foreshortened.

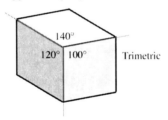

Trimetric

B

BACKFACE CULLING Action ensuring that a model's polygonal faces whose normals point away from the viewer are not rendered, also called *backface elimination*. In most rendering techniques, all surface geometry and properties are used; for example, to account for interobject reflections, global illumination, and so forth. See also **CULLING**.

Read more about this:
Watt, A. and M. Watt, *Advanced Animation and Rendering Techniques*

BACKGROUND LIGHT Lights the background of a scene, enhancing the distinction between the subject and the background. In three-point lighting, background lighting is placed last, usually directly behind the subject and aimed at the background. In film, background lighting is usually of lower intensity, and more than one source may be necessary to uniformly light a background or to highlight points of interest. In video and television, background lighting intensity is similar to key lighting intensity, because video cameras are less able to handle high-contrast lighting ratios. To provide distinction between subject and background, the background lighting requires a color filter, blue for example, to make the foreground stand out. The figure shows the relationships between the subject, camera, key light, and background light. See also **BACKLIGHT**, and **LIGHT PLACEMENT**.

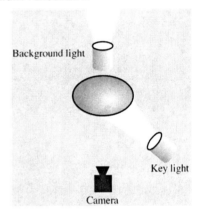

BACKGROUND MATTING Matching the background of an image or graphics object to that of a web page background.

Read more about this:
O'Rourke, Michael, *Principles of Three-Dimensional Computer Animation*

BACKGROUND PLATE A sequence of frames digitized from live-action film or video, onto which are added computer graphics generated objects or scene elements.

BACKGROUND TRANSPARENCY Allows the placement of a graphics object against a Web page background.

BACKLIGHT A photographic and cinematic technique in which a light is placed behind or at right angles to an object (relative to the camera or viewpoint), person, or scene to augment the effect of depth, or to enhance the visual separation of subject and background. Usually, the backlight source and the viewer face each other, with the subject in between. Thus, the backlight is usually placed directly behind the subject. This arrangement produces a glow around the edges of the subject, while the other areas remain darker. Note that backlight lights foreground elements from the rear, while background light lights background elements, such as scenery.

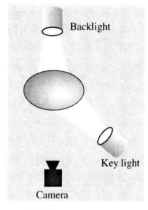

Read more about this:
Birn, Jeremy, [digital] *Lighting & Rendering*

BALANCE Designing the position and size of the anatomical elements of an animated human or animal form so that there is a smooth transition between sequential positions of equilibrium and stability.

Read more about this:
Ratner, Peter, *3-D Human Modeling and Animation*

BALL JOINT A constrained mechanical link between two objects, consisting of a ball-like end on one object that is held captive within a concave spherical socket on the other, allowing three-dimensional rotational movement between them.

BANDING The appearance of distinct bands of color in an image, an undesirable condition altering what should appear to be continuous shading in a rendered image. Two common causes of banding are over processing an image, and converting a reduced bit-depth image back to a full color mode; also called *color banding*, *contouring* and *posterization*. This effect can be created intentionally or accidentally. The figure shows the effects of bit depth and dithering.

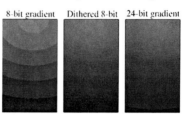

Wikipedia public domain: Phlake (2004)
Shows best in color edition.

BANK A particular rotation that an object or camera may perform as it moves along a path; also called *roll* and *tilt*. For a camera, the rotation axis is through the lens along its aiming direction. See also **CAMERA BANK**.

BARREL DISTORTION A decrease in image magnification with distance from the focal point or optical axis of a camera or projector, usually radially symmetric. See also **DISTORTION** and **PINCUSHION DISTORTION**.

BASE COLOR The color of an object underlying a colored transparent object. See also **BLEND COLOR**, **COLOR BURN**, and **COLOR DODGE**.

Base color

BASE FEATURE A simple starting shape used when beginning the design of a more complex 3D object.

BASIS DEFORMATION A way to deform a 3D model by deforming its coordinate system basis. If the initial coordinate system is defined by the unit orthogonal basis vectors **i, j,** and **k,** then shapes defined in it are deformed with respect to a transformed basis **l, m,** and **n,** which are not necessarily unitary or orthogonal

Here is an example of a deformation in the xy-plane, where the vectors **m** and **n** are given by $\mathbf{m} = a\mathbf{i} + b\mathbf{j}$ and $\mathbf{n} = c\mathbf{i} + d\mathbf{j}$. Simple vector algebra produces $x_i' = ax_i + cy_i$ and $y_i' = bx_i + dy_i$.

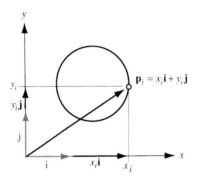

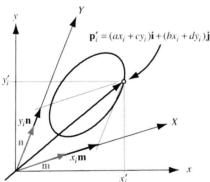

Read more about this:
Mortenson, Michael E., *3D Modeling, Animation, and Rendering*
_____, *Geometric Transformations for 3D Modeling*

BASIS FUNCTIONS Mathematical functions that blend the contributions of control points to the shape of a curve or surface; sometimes called *blending functions*. Bézier, for example, started with the requirement that

any point on a curve segment must be given by a parametric function of the following form:

$$\mathbf{p}(u) = \sum_{i=0}^{n} \mathbf{p}_i f_i(u)$$

where $u \in [0,1]$, and here the vectors $\mathbf{p}_i$ represent the $n+1$ vertices of a *characteristic polygon* (the vertices are the *control points*).

Bézier then set forth the properties that the $f_i(u)$ basis functions must have and looked for specific functions to meet these requirements. Here is a summary of these properties and the reasons for them.

1. The functions must interpolate the first and last vertex points; that is, the curve segment must start on $\mathbf{p}_0$ and end on $\mathbf{p}_n$.

2. The tangent at $\mathbf{p}_0$ must be given by $\mathbf{p}_1 - \mathbf{p}_0$, and at $\mathbf{p}_n$ by $\mathbf{p}_n - \mathbf{p}_{n-1}$.

3. Requirement 2 is generalized for higher derivatives at the curve's end points. Thus, the second derivative at $\mathbf{p}_0$ must be determined by $\mathbf{p}_0$, $\mathbf{p}_1$, and $\mathbf{p}_2$. In general, the rth derivative at an end point must be determined by its r neighboring vertices.

4. The functions $f_i(u)$ must be symmetric with respect to u and $(1-u)$. This means that the sequence of the vertex points defining the curve can be reversed without changing the shape of the curve. This reverses the direction of parameterization.

Bézier chose a family of functions called *Bernstein polynomials* to satisfy these properties. These functions, then, are the basis functions for the curves that bear his name:

$$B_{i,n}(u) = \left(\begin{array}{c} n \\ i \end{array} \right) u^i (1-u)^{n-i}$$

where $\left(\begin{array}{c} n \\ i \end{array} \right)$ denotes the familiar binomial coefficient function, or binomial distribution from probability and statistics:

$$\left(\begin{array}{c} n \\ i \end{array} \right) = \frac{n!}{i!(n-i)!}$$

Read more about this:
Mortenson, Michael E., *Geometric Modeling*

BASIS VECTORS A set of n vectors in an n-dimensional space whose linear combination can express any other vector in that space A set of basis vectors need not be orthogonal or unitary. In three-dimensional Cartesian vector space any three linearly independent vectors form a basis. The unit vectors **i, j,** and **k** form such a basis because **i** = [1 0 0] **j** = [0 1 0], and **k** = [0 0 1] are linearly independent. The components of a vector depend on the basis chosen, and, in general, the components change if the basis changes.

In three dimensions, a set of basis vectors $\mathbf{e}_1, \mathbf{e}_2, \mathbf{e}_3$ emanating from a common point O, the origin, defines three families of parallel lines and forms a Cartesian system. The three lines X_1, X_2, X_3 concurrent at O and collinear with $\mathbf{e}_1, \mathbf{e}_2, \mathbf{e}_3$, respectively, define the coordinate axes.

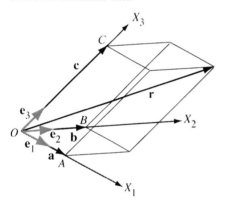

For any point (position vector) **r** in this system, the coordinates (or components) are found as follows: Construct a parallelepiped with O at one vertex, **r** as a body diagonal, and concurrent edges lying collinear with the basis vectors. The three directed line segments corresponding to edges OA, OB, and OC define the vector components of **r** in this basis system. Denote these as **a, b,** and **c**, respectively. The very nature of this construction technique ensures that the parallelogram law of vector addition applies. Thus,

$$\mathbf{r} = \mathbf{a} + \mathbf{b} + \mathbf{c}$$

or

$$\mathbf{r} = r_1\mathbf{e}_1 + r_2\mathbf{e}_2 + r_3\mathbf{e}_3$$

where $r_1, r_2,$ and r_3 are the components or coordinates of **r** with respect to the frame of reference defined by the basis vector $\mathbf{e}_1$, $\mathbf{e}_2$, and $\mathbf{e}_3$.

$$r_1 = \frac{|\mathbf{a}|}{|\mathbf{e}_1|}, r_2 = \frac{|\mathbf{b}|}{|\mathbf{e}_2|}, r_3 = \frac{|\mathbf{c}|}{|\mathbf{e}_3|}$$

Read more about this:
Mortenson, Michael E., *Geometric Transformations for 3D Modeling*

BEAUTY PASS The primary rendering of an image, including color, texture, and diffuse illumination effects, but not including reflections, highlights, or shadows, which are rendered in separate passes. See also **RENDERING IN PASSES.**

Read more about this:
Birn, Jeremy, [digital] *Lighting & Rendering*

BEHAVIORS In animation, standardized object actions and reactions, either natural (as in natural force behavior) or artificial. Some common stock behaviors include inverse kinematics, where a mechanism moves according to its links and joints constraints, tracking that causes an object to follow the motions of another object not mechanically linked to it, bounce, response to damping forces, and so on.

BEND A shape-changing transformation of an object, like a tree or pole bending in a strong wind. A designer applies a bend transformation to mechanical parts or structural shapes to introduce an overall curving deformation. The transformation operates by inducing bending in a special coordinate system, or deformation grid, embedded in the object, which in turn is embedded in the world coordinate system.

Read more about this:
Giambruno, Mark, *3D Graphics and Animation*
Mortenson, Michael E., *Geometric Transformations for 3D Modeling*

BENDY BOX A shape deformation controller used in animation applications.

BETA SPLINE A variation on the B-spline basis function, defined over a uniform knot sequence. It adds two parameters, β_1 and β_2, that provide for global control over certain characteristics of a B-spline curve's shape. Relaxing the requirement of parametric continuity while preserving geometric continuity creates these two extra degrees of freedom. (Brian A Barsky developed this variation to the B-spline, 1981)

β_1 and β_2 are the so-called *bias* and *tension* parameters, respectively. Both affect the flatness of the curve. Manipulation of β_1 affects the tangent vector on the parameter-increasing side of each control point, and increasing β_2 pulls the curve closer to the sides of the control polygon. As β_1 is increased, the curve asymmetrically shifts to one side of the control polygon. When β_2 is increased, the curve uniformly flattens and more closely approaches and approximates the control polygon.

Read more about this:
Mortenson, Michael E., *Geometric Modeling*

BEVEL A narrow, flat or rounded surface forming a transitional surface between two flat faces of an object otherwise forming a hard edge at their intersection; sometimes called a chamfer; a small transitional plane between two larger planar surfaces of a 3D object. Adding beveled or rounded edges to otherwise hard-edged objects in a computer graphics scene can produce a more realistic look. Bevels are used in engineering design for aesthetic as well as practical reasons. For example, bevels reduce stress concentrations at both inside and outside corners of structural or mechanical parts and also reduce the probability of chipping and cracking.

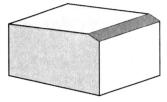

BEZIER CURVE A special curve defined by a set of control points, $\mathbf{p}_i$ the number of which determines the degree of its polynomial parametric equations. A Bézier curve (pronounced *bay zee ay*) is an approximation spline that passes through its first and last control points and is tangent to the first and last sides of the open polygon defined by its control points. It does not allow local

shape control, because changing the position of any control point produces shape change throughout the curve.

$$\mathbf{p}(u) = \sum_0^n \mathbf{p}_i B_{i,n}(u) \text{ where } u \in [0,1]$$

and $B_i(u)$ are the basis functions.

The most common form of Bézier curve is one based on cubic polynomial Basis functions. This is the simplest form that allows a curve to have an inflection point (take on an "S" shape) and twist in 3D space (not constrained to lie in a plane).

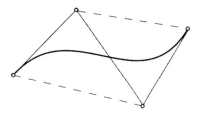

Four control points or a control point and tangent vector at each end of the curve segment define a cubic Bézier curve. This curve is always contained within the convex hull of its control points. In most 3D modeling applications, the end points are called *anchor points* and the tangent vectors are represented by control handles. The size and shape of a Bézier curve are adjusted by moving the anchor points and control handles. Control handles connect to anchor points with control-handle lines.

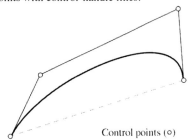

Control points (○)

A control handle works like a magnet, pulling the curve toward it, exerting the greatest influence over that part of the curve nearest to it. If there is only one control handle, then the curve is reshaped closer to the end with the control handle than the other end. The farther a designer moves a control handle from its anchor point, the more the curve near that anchor point pulls away from a line between the curve's two anchor points.

Anchor point (□)

If the control handles are on different sides of the curve, then the curve exhibits an S-shape. If the control handles are on the same side, the curve is somewhat U-shaped.

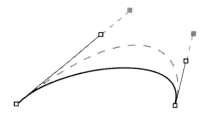

Modify shape (▧)

Two Bézier curves may be joined end-to-end at their anchor points to create a more complex composite curve. If two control-handle lines at the common anchor point are collinear, then a smooth curve is produced through that point. Additional curves may be joined to produce even more complex curves.

Read more about this:
Giambruno, Mark, *3D Graphics and Animation*
Mortenson, Michael E., *Geometric Modeling*
_____, *Mathematics for Computer Graphics Applications*
O'Rourke, Michael, *Principles of Three-Dimensional Computer Animation*
Watt, A. and M. Watt, *Advanced Animation and Rendering Techniques*

BEZIER SURFACE The Bézier surface is a direct extension of the Bézier curve. Points on a Bézier patch are given by the following tensor product, again, a simple extension of the general equation for points on a Bézier curve:

$$\mathbf{p}(u,w) = \sum_{i=0}^{m}\sum_{j=0}^{n}\mathbf{p}_{ij}B_{i,m}(u)B_{j,n}(w)$$

where $u, w \in [0,1]$. The $\mathbf{p}_{ij}$ comprise a $(m+1)\times(n+1)$ rectangular array of control points defining the vertices of the characteristic polyhedron of the Bézier patch, which lies entirely within its convex hull.

$B_{i,m}(u)$ and $B_{j,n}(w)$ are the basis functions, defined in the same way as for Bézier curves.

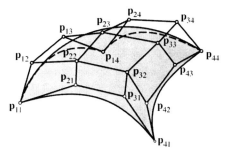

Read more about this:
Mortenson, Michael E., *Geometric Modeling*

BIAS CONTROL The capability to change the shape of certain spline curves. Bias control can adjust the location of a maximum or minimum extreme point (peak or valley) of the motion path or control curve in relation to the keyframe, through a TCB controller. See also **BETA SPLINE.**

Read more about this:
Giambruno, Mark, *3D Graphics and Animation*
Mortenson, Michael E.,

BICUBIC SURFACE The tensor product of two cubic functions. The bicubic surface is an extension of the parametric cubic curve. The following tensor product defines a bicubic Hermite surface, sometimes called a *patch*.

$$\mathbf{p}(u,w) = \sum_{i=0}^{3}\sum_{j=0}^{3}\mathbf{a}_{ij}u^{i}w^{j}$$

where $u, w \in [0,1]$.

There are four defining vectors at each corner of the patch: a vector defining the corner point coordinates, two tangent vectors, and a twist vector (not shown). The $\mathbf{a}_{ij}$ can be expressed in terms of these vectors.

Read more about this:
Mortenson, Michael E., *Geometric Modeling*

BIDIRECTIONAL ASSOCIATIVITY Changes and updates to a 3D model and its 2D drawing representation affect each other, independently of where the change was made.

BIDIRECTIONAL REFLECTANCE DISTRIBUTION FUNCTION (BRDF) A four-dimensional mathematical function defining how light is reflected. It takes the direction of incoming light, defined by θ_i and ϕ_i, and some outgoing direction, defined by θ_r and ϕ_r, and produces the ratio of reflected radiance to incident irradiance. The function can be expressed in several different ways, for example; $\rho(\theta_i,\phi_i,\theta_r,\phi_r)$, corresponding to the figure below.

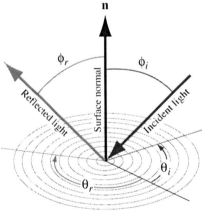

Read more about this:
Watt, A. and M. Watt, *Advanced Animation and Rendering Techniques*

BILLBOARDING Integrating a 2D image into a larger scene; in three-dimensional scenes, a technique used to represent 3D objects by their projected two-dimensional images applied to a single polygon, which is kept perpendicular to the line of sight. Such objects appear to be drawn on a "billboard." This has been used to improve graphics performance and works best when the object in question is distant enough so that it can be replaced with a billboard. See also **SPRITE**.

Read more about this:
Birn, Jeremy, [digital] *Lighting & Rendering*

BINARY SPACE PARTITIONING The recursive subdivision of space into convex sets by planes, producing a tree data structure known as a *BSP tree*. It also can be used to break up complex polygons into smaller and simpler polygons, all of which are convex. This technique is used in 3D computer graphics to increase rendering efficiency. Other applications include constructive solid geometry, collision detection in robotics 3D computer games, and any other applications with object-rich and spatially complex scenes.

BINARY TREE A type of graph-based model used in constructive solid geometry. A tree is a connected graph without closed circuits (i.e., a sequence of nodes connected by a path that loops back on itself). A binary tree has the following characteristics:
1. There is a unique root node, with no entering branches (i.e., no parent node).
2. Every node except the root node has just one entering branch.
3. Each node, except leaf nodes (i.e., terminal nodes of a branch), has two descendants (i.e., two exiting branches).
4. There is a unique path from the root node to each other node.

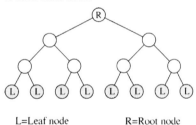

L=Leaf node   R=Root node

Read more about this:
Mortenson, Michael E., *Mathematics for Computer Graphics Applications*

BIRD'S EYE SHOT In cinematography and animation, a shot looking directly down on the subject, distorting perspective through foreshortening, making the subject appear short and squat. A bird's eye shot is often used as the establishing shot of a scene, or to emphasize the insignificance of the subject. For a scene that needs a large area shot, the camera may be mounted on a crane or scaffolding, or located as a virtual camera in an animated scene.

BIT A binary digit, the smallest unit of information used by and stored in a computer. A bit has one of two values: 0 or 1. Bits may be combined into larger units, like a byte, which consists of 8 consecutive bits.

BIT DEPTH The number of bits (binary digits) of information available for each pixel in an image, used to define the pixel color and transparency.

BITMAP A rectangular array in computer memory representing dots or pixels that creates a bitmap image. A graphics application assigns each element in the array a value consisting of one or more bits of information, which in turn indicate the state of a dot or pixel: whether it is on or off, what color it is, and so forth.

BITMAP IMAGE An image stored as an array of pixel intensities (also called a *raster image*), unlike a vector graphics image that stores equations that represent shapes. A standard bitmap is an ordered rectangular array of intensities. Raster images are stored in image files. This kind of image is resolution dependent, and cannot be scaled arbitrarily without loss of quality.

BIVARIATE DEFORMATION Changing a object's shape by embedding it in a curved 2D space.

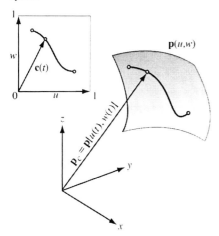

Deformations of this space are passed on to the object. For example, given a Hermite, Bézier, or B-spline curve, $c(t)$, defined and embedded in a normalized parametric plane, and a bivariate surface, $p(u, w)$, in the x, y plane, or in x, y, z space, then the changed curve is mapped as
$$p_c = p[u(t), w(t)] .$$
See also **TRIVARIATE DEFORMATION**.

Read more about this:
Mortenson, Michael E., *Geometric Modeling*

BLEED See *color bleeding*.

BLEND COLOR The initial color of a transparent object overlying another object. See also *base color*, *color burn*, and *color dodge*.

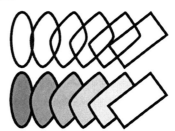

Blend color

BLENDING The gradual, continuous change in some attribute, such as shape, color, or texture, between an initial and final condition. The entire sequence of states of a blend operation is rendered, unlike morphing where only the final deformed object is rendered.

BLENDING GROUP Defines how a selected set of metaballs should fuse in a given model or model segment; sometimes called *fusion group*.

Read more about this:
O'Rourke, Michael, *Principles of Three-Dimensional Computer Animation*

BLENDING FUNCTIONS Also called *basis functions*.

BLEND SURFACE A secondary surface forming a locally smooth transition between two or more primary surfaces, which may or may not intersect. Function and aesthetics dictate the use and shape of a blending surface. Blend-surface construction methods include rolling ball, spline, tramline, and polygonal. Not only are the coincident curves identical, but also the tangent vectors across these boundary curves must match (at least their unit tangent vectors).

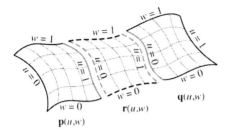

Read more about this:
Mortenson, Michael E., *Geometric Modeling*

BLINN-PHONG SHADING MODEL An optimization of the original Phong model for specular reflection, including an ambient term, a diffuse term and a specular term. The ambient and diffuse terms are identical to the original Phong model. The difference between the Blinn and Phong models lies in the way specular highlights are computed. Instead of computing the reflection vector of the incoming light vector and the surface normal as in the Phong model, the Blinn model computes an angle half way between the light vector and the view vector. This angle is used in place of the reflection vector to calculate the final result. The images below compare renderings with Blinn-Phong (left) and Phong (right) shading models.

Wikipedia, Brad Smith, 2006. Shows best in color edition.

The advantage of the Blinn model over the Phong model is achieved only if a directional light source is used, where the light vector is the same for every point on the surface. Then it is possible to compute the half angle once for the entire scene, because computing the half angle only requires a constant light vector and view vector that don't change from one point to another within the scene. The reflection vector in the Phong model is computed for every point because it is dependent on the surface normal. The advantage of this model cannot be

realized when using point lights or spot lights since the light vector is different for each point in the scene.

BLOBBY MOLECULES Another name for *metaballs*.

BLOCK A common geometric primitive used in CSG systems; a rectangular solid. An instance of a block is defined by specifying its length, width, and height.

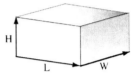

BLOCKING The plan defining the movement of characters, cameras, and lighting within a scene.

BLOOM The bright hazy glare or obscuring halo perceived around extremely bright objects in a scene and blurring their contours, caused by the scattering of light upon entering the viewer's eyes. This effect is used in animation, virtual reality cinematography, demos, and high dynamic range (HDR) rendering to simulate an imaging artifact of real-world cameras, producing fringes (or feathers of light around very bright objects in an image. The computer-generated image below is an example of bloom used in the film *Elephant's Dream*,

T. Roosendaal, et al (2006). Shows best in color edition.

The physical basis of bloom is that, in the real world, a lens never focuses perfectly. Even a perfect lens will mix portions of the incoming light rays reflected from an object image to form a diffraction pattern at its edges. This effect isn't noticeable under normal conditions; but an intensely bright light source will cause the image of a brightly lighted object to bleed beyond the edges of its boundary.

BLUE FILL A lighting technique used in film making and computer graphic scenes to simulate the darkness of night using a dark blue fill light, which provides just enough light to discern muted scene details.

Read more about this:
Birn, Jeremy, [digital] *Lighting & Rendering*

BLUE SPILL Intrusion of background color into the color of a foreground object; also known as *color spill* or *fringing*.

BLUESCREEN Also known as *chroma key* or *color keying*; uniform blue background against which actors or characters are filmed or animated, which is later replaced with a different background. This process mixes two images or frames together. Then a specific color from one image is removed, exposing another image behind it. Other colors may be used: green, orange, or grey ... called *greenscreen*, *orangescreen*, or *greyscreen*. For example, bluescreen is typically used for television weather forecasts. The presenter appears to be standing in front of a large weather map, while in fact, there is just a large blue background screen behind the presenter.

Read more about this:
Giambruno, Mark, *3D Graphics and Animation*
O'Rourke, Michael, *Principles of Three-Dimensional Computer Animation*

BLURRING Changing an initial crisply focused image by rendering it obscure, dim, or indistinct, as if seen through a haze or fog or at a great distance; in film and animation, an effect indicating motion. See also **MOTION BLUR**.

Read more about this:
O'Rourke, Michael, *Principles of Three-Dimensional Computer Animation*

BONES DEFORMATION A way to control the shape and motion of a 3D model using a simple secondary model consisting of an assemblage, or "skeleton," of links and joints embedded in the primary object. Motions of the skeleton are automatically translated into motions and deformations of its primary.

Read more about this:
Giambruno, Mark, *3D Graphics and Animation*

BOOLEAN MODEL A combination of two or more simpler objects (*primitives*), to produce a more complex object, using the Boolean operators union, difference, intersection, and others. Constructive solid geometry uses Boolean model-building techniques. The figure below shows four examples of a Boolean model, showing how two primitives are reshaped by nonuniform scaling transformations, placed into a common coordinate system, and subjected to a Boolean operation, producing a final model.

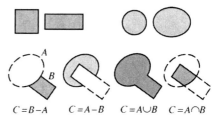

$$C = B - A \qquad C = A - B \qquad C = A \cup B \qquad C = A \cap B$$

Read more about this:
Giambruno, Mark, *3D Graphics and Animation*
Mortenson, Michael E., *3D Modeling, Animation, and Rendering*
_____, *Geometric Modeling*
_____, *Mathematics for Computer Graphics Applications*
O'Rourke, Michael, *Principles of Three-Dimensional Computer Animation*

BOOLEAN OPERATOR A solid modeling tool: union (addition), difference (subtraction) and intersection (points-in-common). A modeler uses them to combine simple geometric solids to create complex solids. These operators are based on rules of logical operations developed by George Boole (1815-1864). See also **CONSTRUCTIVE SOLID GEOMETRY**.

Read more about this:
Giambruno, Mark, *3D Graphics and Animation*
Mortenson, Michael E., *3D Modeling, Animation, and Rendering*
_____, *Geometric Modeling*
_____, *Mathematics for Computer Graphics Applications*
O'Rourke, Michael, *Principles of Three-Dimensional Computer Animation*

BOOM AND CRANE SHOTS Overhead camera shots and moves executed using a mechanical boom or crane, or simulating these moves with computer-graphics animation techniques. These shots allow a director to view action from unique angles and points of view.

BOTTOM LIGHTING Compositing a light onto film by using a mask and a light source from below.

BOUNCE The rebound or reaction after a collision; the response and natural force behavior of an elastic object when dropped, like a ball. Each succeeding bounce reaches a lower height than the previous bounce as the result of damping forces.

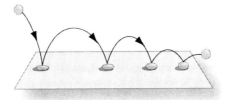

BOUNCE LIGHTS Extra fill lights added to a scene to simulate reflected light, used when global illumination software capabilities are limited or absent, or to reduce rendering time; also called *simulated radiosity*.

Photographers and filmmakers use walls, ceilings and even entire rooms as reflectors, especially for interior scenes that may not be adequately lighted. In the photo, a reflector is positioned to bounce sunlight onto a model.

Mila Zinkova (2009). Shows best in color edition.

A similar technique is used in cinematography where reflecting walls or screens positioned off-camera light the scene, providing illumination similar to that of a large window. Light bounced off a ceiling resembles that of fluorescent tubes. Flat lighting is like an overcast day; so a more realistic interior illumination can be achieved by reducing the power of additional lighting relative to the available light.

Read more about this:
Birn, Jeremy, [digital] *Lighting & Rendering*

BOUNDARY CONDITIONS Mathematical, geometric, or physical constraints on a model at the ends or edges of geometric elements; for example, the tangent direction and radius of curvature at the endpoints of a curve segment are boundary conditions.

BOUNDARY EVALUATION Procedures using Boolean operations on boundary representations to determine the valid boundary of an object.

BOUNDARY REPRESENTATION (B-REP) A solid modeling technique in which an object's surface geometry is represented by edges, faces, and vertices. A boundary is constructed as a union of faces (surfaces), bounded by edges (curves), which in turn are bounded by vertices (points). A face is a bounded region of a more extensive surface, an edge is a segment of an unbounded curve, and vertices are edge endpoints. A boundary model consists of the mathematical data of the surface geometry on which each face lies, the curve geometry of each edge (a closed circuit of which bounds each face), and the point geometry (the coordinates) of the vertices. The simplest form of a b-rep is a polyhedral model. B-reps are a logical extension of wireframe models. A b-rep models an object's surface, using polygonal planes rather than just an object's edges, as in wireframe models.

Read more about this:
Mortenson, Michael E., *Geometric Modeling*
_____, *Mathematics for Computer Graphics Applications*

BOUNDING BOX A wireframe box automatically constructed just large enough to contain a selected geometric construction, a modeled object, camera, light, or combination of these; an interactive aid, not part of the 3D model itself, but extracted from its geometry and displayed as a temporary stand-in. For example, a bounding box is substituted for a complex object during translations or rotations to relieve the computational demands of continuously updating a fully drawn display. Using a bounding box expedites visualizing the moving object. Note that these movements are used in the model-creation process or scene setting and are not part of the final animation.

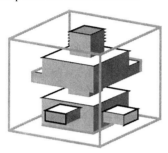

The minimum bounding box of a set of points is the same as the minimum bounding box of its convex hull, a fact that may be used to speed up computation.

The term "box" comes from its application within a Cartesian coordinate system, where it is a rectangle in a two-dimensional coordinate system, and a rectangular parallelepiped, or "box," in a three-dimensional system.

The axis-aligned minimum bounding box for a given point set is its minimum-bounding box subject to the constraint that the edges of the box are parallel to the Cartesian coordinate axes. The bounding box idea is used to approximate the location of an object and is a simple descriptor of its shape. For example, bounding boxes can expedite finding intersections between objects in a scene, where the initial computation looks for possible intersections between their minimum bounding boxes. Since it is computationally very easy to check for this kind of intersection, pairs of objects distant from each other can be immediately excluded from further computational consideration.

Read more about this:
Giambruno, Mark, *3D Graphics and Animation*
Mortenson, Michael E., *3D Modeling, Animation, and Rendering*
O'Rourke, Michael, *Principles of Three-Dimensional Computer Animation*

BOUNDING SPHERE Analogous in function to a **BOUNDING BOX**.

Read more about this:
Giambruno, Mark, *3D Graphics and Animation*
Mortenson, Michael E., *3D Modeling, Animation, and Rendering*
O'Rourke, Michael, *Principles of Three-Dimensional Computer Animation*

BOUNDING VOLUME A closed volume that completely contains a specified collection of objects. Using simple volumes to contain more complex objects improves the efficiency of geometrical computations. Normally, simpler volumes have simpler ways to test for intersections.

In a ray tracing, 90% of the rendering time can be spent in finding the points of intersection between each ray and each object in a scene. However, in a typical scene a given ray will not intersect most of the objects in it, so it is more efficient to begin by testing bounding volumes for intersections. Since bounding volumes are simple shapes, this calculation is fast. If the ray intersects the bounding volume, only then are intersections with the object tested.

Read more about this:
Mortenson, Michael E., *3D Modeling, Animation, and Rendering*

BOUNDING VOLUME HIERARCHY (BVH)
An organized structure of bounding volumes used to speed up ray tracing. For example, given an object defined by several hundred primitives, a bounding volume is created for the entire object. Then this is subdivided into two or more new bounding volumes. These are further subdivided, and at each step in this process the volumes become smaller and contain fewer primitives. This subdivision stops when each of the volumes contains some minimum number of primitives. The resulting data structure is a tree of bounding volumes, of decreasing size pro-

gressing from root to leaf nodes. This data structure defines a bounding volume hierarchy, or BVH. Intersections of a ray with the object, begin by first testing it against the root volume. If an intersection is found, then intersection computations proceed through the hierarchy of subvolumes until the search is narrowed to only a few small bounding volumes. Thus, the task of searching for intersections with hundreds of primitives is reduced to that of searching for intersections with only a few dozen.

Read more about this:
Mortenson, Michael E., *3D Modeling, Animation, and Rendering*

BRDF The acronym for **BIDIRECTIONAL REFLECTANCE DISTRIBUTION FUNCTION**.

BRESENHAM LINE ALGORITHM Determines which points in an *n*-dimensional raster to plot to form a close approximation to a straight line between two points. It is used to draw lines on a computer screen, using only integer addition, subtraction and bit shifting, all of which are very cheap operations in standard computer architectures. It is one of the earliest algorithms developed in the field of computer graphics. A variation of the algorithm applies to drawing circles.

BRIDGING SHOT Connects two scenes separated by time or space.

BRIGHTNESS The lightness or darkness of a color, apart from its hue or saturation. Pure white has maximum brightness, and pure black minimum brightness; sometimes called *value*. Negative brightness can be used to simulate shadows. For example, the spot of a spotlight may be darkened to create a shadow under a ball without requiring the time-consuming true shadow computation. See also **HSB**.

Brighter ——————————————▶

Shows best in color edition.

Read more about this:
Demers, Owen, [digital] *Texture & Painting*
Giambruno, Mark, *3D Graphics and Animation*
O'Rourke, Michael, *Principles of Three-Dimensional Computer Animation*

BRIGHTNESS TEMPERATURE A measure of the intensity of thermal radiation emitted by an object, given as a temperature because there is a relationship between the intensity of the radiation emitted and the physical temperature of the radiating body. See also **COLOR TEMPERATURE**.

B-SPLINE CURVE A piecewise polynomial curve defined by a set of control points through which the curve ordinarily does not pass (therefore it is an *approximating spline*). The degree of its polynomial parametric equations is defined independently of the number of control points. Local control of curve shape is possible because changes in control point location do not propagate shape change globally, and control points influence only a few nearby curve segments. The so-called *nonrational form* is given by

$$\mathbf{p}(u) = \sum_{i=0}^{n} \mathbf{p}_i N_{i,K}(u)$$

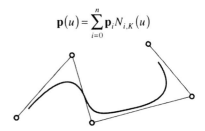

Read more about this:
Giambruno, Mark, *3D Graphics and Animation*
Mortenson, M. E., *Geometric Modeling*
O'Rourke, Michael, *Principles of Three-Dimensional Computer Animation*
Watt, A. and M. Watt, *Advanced Animation and Rendering Techniques*

B-SPLINE SURFACE An extension of the mathematics of B-spline curves to produce surfaces using tensor product basis functions.

$$\mathbf{p}(u,w) = \sum_{i=0}^{m} \sum_{j=0}^{n} \mathbf{p}_{ij} N_{iK}(u) N_{jL}(w)$$

Read more about this:
Mortenson, Michael E., *Geometric Modeling*

BUILDING-BLOCK GEOMETRY Also called **CONSTRUCTIVE SOLID GEOMETRY (CSG)**.

BULLET TIME PHOTOGRAPHY Extreme slow motion, allowing greater flexibility in controlling the movement of characters and objects within a scene.

BUMP A localized shape-changing transformation of a bounding surface.

BUMP MAPPING A shading function used to render a textured surface, using a grayscale image to vary the apparent surface roughness of an object by randomly perturbing its surface normals to affect light-reflection calculations, adding texture and detail without increasing the number of polygons. For example, the rough-tiled or plated look of alligator skin or dimpled appearance of an orange or a golf ball can be achieved using bump mapping. A color image with good contrast may work as well as a grayscale bump-map image. Diffuse illumination varies over a bump-mapped surface just as though bumps were actually present; specular highlights are appropriately scattered, and reflection and refraction effects are also correctly achieved by bump maps. The image below shows a cube with bump mapped textured surfaces,

B. Haley, Ohio State University (no date available).

When a bump or depression appears on the silhouette of an object it may not be rendered as such. Because these features are not part of the model per se, they are not ordinarily part of the silhouette computation.

Other problems include: the shadows of bump-mapped objects correspond to the geometry of the original (non-bump mapped) objects; shadows of other objects cast onto bump-mapped surfaces are smooth; bump-mapped surfaces do not cast attached shadows; and the curve of intersection between two surfaces will not show the effect of any bump mapping on those surfaces.

Read more about this:
Birn, Jeremy, [digital] *Lighting & Rendering*
Demers, Owen, [digital] *Texture & Painting*
Giambruno, Mark, *3D Graphics and Animation*
Mortenson, Michael E., *3D Modeling, Animation, and Rendering*
O'Rourke, Michael, *Principles of Three-Dimensional Computer Animation*
Watt, A. and M. Watt, *Advanced Animation and Rendering Techniques*

C

CAD The acronym for *computer-aided design*. Standing alone the term encompasses more applications than the "CAD" in CAD/CAM. However, both CAD and CAD/CAM systems usually provide two ways to construct a geometric model: by solid modeling and by surface modeling.

CAD/CAM The acronym for *computer-aided design/computer-aided manufacturing*, referred to together because most sophisticated engineering and manufacturing 3D modeling programs combine the two functions through smooth down- and up-stream data interfaces.

CAE Acronym for **COMPUTER-AIDED ENGINEERING**.

CAMERA An electro-mechanical device for recording still or moving images on film, video tape, or digitally; a *virtual camera* used in 3D modeling, animation, and rendering, simulating the effects of a real camera and defining the viewer's position and orientation.

Read more about this:
Giambruno, Mark, *3D Graphics and Animation*
Mortenson, Michael E., *3D Modeling, Animation, and Rendering*

CAMERA ANGLE The aiming direction of a camera from a location within or just outside a scene. A scene may be shot from several camera angles; for example, Dutch angle, high-angle and low-angle shots, perspective, point of view (POV), bird's-eye shot, and relative to the line of action.

The camera's location with respect to the subject greatly affects how the viewer perceives that subject. A high-angle shot makes the subject look small or weak, a low-angle shot makes the subject look powerful or threatening, a Dutch angle shot gives the viewer a feeling of a world out of balance or psychological unrest, and a neutral shot has little psychological effect on the viewer.

Read more about this:
Demers, Owen, [digital] *Texture & Painting*
Mortenson, Michael E., *3D Modeling, Animation, and Rendering*

CAMERA ANIMATION Position and orientation transformations of the camera to achieve a time-varying camera location and aiming direction. The camera is treated just like any other object in an animated scene insofar as motion control. However, there are specially defined camera movements, including dolly, pan, aim, track and orbit.

Read more about this:
Mortenson, Michael E., *3D Modeling, Animation, and Rendering*
O'Rourke, Michael, *Principles of Three-Dimensional Computer Animation*

CAMERA BANK The rotation of a camera about an axis through its lens and in the direction it is aiming; also called *roll*. If the camera is animated to move along a curved path, while introducing a coordinated tilt, a banking effect is produced.

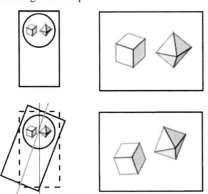

Bank angle

CAMERA COORDINATE SYSTEM See *view coordinate system*.

CAMERA DIRECTION Where the camera is pointing, in scene composition and rendering. There are several ways to specify the camera direction: by specifying a viewing direction vector, by specifying rotations about axes through the camera position, or by giving a point at which to aim. See also **AIM POINT**, **CAMERA MOVES**, **CAMERA POSITION**, and **EYE POINT**.

CAMERA EFFECTS In scene rendering, the simulation of visual effects that can be produced with a camera, such as lens flare, defocus, central focus, depth of field, and colored filters.

CAMERA MOVEMENTS Standard motions in scene composition and rendering, including aim, dolly, orbit, pan, rack focus, tilt, track,

and zoom. Only dolly and tracking moves change the camera location. Otherwise, it is in a fixed position, and the moves change its aiming direction.

Read more about this:
Mortenson, Michael E., *3D Modeling, Animation, and Rendering*
O'Rourke, Michael, *Principles of Three-Dimensional Computer Animation*

CAMERA POSITION Locates the camera in a scene; also called *eyepoint* or *reference viewpoint*.

Read more about this:
Mortenson, M. E., *3D Modeling, Animation, and Rendering*
_____, *Mathematics for Computer Graphics Applications*

CAMERA SHAKE The rapid up-and-down or side-to-side motion of a camera to emphasize impacts, explosions, earthquakes, and the like. A virtual camera can be animated in a way to simulate this effect.

CAMERA TARGET A displayed geometric icon, usually a small wireframe cube or similar shape linked to a virtual camera that indicates the center of the camera's field of vision; an aid to setting up the desired viewpoints of a scene to be rendered.

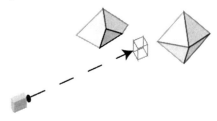

Read more about this:
Giambruno, Mark, *3D Graphics and Animation*

CARDINAL SPLINE A type of interpolating spline curve. The curve passes through all of its control points except the first and last, to provide more control of the curve's shape at and near its actual bounding points.

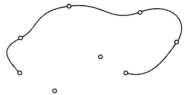

Read more about this:
Mortenson, Michael E., *Geometric Modeling*
O'Rourke, Michael, *Principles of Three-Dimensional Computer Animation*

CARTOON A 2D characterization of people, animals, and objects. The original meaning was in fine art, and meant a preparatory drawing for a piece of art. The modern meaning is that of humorous illustrations in magazines and newspapers. Most recently there are now several contemporary meanings, including creative visual work for print media, for electronic media, and even animated films and animated digital media. The following image is a frame of an animated cartoon horse, drawn by rotoscoping from Eadweard Muybridge's 19th century photos

Rotoscoping from E. Muybridge

Read more about this:
Mortenson, Michael E., *3D Modeling, Animation, and Rendering*

CARTOON PHYSICS An animation technique that allows the laws of physics to be exaggerated or ignored to produce a humorous or dramatic effect. For example, when a cartoon character runs off a cliff, gravity appears to have no effect until the character notices its predicament and reacts. Here are two more examples: a character is seen passing through a solid wall leaving a hole in the shape of its silhouette, and holes that are portable. See also **RAGDOLL PHYSICS**.

CASTING A highly constrained shape, created by a manufacturing process of the same name, used in CAD/CAM solid modeling; an object made by pouring a liquefied material into a mold, which then cools or cures and hardens. Casting also describes the process of choosing actors to play various roles in a theatrical or motion picture production.

CAST SHADOW A shadow formed by a lighted object onto another object or background in a scene. The shadow-rendering pass captures this lighting effect.

CAUSTICS An effect of specular highlight transmission; a focusing effect on reflected or refracted light caused by a curved surface of either a mirror-like or transmitting medium interface. Below is a computer-generated image showing caustic effects

Wikipedia, T-tus (2006). Shows best in color edition.

Under the right conditions, the concentration of light in caustic transmission can burn a surface on which it is focused. This is especially true of caustics caused by sunlight. The word *caustic* comes from the Greek via the Latin *causticus*, burning. Most rendering systems support caustic effects, and some of them support volumetric caustics. Ray tracing the possible paths of the light beam through the glass, accounting for the refraction and reflection, achieves this latter capability.

Read more about this:
Birn, Jeremy, [digital] *Lighting & Rendering*
Watt, A. and M. Watt, *Advanced Animation and Rendering Techniques*

CEL A single rendered frame of an animation sequence; a sheet of transparent acetate or celluloid on which the drawings of animated cartoons are traced or painted. The word *cel* comes from *celluloid*, the material used for animation in the early days of filmmaking. Because celluloid burned easily and suffered from spontaneous decomposition, cellulose acetate plastics eventually replaced it.

Traditionally, the characters were drawn on cels and then laid over a static background drawing. This reduced the number of times an image had to be redrawn . With the advent of computer assisted animation production, the use of cels has been practically abandoned in major productions.

Read more about this:
O'Rourke, Michael, *Principles of Three-Dimensional Computer Animation*

CELL DECOMPOSITION The subdivision of a solid into smaller, more easily modeled, parts.

Read more about this:
Mortenson, Michael E., *Geometric Modeling*

CENTRAL FOCUS That part of an image or scene lying on or very near the optical axis of the virtual camera, at the camera aim point, consequently in sharp focus.

CENTRIFUGAL DEFORMATION Shape change imposed by radial forces acting on an object spinning about an axis.

Read more about this:
Mortenson, Michael E., *3D Modeling, Animation, and Rendering*

CGI The acronym for *computer-generated imagery*.

CHAIN A series of hierarchically linked objects, in animation or mechanism design.

CHANNEL Digital images are made of pixels. A pixel is made up of a set of different primary color elements, each element requiring a specific number of bits, a so-called channel, to define its state. A grayscale image of the same size as a corresponding color image requires just a single channel for each pixel. For example, the image from a standard digital camera has a red channel, a green channel, and a blue channel; the corresponding grayscale image requires just one channel. There are several commonly used color models, each with specific channel requirements: The first image is 24-bit RGB; the second is the red channel of the original RGB image (converted to grayscale); the third is the green channel of the original RGB image (converted to grayscale); and the fourth is the blue channel of the original RGB image (converted to grayscale). The subtle differences in the last three images are not easy to detect at the scale shown, but look at the shadows on the bench back, the shading on the child's stroller, and elsewhere.

Gutza (2004). Shows best in color edition.

Read more about this:
Giambruno, Mark, *3D Graphics and Animation*

CHANNEL ANIMATION Animation controlled by data passed through channels designed for that purpose. Data contained in these channels are used to control aspects of an animation sequence: the intensity of a light source, the density of a texture, the force of gravity, or the motions of an object. Channel animation introduces a powerful way to create an animation sequence in real time, without key frames, by manipulating one or more input device.

Read more about this:
O'Rourke, Michael, *Principles of Three-Dimensional Computer Animation*

CHARACTER ANIMATION The technique of animating an object so that, not only does it move, but it also acquires a distinct personality, endowing the object with a life-like appearance. The two main methods of character animation are the *kinematic model* and the physics-based model, called *physics-based animation* or natural-force behavior. The kinematic method uses position and motion capture to direct animation. Physics-based animation simulates the effects of applied forces: from internal sources such as muscles, and from external forces such as wind and gravity, all with the constraints of some form of skeletal system, to determine motions. Physics-based animation requires more computational power, but is more flexible and achieves more realistic results.

Character animation is enhanced by special effects animation, which creates anything that is not a character; most commonly vehicles, machinery, and natural phenomena such as rain, snow, lightning and water, as well as the "non-natural" effects often seen in science fiction films. Sometimes even special-effects animation uses the principles of character animation.

Read more about this:
Giambruno, Mark, *3D Graphics and Animation*

CHARACTERISTIC POLYGON A polygon whose vertices are the control points of a Bézier curve. If the curve is nonplanar, then the four points do not lie in a common plane. See also **CONVEX HULL**.

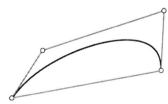

Read more about this:
Mortenson, Michael E., *Geometric Modeling*

CHARACTERISTIC POLYHEDRON A polyhedron whose vertices are the control points of

a Bézier surface. The control points defining a "face" ordinarily will not lie in a common plane. See also **CONVEX HULL**.

Read more about this:
Mortenson, Michael E., *Geometric Modeling*

CHARACTER RIGGING Creating a motion control skeleton for a static character mesh so that the character can be animated.

CHEAP MESH A 3D model with a low polygon count, making it fast and efficient to render; used in early computer games to speed up the interaction, consequently producing poor quality graphics by current standards.

Read more about this:
Giambruno, Mark, *3D Graphics and Animation*

CHEATING Shifting elements in the frame to balance a scene composition; enhancing lighting in a scene.

CHIAROSCURO The effect of distance and the condition of the intervening atmosphere on the image of an object; an atmospheric effect. The greater the distance and the greater the atmospheric density, the dimmer the colors of an object appear and the less sharp its image. Artists routinely take advantage of this effect when painting landscapes; for example, by muting the colors of distant hills, mountains, or other subjects and blurring their image. Notice that the chiaroscuro effect blurs the image of the distant sphere.

Shows best in color edition.

Read more about this:
O'Rourke, Michael, *Principles of Three-Dimensional Computer Animation*

CHILD NODE In animation and mechanism design, the hierarchical relationship between two linked objects, where the object that is closest to the beginning or root of the hierarchical tree is the parent node and the other the child node. Brother or sister nodes share the same parent node. A node that is connected to all lower-level nodes is an ancestor node.

Read more about this:
Mortenson, Michael E., *Mathematics for Computer Graphics Applications*
O'Rourke, Michael, *Principles of Three-Dimensional Computer Animation*

CHOKE A kind of *trap* where a light background overlaps a dark-colored object or area within it. See also **SPREAD**.

CHOKER An extreme **CLOSE-UP SHOT**.

CHORD A line segment whose end points lie on a curve.

CHORDAL DEVIATION The maximum distance between a point on a curve and a line (called the *chord*) whose end points also lie on the same curve, where the first point lies somewhere between the end points of the chord; the maximum distance that an approximating polygonal face deviates from the true surface.

CHOREOGRAPHY The art of composing a scene, including position, motion, and lighting.

CHROMA The purity of a color; the higher the chroma value of a color the more hue present, which means the more saturated the color is. See also **COLORFULNESS** and **VALUE**.

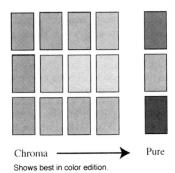

Chroma ⟶ Pure
Shows best in color edition.
Read more about this:
Giambruno, Mark, *3D Graphics and Animation*

CHROMA KEY A process that replaces a solid color (usually blue or green) with another image; used to composite actors into virtual environments. More generally, chroma key is a technique for mixing two images or frames together, in which a color (or a small color range) from one image is removed (or made transparent), revealing another image behind it. See **BLUESCREEN**.

CHROMATIC ABERRATION An optical effect caused by the failure of a lens to focus all colors to the same point, producing colored fringes at the edges of optically created images. This effect occurs because lenses have a different refractive index for different wavelengths of light, which decreases with increasing wavelength.

Read more about this:
Birn, Jeremy, [digital] *Lighting & Rendering*

CHROMATICITY The quality of a color as determined by its dominant wavelength and its purity. See also **CHROMA**.

CHROME REFLECTION MAPPING A view-dependent mapping technique; an approximation of ray tracing, that approximates the reflection of the environment in a shiny surface. The approximation works because most reflecting surfaces are not perfectly smooth, so that the reflection itself does not have to be perfectly rendered.

Read more about this:
Watt, A. and M. Watt, *Advanced Animation and Rendering Techniques*

CIE LAB COLOR MODEL A device-independent standard color model established by the Commission International d'Eclairage.

CINEMATOGRAPHY The art and science of making and reproducing motion pictures, with emphasis on composition, staging, camera use, and framing; the way a shot is recorded by the camera, including lens selection, focus setting, depth-of-field, zoom, camera movement, and so forth.

Read more about this:
Birn, Jeremy, [digital] *Lighting & Rendering*

CLAMPING The process of limiting a position to a specific area. Unlike wrapping, clamping merely moves the point to the nearest available value. One of the many uses of clamping in computer graphics is the placing of a detail inside a polygon, such as a bullet hole on a wall. It can also be used with wrapping to create a variety of effects.

CLASSICAL CUTTING An inconspicuous film editing style that focuses on the action of the characters.

CLASSICAL WAVE THEORY Describes how light is transmitted, reflected, diffracted, refracted, and absorbed; in physics and physical optics, the theory of the propagation and behavior of light. It was developed in the nineteenth century, before the advent of relativity and quantum physics, which further refined our understanding of light. The classical wave theory is still applicable to all but very special lighting effects.

CLAYMATION Animation of clay figures to create cartoons or other film productions. The clay figures are reshaped and repositioned manually for each frame. It is one of many forms of stop- motion animation.

CLIP To cut off part of an image outside a specified boundary (see also **CLIPPING**); also a short segment of film, video, or animation. In rendering, clipping refers to an optimization where the computer draws only objects that might be visible to the viewer.

CLIP MAPPING Creating the visual effect of a hole in an object and making other objects or surfaces visible through the hole; also called *visibility mapping*; a form of transparency mapping.

CLIPPING Determines which part of a scene is fully rendered and displayed, within defined spatial boundaries. A bounded 3D space, the view volume, defines the space that is visible to the camera. This is usually the frustum of a pyramid whose bounding planes are the clipping planes. Only objects in this space are displayed. It is also the limiting or truncating of subtle variations in hue and tone that occurs when rendering a scene with areas of extreme contrast between highlights and shadows.

Read more about this:
Mortenson, M. E., *Mathematics for Computer Graphics Applications*
Watt, A. and M. Watt, *Advanced Animation and Rendering Techniques*

CLIPPING PATH In 2D computer graphics, a closed vector path, or shape, used to select an image. Anything inside the path will be included; anything outside will be omitted from the output. A clipping path produces a hard edge.

CLIPPING PLANE A boundary plane on one side of which objects or parts of objects are displayed and those on the other side are not displayed. The near and far clipping planes define a region within the field of view of a scene and within which objects are rendered and displayed. Additional planes, or perhaps other surfaces, form the enclosing sides. A clipping plane prevents a renderer from calculating surfaces at extreme distances from the viewer. It is perpendicular to the camera, a set distance away (the threshold), and occupies the entire viewport. Used in real-time rendering, clipping planes help preserve processing for objects within clear sight.

Clipping planes can, under certain circumstances, detract from the realism of a scene. A viewer may notice that some objects at the boundary of a clipping plane are incorrectly rendered or seem to appear or disappear spontaneously. The addition of fog—a variably transparent region of color or texture just before the clipping plane—can help soften the transition between what should be in plain sight and opaque, and what should be beyond notice and fully transparent, and therefore does not need to be rendered.

Read more about this:
Giambruno, Mark, *3D Graphics and Animation*
Mortenson, Michael E., *3D Modeling, Animation, and Rendering*
O'Rourke, Michael, *Principles of Three-Dimensional Computer Animation*
Watt, A. and M. Watt, *Advanced Animation and Rendering Techniques*

CLOSED PATH A curve that closes back upon itself to form a continuous path, such as a circle. See *path*.

CLOSED SET Also called *closed interval*. See **OPEN SET**.

CLOSED SHAPE In three-dimensional space, a shape that has an inside and an outside, separated by a bounding surface; in two-dimensional space, a shape whose boundary is defined by a closed curve.

CLOSE-UP A shot that frames a small part of a scene; for example, the shot of a catcher's hand signal to a pitcher in a baseball game. Close-up shots create drama and intimacy, bringing the viewer into the action. A close-up requires only a minimal background, because the subject should almost fill the image area. This means less background geometry, less lighting, and less motion are required in animation sequences, as well as less rendering. Close-ups are sometimes used as cutaways or zoom-in from a distant shot to show detail, such as a character's expression or emotion.

There are several kinds of close-up shots. For a human character these are the so-called medium close-up that frames the head and shoulders, the close-up that frames the head, and the extreme close-up that might include only the eyes.

Read more about this:
Demers, Owen, [digital] *Texture & Painting*

CLOTH MODELING Simulating realistic cloth-like appearance, deformations, and dynamic responses. A cloth model may exhibit a two-dimensional catenary action of draping under the influence of its own weight, or flutter like a flag in a breeze. Three technical problems must be resolved: geometry, texture, and physics. Geometry describes the shape of the cloth piece. Texture describes its surface appearance. Physics describes how the cloth responds to gravity, wind, the shape and movement of the wearer of a piece of clothing, how the cloth behaves when wet, and many other forces and environments.

Read more about this:
Watt, A. and M. Watt, *Advanced Animation and Rendering Techniques*

CLOUD BOW Similar to a *fogbow*.

CLOUD OF POINTS A large set of points that is distributed over the surface of some physical object. The coordinates of the points are obtained from a 3D scanner or digitizer. These data are used to define a continuous bounding surface of a 3D model of the object. This technique is used in reverse engineering applications. It differs from a *point cloud* used in scientific visualization, which conveys three-, or more, dimensional data.

CLOUD PRIMITIVE A simple environmental shape used to model clouds. Cloud modeling may include controls for the following characteristics: number of clouds, size, color, opacity, pattern, and edge appearance. See also **PRIMITIVE**.

CLOUDS Atmospheric phenomena; a region of fine water droplets or vapor, with distinct boundaries and structure that vary over time. There are three general categories of cloud types: cumulus, stratus, and cirrus. Cumulus clouds form puffy, towering mounds with flat bases and great vertical development whose tops may look like heaps of whipped cream. Stratus clouds form extensive layers, and cirrus form fibrous strands at high altitudes. Clouds may be modeled and rendered for a scene, or footage of real clouds may be incorporated into a scene using compositing techniques. In either situation, an understanding of atmospheric dynamics and attentive observation of the changes constantly occurring in the sky overhead is necessary. Good cloud modeling animation must capture the motion and form changes. Rain and snow effects must be associated with the right kinds of clouds.

Read more about this:
Naylor, John, *Out of the Blue*
O'Rourke, Michael, *Principles of Three-Dimensional Computer Animation*

CLOUDS AT SUNSET Add to the dramatic effect by reflecting the rusty and rosy hues of sunlight and cast ray-like shadows across the sky. As the sun sets and continues to fall farther and farther below the horizon, clouds reflect ever-changing colors. The types and altitude of the clouds further vary the effects.

Image source unknown. Shows best in color edition.

Read more about this:
Naylor, John, *Out of the Blue*

CMYK COLOR MODEL An acronym for the colors cyan, magenta, yellow, and black; sometimes referred to as CMY (cyan, magenta, and yellow); the colors of ink in a four-color printing process and a color model used in computer graphics illustrations and rendering; a color model based on the light-absorbing properties of ink printed on paper. Cyan, magenta, and yellow are the complements of red, green, and blue, respectively. CMY are so-called *subtractive primaries* because they subtract color from white light.

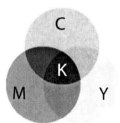

Shows best in color edition.

The combination of pure cyan, magenta, and yellow produces black. In the CMYK color model, specific colors are determined by what is removed from white light. For example, cyan subtracts red from reflected white light, itself the sum of red, green, and blue. In terms of the *additive primaries*, red, green, and blue (RGB), cyan is blue plus green.

Certain colors in the RGB and HSB color spaces are not reproducible in the CMYK system; neon colors, for example, while pure cyan and pure yellow are not available in the RGB system. See also **COLOR SPACES**.

Read more about this:
Demers, Owen, [digital] *Texture & Painting*
Giambruno, Mark, *3D Graphics and Animation*

COAXIAL A geometric relationship between two 3D objects where the axis of a rotational feature of one 3D object lies along a common line with the axis of a rotational feature of the other object. More specific than alignment, it is the three-dimensional linear analog of *concentric*.

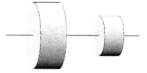

COLLAGE A film style that assembles images from a variety of sources, often juxtaposing staged fictional scenes with newsreel, animation, or other material; an artistic composition made up of different combined materials; from the French word *coller* (to stick). Traditionally, a collage is a work created by gluing material to a surface. By doing so, the artist incorporates fragments of the real world.

COLLECTIVE ANIMAL BEHAVIOR Describes the coordinated behavior of large groups of similar animals, including flocking of birds, schooling of fish, and herding of cattle. Each group has its own distinctive pattern of movement, which can be modeled, animated, and rendered.

Starlings flocking, T. Hansen (2006).

Fish schooling, Mila Zinkova (2004).

COLLINEAR A geometric relationship between 3D models where a linear feature of one lies along a common line with a linear feature of another model. See also **ALIGN** and **COAXIAL**

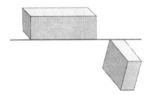

COLLISION In the real world, collisions occur when two objects moving through space make physical contact. Modeling this behavior requires a mathematical description of the objects and their motions and a geometric procedure to determine if, indeed, contact has occurred. After the details of geometric contact are determined, the physical forces that affect the motions of the objects after the collision are accounted for. Here friction and the elastic properties of the colliding objects come into play, influencing object deformation and rebound. Finally, secondary and subsequent collisions must be computed.

The collision of two moving bodies produce forces that in turn produce change in speed and direction. Collisions can be elastic or inelastic. In elastic collisions, shape changes

from impact are temporary, and the colliding bodies soon return to their pre-collision shapes. For inelastic collisions, the bodies are permanently deformed. The assumption of conservation of momentum as well as conservation of kinetic energy makes it possible to calculate the final velocities in two-body collisions.

Read more about this:
Mortenson, Michael E., *3D Modeling, Animation, and Rendering*

COLLISION DETECTION Determining if two moving objects come into contact with one another; a computational geometry problem arising in 3D modeling and animation that may be referred to as *collision detection and avoidance*, especially in animation, kinematics, natural force behavior, and assembly modeling. This is similar to *motion planning* techniques used in robotics (also known as the *navigation problem*, or the *piano mover's problem*).

Read more about this:
Mortenson, Michael E., *3D Modeling, Animation, and Rendering*
O'Rourke, Michael, *Principles of Three-Dimensional Computer Animation*

COLOR A property of light determined by the frequency or wavelength (the reciprocal of frequency multiplied by the speed of light) of the light emitted from or reflected by an object, affected by the medium through which it passes and the surfaces of objects it strikes or passes through. Most light sources emit a mix of wavelengths, called a *spectrum*. The color of an object is a result of selective absorption of some of the incident light; objects made of different materials absorb different wavelengths of the light striking their surface. So the surface color of an object is determined by the reflection and re-emission of part of the spectrum of the incident light. In computer graphics, color is computed and specified as a combination of hue, saturation, and brightness in the HSB color model, or red, green, and blue color levels in the RGB model.

The use of color in scenes and renderings can have dramatic effects on mood, the perception of depth (absolute and relative), and the impression of natural color and light as opposed to simple artificial cartoon worlds. An object with red hues is usually perceived by a viewer as being warmer and closer than one with blue hues.

Shows best in color edition.

A well-thought-out color scheme establishing the tone and mood of a rendering is the hallmark of professional-quality workmanship. See also **LUMINANCE, SATURATION, DIFFUSENESS, TEMPERATURE, CHROMATICITY, CMYK MODELS,** and **COLOR PALETTE**.

Read more about this:
O'Rourke, Michael, *Principles of Three-Dimensional Computer Animation*

COLOR (24-BIT) The number of different colors a monitor is capable of displaying. A 24-bit color monitor can display approximately 16.7 million separate colors. Eight bits are allocated to each color (red, green, and blue), permitting 256 levels of intensity per color. This translates into the ability to produce 256x256x256 = 16,777,216 different colors. 32-bit color adds an extra eight bits to describe pixel transparency or compositing masks. These extra bits define an alpha channel.

COLOR BALANCE Determines the color of light that is perceived as white light on photographic film; in rendering, color balance simulates photographic effects. Film color balanced for indoor photography reproduces colors accurately for scenes with typical indoor lighting (incandescent light bulbs, etc.). But if indoor film is used to photograph outdoor scenes in daylight, the result exhibits a bluish tint. Film color balanced for outdoor photography, if used indoors, produces yellow or orange tinted photos. A similar light and color adjustment is used in video cameras, called *white balance*.

In photography and image processing, color balance is a global adjustment of color intensity (typically red, green, and blue primary colors). An important goal of this adjustment is to render specific colors – particularly neutral colors – correctly; hence,

the general method is sometimes called gray balance, neutral balance, or white balance. Color balance changes the overall mixture of colors in an image and is used for color correction; generalized versions of color balance are used to get colors other than neutrals to also appear correct or pleasing.

Read more about this:
Birn, Jeremy, [digital] *Lighting & Rendering*

COLOR BANDING A problem of inaccurate color presentation in computer graphics display. In 24 bit color modes, 8 bits per channel should be enough to render images in the full visible spectrum, but in some cases there is a risk of producing abrupt changes between shades of the same color. For example, displaying natural gradients (like sunsets, dawns or clear blue skies) can show minor banding. Possible solutions include introducing dithering and increasing the number of bits per color channel. See also **BANDING** and **POSTERIZATION**.

COLOR BLEEDING The unintentional and undesirable overlapping or blending of two adjacent colors along and beyond their common border; the effect of light on the color of a surface, when that light has first reflected off other surfaces of different colors, transferring color from one object to another via reflected light, often seen in radiosity renderings.

Shows best in color edition.

Read more about this:
Watt, A. and M. Watt, *Advanced Animation and Rendering Techniques*

COLOR BURN A process that darkens the base color to reflect the blend color of overlapping semi-transparent objects. See also **COLOR DODGE**.

COLOR CALIBRATION To measure or adjust the color response of a graphics device (input or output) to establish a relationship to a standard color space. The device to be calibrated is called the *calibration source*; the color space that serves as a standard is the *calibration target*.

COLOR CONTRAST A technique using the juxtaposition of two or more colors to highlight an object or particular part of a scene, used to get the viewer's attention. See also **COMPLEMENTARY COLORS** and **COLOR EXCLUSIVITY**.

COLOR CORRECTION Changing the RGB values of a group of pixels to match elements within a shot to background plates, or to match throughout a series of shots. Primary color correction is used to adjust the intensity of red, green, blue, gamma (mid tones), shadows (blacks) and highlights (whites). Secondary correction is used to adjust luminance, saturation and hue in six colors (red, green, blue, cyan, magenta, yellow). The objective of secondary controls is to adjust values within a narrow range, with little or no effect on the remainder of the color spectrum. Digital grading allows objects and color ranges within the scene to be isolated with precision and then adjusted. Color tints can be manipulated and visual treatments pushed to extremes not physically possible with laboratory processing. Special digital filters and effects can also be applied to the images.

COLOR DEPTH A measure in bits of the number of colors a monitor can display. A 24-bit color monitor is capable of displaying millions of colors. A 16-bit color monitor can display thousands of colors, while an 8-bit monitor can display only 256 different colors. It is also described as bits per pixel (bpp), particularly when specified along with the number of bits used. Thus, the higher color depth the broader the range of distinct colors available for an image. However, color depth is only one aspect of color representation. Note that the RGB color model cannot produce highly saturated colors such as yellow. See also **GAMUT**.

COLOR DODGE A process that lightens the base color to reflect the blend color of overlapping semi-transparent objects. This decreases the contrast to make the bottom layer reflect the top layer: the brighter the top layer, the more its color affects the bottom layer. Blending with white gives white. Blending with black does not change the image. This effect is similar to changing the white point. See also **COLOR BURN**.

COLORED SHADOWS Shadows cast by an object illuminated by more than one light source. Sometimes the combination of sunlight and airlight produces colored shadows. For example, shadows on snow appear blue, and shadows at some distance may exhibit a bluish color. Another example is the shadow of an object formed by the light entering a room from a north-facing window on a clear and bright day: the shadow will look yellow if the object is also lit by an artificial light from another direction, which produces a blue shadow. The human visual system and mechanisms of perception contribute to this effect as well.

Flkr.com, slithy-toves (2009). Shows best in color edition.

Read more about this:
Naylor, John, *Out of the Blue*

COLOR EXCLUSIVITY Using a unique color on the primary object in a scene, enhanced by color contrast with its immediate surroundings.

COLOR FILTER In photography, a specially coated glass placed over the lens to enhance or diminish the effects of a specific color or narrow range of colors, which effects may be simulated in rendering programs.

COLORFULNESS Relating to the perceived intensity of a specific color in an image, in contrast to a grayscale image. A colorful image appears vivid and often intense. A less colorful image appears as muted and closer to gray. The absence of colorfulness in an image puts it in the gray category (an image with no colorfulness in any of its colors is called *grayscale*). With three attributes—colorfulness (or chroma or saturation), lightness (or brightness), and hue—any color can be described.

COLOR GEL A transparent colored material that is used in theatre, event production, photography, videography and cinematography to color light and for color correction. Modern gels are thin sheets of polycarbonate or polyester, placed in front of a light source.

COLORIMETRY The technology used to quantify and describe human color perception. It is similar to spectrophotometry.

COLORIMETRIC, ABSOLUTE A rendering intent specifying a change in color space that leaves unchanged the colors that fall within the new color space.

COLORIMETRIC, RELATIVE A rendering intent specifying a change in color space based upon a comparison between an extreme highlight (or white point) within the initial color space to the new color space.

COLOR INTERPOLATION A method of finding and rendering an average or transitional color for a 3D region bounded by regions of other colors. When color is used to represent the quantitative values of some physical state, like the temperature at various points throughout some solid, color interpolation is a method that finds appropriate colors for intermediate points. It is used in volume rendering.

COLOR LOOK-UP TABLE Used in 8-bit color depth monitors, to describe a specific color of the 256 colors available; a mechanism to transform a range of input colors into another range of colors. It may be a hardware device built into an imaging system or a software function built into an image processing application. The hardware color look-up table will convert the logical color (pseudo-color) numbers stored in each pixel of video memory into physical colors, normally represented as RGB triplets, that can be displayed on a computer monitor. The palette is a block of fast RAM, which is addressed by the logical color and whose output is split into the red, green, and blue levels that drive the actual display device.

COLOR MAPPING The pixel colors of the 2D image transferred and rendered onto the surface of a 3D object.

Read more about this:
Demers, Owen, [digital] *Texture & Painting*

COLOR MODEL A method for producing a new color by mixing a small set of standard colors; sometimes called a *color system*. The range of colors that can be produced by a color model is the color space of the model. The most common color models are:

Grayscale: white to black, with all shades of gray in between.

RGB (red, green, and blue): this is an additive color model used by computer monitors, which depends on a light source to produce color. RGB values are specified as percentages or as values from 0 to 255.

HSB (Hue, saturation, and brightness): an RGB-derived color model.

CMYK (Cyan, magenta, yellow, and black): a subtractive color model with typical printing process colors, dependent on the light-absorbing properties of ink on paper.

Others include the Chevreul, Munsell, and Rood systems.

COLOR PALETTE A menu of color options and mixing controls for producing a desired hue. .See also **COLOR SPACES**.

COLOR PASS Also called **BEAUTY PASS**.

COLOR PROFILE A mathematical description of a graphics device's color space, allowing its conversion to another color space.

COLOR SCHEME The total set of colors used in a rendering, to set the mood for the scene; the choice of colors used in a design for a range of media; for example, using a white background with black text.

Read more about this:
Demers, Owen, [digital] *Texture & Painting*

COLOR SEPARATION Separating the colors of an image into its base components, for example, red, green, and blue. This expedites the conversion between color models.

COLOR SPACE The range of colors that can be displayed or printed; also called *color gamut*. A computer monitor can display most of the RGB color space. Pure cyan and pure yellow are among the few colors that cannot be accurately displayed on a monitor. The CMYK color space is a large subset of the RGB space plus the pure cyan and yellow and others that are outside the RGB space.

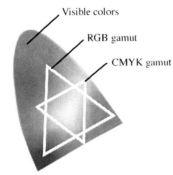

Shows best in color edition.

Read more about this:
Demers, Owen, [digital] *Texture & Painting*

COLOR SPILL Also known as *blue spill*.

COLOR TEMPERATURE A characteristic of visible light measured in degrees Kelvin, used to differentiate between near-white light sources, to describe the color balance of film, and to describe the color of light. Note that 0° Kelvin corresponds to -273° Centigrade, so adding 273° to a temperature in degrees K produces the equivalent temperature in degrees C.

Some colors are perceived as warmer or cooler than others. For example, most people consider red colors warmer, and blues cooler. However, these psychological descriptions are the reverse of their temperature specification in degrees Kelvin. The color temperature of a light source refers to its visible color and not to the temperature at which its filament burns.

The color temperature of a light source is found by comparing its chromaticity with that of an ideal blackbody radiator. The temperature at which the heated blackbody radiator matches the color of the light source is that source's color temperature.

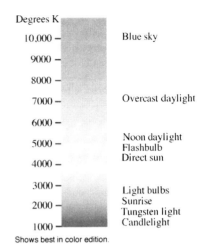

Shows best in color edition.

Read more about this:
Birn, Jeremy, [digital] *Lighting & Rendering*

COLOR TIMING Settings different exposure times for red, green, and blue light in developing a film negative. The process of color grading alters the color of motion picture and television images, either electronically, photo-chemically, or digitally. The photochemical process, also called color timing, is done in a photographic lab, where, for example, the red, green, and blue components of an image are subject to different development times.

COLOR VALUE The brightness of a color; a measure of the lightness/darkness of a color that approximates its subjective perception .

COLOR VISION The ability to distinguish objects based on the wavelengths of the light they reflect or emit. The mechanisms of the perception of color are complex, involving the physiological pathways from eye to brain and the psychological interpretation by the mind. For example, a red apple does not emit red light. Rather, it absorbs all the frequencies of visible light shining on it except for a group of frequencies that is reflected and perceived as red.

COLOR WHEEL A graphic interpretation of the HSB color model, where hue is expressed in degrees from 0° to 360° and saturation varies from 0% at the wheel's center to 100% at its outer edge; a graphic representation of the CMYK color model, where the primary colors are 120° apart, a secondary color is opposite each primary, and tertiary colors and the remaining colors fill out the spectrum.

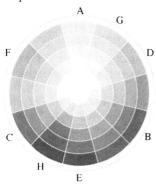

A, B, C = Primary
D, E, F = Secondary
AE, GH, DC, BF = Complementary

Shows best in color edition.

COMBINATORIAL STRUCTURE The topological organization of a solid object's bounding surface that has been segmented to facilitate some computational purpose.

COMPLEMENTARY COLORS A pair of colors located opposite each other on the color wheel; used to highlight an object. Complementary colors added together in equal amounts produce white. In the RGB color model (and derived models such as HSV), primary colors and secondary colors are paired in this way: red and cyan, green and magenta, and blue and yellow.

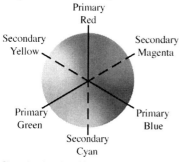

Shows best in color edition.

Read more about this:
Demers, Owen, [digital] *Texture & Painting*

COMPONENT PLACEMENT Rigid-body transformations to position an object within an assembly of other objects; semi-automated or guided process of modeling an assembly.

COMPOSITE CURVE Two or more curves joined end-to-end.

COMPOSITING A process in which separate images are combined to form a single final image; for example, combining live action scenes with animation, or combining the main image rendering with its separate shadow and highlights renderings. Most compositing is done by digital methods. See also **CROSS-DISSOLVE** and **MATTING**.

Read more about this:
Birn, Jeremy, [digital] *Lighting & Rendering*
O'Rourke, Michael, *Principles of Three-Dimensional Computer Animation*

COMPOSITION The overall layout of each rendering, including light and shadow, color, background, and placement of foreground subjects. Elements of composition are:

1. Line: the visual path that enables the eye to move within the piece

2. Shape: areas defined by edges within the piece, whether geometric or organic

3. Color: hues with their various values and intensities

4. Texture: surface qualities that translate into tactile illusions

5. Direction: visual routes that take vertical, horizontal, or diagonal paths

6. Size: the relative dimensions and proportions of shapes to one another

7. Perspective: the expression of depth: foreground, middle ground, background

8. Space: the space taken up by (positive) or in between (negative) objects

COMPOSITIONAL TECHNIQUES Procedures used to satisfy aesthetic goals. Not all techniques are compatible, because not all artists share the same goals. Here are some:

1. The *rule of thirds*, the main subject should be slightly off center of the frame.

2. The *rule of odds* frames the main subject with an even number of surrounding secondary subjects.

3. The *rule of space*, or *lead room*, calls for leaving more space in the direction of the subject's movement or gaze.

4. *Simplification* calls for minimizing the viewer's distraction from the main subject by minimizing the number of secondary subjects and actions.

5. *Limiting focus* or depth of field puts everything but the main subject out of focus.

COMPOUND ANGLE An angle measured by a vector with three nonzero components. A plane, or features on a plane, not perpendicular to at least one of the three principal coordinate planes is constructed using a compound-angle relationship to its coordinate system.

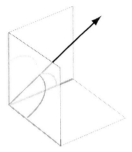

COMPRESSION A process used to reduce the size of digital files, particularly graphics files, for faster transmission, lower storage requirements, and more efficient manipulation. Compression may be lossless or lossy (for example, JPEG). Image quality may be affected by the compression technique used and the level of compression applied.

COMPUTATIONAL FLUID DYNAMICS An analytical technique using a finite-element model to determine the behavior of water or other liquid. A very large number of simultaneous equations must be solved for each time interval of an animation sequence incorporating such behavior. See also **HYDRODYNAMICS** and **NATURAL FORCE BEHAVIOR**.

COMPUTATIONAL GEOMETRY A branch of computer science and mathematics that focuses on the development of algorithms that are stated in geometric terms, usually to solve geometric problems. Most of these problems are in the fields of computer graphics, CAD/CAM, geometric modeling, robotics, geographic information systems, integrated circuit design, and computer-aided engineering.

The major subdivisions of computational geometry are:

1. Combinatorial computational geometry, or algorithmic geometry, operates with geometric objects assumed as discrete entities.

2. Numerical computational geometry (machine geometry, computer-aided geometric design or geometric modeling) represents 3D solid objects in mathematical forms suitable for computer computations.

COMPUTER-AIDED DESIGN (CAD) An integrated set of computer and computer graphics applications used to create a mathematical model of an engineering design or a real object's shape. Many CAD applications include 3D modeling and 2D drafting, where the emphasis is on the engineering design, with interfaces to analysis (CAE) and manufacturing (CAM) applications. Specialized CAD applications support mechanical and structural design, circuit design, and assembly processes, among others.

COMPUTER-AIDED ENGINEERING (CAE) An integrated set of computer and computer graphics applications that may include structural analysis, aerodynamic analysis, and thermodynamic analysis, among others. Most of these applications rely on a finite-element model, which is derived from a CAD 3D model.

COMPUTER-AIDED MANUFACTURING (CAM) An integrated set of computer and computer graphics applications that may use the CAD model of a mechanical part or a circuit design to generate instructions for automated machines to produce the object.

COMPUTER ANIMATION The use of computers to create moving images. It is a hybrid subdiscipline of computer graphics and animation. The image shows an example of computer animation produced in the motion-caption technique

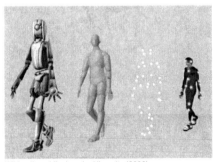

Wikipedia public domain, Hipocrite (2006).

COMPUTER-GENERATED IMAGERY (CGI)

The application of 3D computer graphics to special effects and animation. CGI is used for visual effects because computer generated effects are more controllable than more physically based processes, such as constructing miniatures for effects shots or hiring extras for crowd scenes, and because it allows the creation of images that would not be feasible using any other method. It often allows a single artist to produce content without the use of actors, expensive set pieces, or props.

COMPUTER GRAPHICS The representation and manipulation of pictorial data by a computer and displayed on a computer monitor. Two-dimensional computer graphics is the computer-based creation of digital images from 2D geometric models. The term may stand for the branch of computer science that uses such techniques or for the models themselves. 2D computer graphics began in the 1950s, based on vector graphics devices. Raster-based devices largely supplanted these.

Three-dimensional computer graphics uses a three-dimensional representation of geometric data (a 3D model) that is rendered to produce 2D images. Such images can be for later display or for real-time viewing. Apart from the rendered graphic, the model is contained within a graphical data file. A 3D model is the mathematical representation of any three-dimensional object. A model is not technically a graphic until it is visually displayed.

COMPUTER IMAGING Images in digital form manipulated, composed, and rendered via computer graphics applications and stored in a computer, including digital photography and scanned images.

CONCATENATED Combined; applies to a sequence of transformations of some object, where individual transformations are combined to form a single equivalent transformation.

Read more about this:
Mortenson, Michael E., *Geometric Transformations for 3D Modeling*
O'Rourke, Michael, *Principles of Three-Dimensional Computer Animation*

CONCAVE Describes a solid having a depression in its surface, like a valley or dent; an inwardly curved surface, as in some lenses; the opposite of convex.

CONE A common geometric primitive in constructive solid geometry (CSG); usually a right circular cone. An instance of a cone is defined by specifying its height, base radius, location, and orientation.

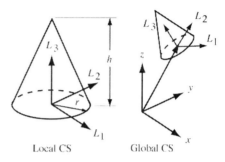

Local CS   Global CS

CONFIGURATION SPACE In mechanical engineering, a multi-dimensional coordinate system or space whose principal axes are time and measures of the various degrees-of-freedom of the links and joints of some mechanism; the space of possible positions that a physical system may attain, possibly subject to external constraints; in engineering and sciences in general, a multi-dimensional system of independent variables whose values at any point represent the state of the system at a specific time..

CONIC CURVE A 2D curve defined by a second-degree implicit equation. Conversely, any second-degree equation defines a conic. The standard form of the conic curve is

$$Ax^2 + 2Bxy + Cy^2 + 2Dx + 2Ey + F = 0$$

which produces an ellipse, hyperbola, or parabola, depending on the values of the coefficients. Coordinate-free definitions of these curves are
1. An ellipse is the set of all points P for which the sum of the distances from two fixed points A and B (called the *focal points*, or foci) is a constant, K, so that $AP + BP = K$. If $AB = 0$, then a circle is produced with a radius $R = K/2$.

2. A hyperbola is the set of all points P for which the difference of the distances from

two fixed points A and B (the foci) is a constant, K, so that $AP - BP = K$.

3. A parabola is the set of all points P that are equally distant from a fixed point A (the focus) and a fixed line l (the directrix), so that $AP - d = 0$.

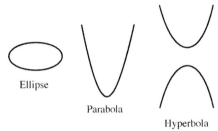

Ellipse

Parabola

Hyperbola

Read more about this:
Mortenson, Michael E., *Geometric Modeling*
———, *Mathematics for Computer Graphics Applications*

CONJUGATE NET A net of curves on a surface where the tangents of the curves of one family of the net at points along each fixed curve of the other family form a developable surface. The two families of the net do not play symmetrical roles in this definition, but the two families are interchangeable. A necessary condition for the parametric net on a patch to be a conjugate net is $\mathbf{p}^{uw} \bullet \mathbf{n} = 0$,

where $\mathbf{p}^{uw}$ is a vector determined by a mixed partial derivative with respect to the parametric variables u and w.

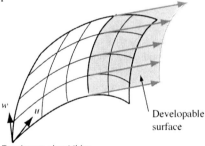

Developable surface

Read more about this:
Mortenson, Michael E., *Geometric Modeling*

CONNECTIVITY A topological property indicating how geometric elements of a model are inter-connected. See also **CONNECTIVITY MATRIX** and **TOPOLOGY**.

Read more about this:
Mortenson, Michael E., *Geometric Modeling*
———, *Mathematics for Computer Graphics Applications*

CONNECTIVITY MATRIX A two-dimensional matrix that describes how vertices are connected to form the edges of a polyhedron. This matrix is always square, which means that there are as many rows and columns as there are vertices. Columns are numbered consecutively from left to right, and rows from top to bottom. A particular element in the table is identified as a_{ij} , where i identifies the row and j the column in which the element is found. If element $a_{ij} = 1$, then vertices i and j are connected by an edge. If $a_{ij} = 0$, then vertices i and j are not connected. The tetrahedron connectivity matrix shown below demonstrates this. For example, since $a_{3,2} = 1$, vertex 2 and vertex 3 are connected.

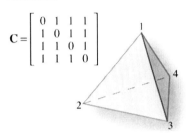

$$C = \begin{bmatrix} 0 & 1 & 1 & 1 \\ 1 & 0 & 1 & 1 \\ 1 & 1 & 0 & 1 \\ 1 & 1 & 1 & 0 \end{bmatrix}$$

A connectivity matrix can also describe how faces are connected. For a cube, the 6×6 matrix shown below is used. By convention, if $i = j$, then $a_{ij} = 0$. Notice that the arrays are symmetrical about the main diagonals and are, therefore, doubly redundant.

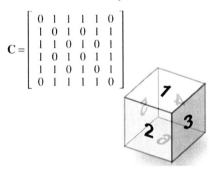

$$C = \begin{bmatrix} 0 & 1 & 1 & 1 & 1 & 0 \\ 1 & 0 & 1 & 0 & 1 & 1 \\ 1 & 1 & 0 & 1 & 0 & 1 \\ 1 & 0 & 1 & 0 & 1 & 1 \\ 1 & 1 & 0 & 1 & 0 & 1 \\ 0 & 1 & 1 & 1 & 1 & 0 \end{bmatrix}$$

Read more about this:
Mortenson, Michael E., *Mathematics for Computer Graphics Applications*

CONSTRAINT A geometric restriction placed on the position or motion of an object with respect to its spatial relationship to one or more other objects. Constraints are also used to guide the creation of a geometric model by restricting the positions or relationships of its geometric elements. Constraints are more restrictive than limits: for example, an object may be constrained to maintain a given rotational orientation, or remain at a fixed distance and direction from some other object that is free to move.

Read more about this:
Giambruno, Mark, *3D Graphics and Animation*

CONSTANT MAPPING See *luminosity mapping*.

CONSTRAINT A geometric restriction placed on the position or motion of an object with respect to its spatial relationship to one or more other objects. Constraints are also used to guide the creation of a geometric model by restricting the positions or relationships of its geometric elements. Constraints are more restrictive than limits: for example, an object may be constrained to maintain a given rotational orientation, or remain at a fixed distance and direction from some other object that is free to move.

Read more about this:
Giambruno, Mark, *3D Graphics and Animation*

CONSTRAINT PLANE See **ASSEMBLY CONSTRAINTS**.

CONSTRUCTION GEOMETRY Points, lines, arcs, planes, spheres and other simple geometric elements used as temporary aids in constructing of a 3D model. These elements can be retained as part of the total model database but are not included in the final rendering.

CONSTRUCTION PLANE A convenient auxiliary plane, used as a working plane or reference plane with respect to which elements of a 3D model are more easily constructed. This plane is only a temporary tool to aid model building and is not part of the model or its final rendering. When activated during a modeling process, the construction of 2D geometric elements of an object occurs in this plane.

Read more about this:
O'Rourke, Michael, *Principles of Three-Dimensional Computer Animation*

CONSTRUCTIVE SOLID GEOMETRY (CSG) A solid modeling method that combines simple solid shapes called primitives to build more complex models, using the Boolean operators union, difference, and intersection. The resulting model is a procedural model stored in the mathematical form of a binary tree, where the leaf nodes are the primitives, correctly sized and positioned, and each branch node is a Boolean operator.

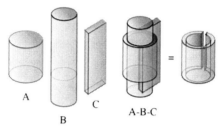

CSG models are guaranteed to be solid if all of the primitive shapes are solid, which is an important characteristic of many manufacturing and engineering computations.

Read more about this:
Mortenson, Michael E., *Geometric Modeling*
_____, *Mathematics for Computer Graphics Applications*
O'Rourke, Michael, *Principles of Three-Dimensional Computer Animation*

CONTACT One of the most difficult physical behaviors to model between two or more moving solid objects is non-penetration contact. Two major problems must be solved to achieve an accurate simulation: first, a collision between two moving objects must be detected, and the positions of the objects and the time of the collision determined; and second, the contact forces between them must be computed. The mathematical tools of computational geometry and robotics are used to solve these problems. The shapes of the objects, their motion trajectories, local spins and oscillations, and their mechanical properties (elasticity, etc) furnish the input.

If the paths of the objects are known (as is usual in robotics), then time-dependent swept surfaces are computed, where the objects' silhouettes in the planes normal to their respective paths act as generator curves. If the swept surfaces produced by the objects intersect and the objects are simultaneously at the intersection, then a collision or contact has occurred (and has been detected). Contact forces then alter the subsequent paths of the objects, and force-determination computations are required to find these new paths. If the paths are not known in advance, then a time-step sequence of computations must be performed to detect intersections.

Contact forces alter the shape of the colliding objects. Elastic deformations are temporary and plastic deformations are permanent (absorbing kinetic energy and converting it into heat). These forces also affect the post-collision paths.

Read more about this:
Mortenson, Michael E., *3D Modeling, Animation, and Rendering*

CONTINUITY In animation and filmmaking, the smooth flow of foreground action and background setting from frame to frame in a scene, including form, function, motion, and visual effects. In a TCB controller, continuity is the parameter used to adjust how smoothly a control curve approaches a control point. It describes the relationship between two curves sharing a common point or between two surfaces sharing a common curve. There are two kinds of geometric modeling continuity: *geometric continuity* and *parametric continuity*.

Read more about this:
Giambruno, Mark, *3D Graphics and Animation*
Mortenson, Michael E., *3D Modeling, Animation, and Rendering*
_____, *Mathematics for Computer Graphics Applications*

CONTINUITY EDITING Cutting procedure to maintain a smooth flow of the action, matching time and space relationships from shot to shot.

CONTINUOUS TONE An unlimited range of colors or shades of gray, as in photographs, as opposed to digitally constructed color or gray images which have a limited number of colors available.

In a continuous tone image, each color at any point is reproduced as a single tone, and not as a combination of discrete halftones, such as one single color for monochromatic prints, or a combination of halftones for color prints. The most common continuous tone images are in color photographs.

A computer monitor is an example of a continuous-tone device. A pixel can represent any color, because its color components are in analog form that can vary continuously, and does not require halftones to produce a color. However, a computer monitor cannot provide infinite tone variations, since it is a digital device. A 24-bit color monitor has 256 discrete steps for each color, for a total of 16,777,216 possible colors. An analog video device (one that has not been manipulated by a computer of any kind) can provide infinite tone variations within its color gamut.

A halftone image uses discrete dots of color that, beyond a minimum distance, approximate the intended color; for example, inkjet printers. Magazines and most printed material use this technique. See also **HALFTONE**.

CONTOURING See **BANDING**.

CONTOUR SURFACE A surface fitted to a set of curves, each of which represents a constant value of some variable, such as curves of equal elevation above sea level in a topographic map.

Read more about this:
O'Rourke, Michael, *Principles of Three-Dimensional Computer Animation*

CONTRAST A measure of the relationship between light and dark tones in an image; the greater the difference between light and dark tones, the greater the contrast, eventually producing a high-contrast image. A histogram reveals a low-contrast image when the frequency-of-occurrence values are closely clustered together. Two or more distinct clusters of values reveal a high-contrast. A shadow adds contrast between two objects with similar tones. Contrast makes the image of objects distinguishable from one another and the background.

Read more about this:
O'Rourke, Michael, *Principles of Three-Dimensional Computer Animation*

CONTRE-JOUR A French term meaning *against daylight*, referring to the kind of image created when the camera is pointing directly toward the source of light and the subject is strongly backlighted.

This effect hides details and produces a stronger contrast between light and dark, creating silhouettes and emphasizing outlines of shapes. The sun, or other bright light source, is seen as a bright spot or strong glare behind and surrounding the subject. Sometimes fill light is used to bring out some detail on the side of the subject facing the camera.

Adrian Pingstone (1970)

CONTROL CURVE Also called *TCB controller*; a curve used to specify the motion of an animated object. See also **TCB CONTROLLER**.

CONTROL HANDLE A small square icon at the end of a line segment that is attached to an anchor point and used to modify the shape of a curve; sometimes called *control handle line* and *direction point*. Dragging the control handle to a new position changes the direction and length of the control handle line, which in turn changes the shape of the curve at the anchor point.

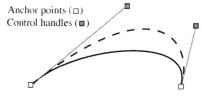

Anchor points (□)
Control handles (■)

CONTROLLED DEFORMATION A shape-modifying technique in 3D modeling and animation; for example using a **CONTROL SKELETON**.

CONTROL POINTS A set of points that defines the shape of certain kinds of curves and surfaces, among them Bézier, NURBS,

and b-spline. Moving, adding, or deleting a control point changes the shape of the curve or surface. Control points are assigned weights, scalar values used to refine the shape of a curve or surface.

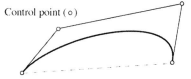

Control point (o)

Read more about this:
Giambruno, Mark, *3D Graphics and Animation*
Mortenson, Michael E., *Geometric Modeling*
_____, *Mathematics for Computer Graphics Applications*
O'Rourke, Michael, *Principles of Three-Dimensional Computer Animation*
Watt, A. and M. Watt, *Advanced Animation and Rendering Techniques*

CONTROL POLYGON Also called a *characteristic polygon*; a polygon formed by connecting in order the control points of a Bézier curve with straight lines. See also **CHARACTERISTIC POLYGON**.

Read more about this:
Mortenson, Michael E., *Geometric Modeling*

CONTROL SKELETON A set of links and joints associated with a 3D model in such a way that their motion is transformed into the motion and shape deformation of the model.

CONVEX A surface that is rounded outward from a solid body, without depressions; a localized bump or raised area on a surface; an outwardly curving surface, as in some lenses; the opposite of concave.

CONVEX HULL In 2D space, equivalent to the convex polygon produced by stretching a rubber band over the vertex points of a concave polygon or polyline. A convex polygon is identical to its convex hull. In 3D space, the convex hull is equivalent to the polyhedron produced by stretching a rubber sheet over a concave polyhedron. A convex polyhedron is identical to its convex hull. Notice, for example, that a Bézier curve is always contained within the convex hull of its control points.

A set of points in space also has a convex hull, again, whose equivalent is produced by stretching a rubber sheet over them. For a concave polyhedron, one or more points will lie inside the convex hull. No point in a set lies outside the convex hull of the set.

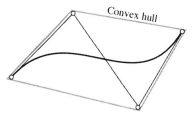

Convex hull

Read more about this:
Mortenson, Michael E., *Mathematics for Computer Graphics Applications*
Watt, A. and M. Watt, *Advanced Animation and Rendering Techniques*

COOKIES Also called *cucoloris* or *gobos*; a device used between a light source and a subject to throw a special light pattern or shadow; used to create a more natural look by breaking up the light from a man made source. For example, cookies can be used to simulate the movement of passing shadows or the light coming through a leafy canopy.

Read more about this:
Birn, Jeremy, [digital] *Lighting & Rendering*

COORDINATES A set of three numbers that locate a point within a reference grid, or co-ordinate system and represent distances along three independent axes from their intersection point.

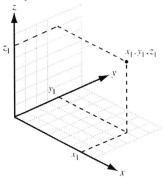

COORDINATE SYSTEM A 3D reference grid parallel to three mutually perpendicular lines, called the *coordinate axes* whose intersection is the origin of the system. 3D models are constructed with respect to some coordinate system. Many overlapping coordinate systems are required to model a complex object or scene. For example, in constructive solid geometry, each primitive is defined in its own local coordinate system

and then combined with other primitives in the world coordinate system to form a more complex object.

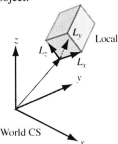

World CS

Some animation effects are also driven within a local coordinate system. The complete modeled object is then placed into a scene coordinate system, which is just another world coordinate system, and in which it can be further animated and even partially rendered.

A coordinate system has either a right-handed or left-handed orientation. Imagine grasping the z-axis with your right hand, its thumb aligned in the positive z direction. For a right-hand coordinate system, your fingers will curl in a manner that brings the x-axis into the y-axis. If not, then it is a left-hand coordinate system.

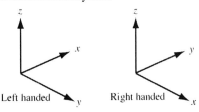

Left handed   Right handed

Other coordinate systems include the view coordinate system, the picture-plane coordinate system, and the display coordinate system, which consists of two parts: a window and a viewport. All of these coordinate systems are mathematically related to one another through the modeling program. Even though the interactive techniques available in most 3D modeling systems make it easy to work with these inter-related coordinate systems (they are often transparent to the user), it is to the user's advantage to have some understanding of their underlying relationships.

Read more about this:
Mortenson, Michael E., *3D Modeling, Animation, and Rendering*
_____, *Mathematics for Computer Graphics Applications*

COORDINATE SYSTEM TRANSFORMATION
A mathematical procedure for changing the frame of reference from one coordinate system to another; for example, from the world coordinate system to the screen coordinate system. In the figure, the point **p** has different coordinates, depending on the coordinate system in which they are measured.

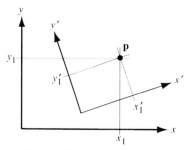

Read more about this:
Mortenson, Michael E., *Geometric Transformations for 3D Modeling*
_____, *Mathematics for Computer Graphics Applications*

COPLANAR Having a common plane. Points in space are coplanar if they all lie in the same plane. Three distinct points are always coplanar; but four points in space are not necessarily coplanar.

CORNER RADIUS The blending of two edges at a vertex of a polygonal shape with a circular arc, or the blending of two planar faces meeting along the edge of a polyhedral shape with a cylindrical surface.

CORONAE A diffraction effect producing pale colored rings around the full (or nearly full) moon when it is seen through a thin veil of altocumulus clouds.

Shows best in color edition.

COVERING SHOT A shot where one character blocks another from the camera's view. In the image, the view of one character is partially covered by another.

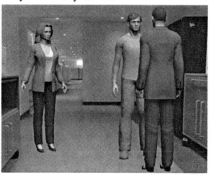

4film,making.com, (no date).

CRACKING PROBLEM The appearance of unwanted gaps in the surface of a rendered object caused by the independent subdivision and polygonization of adjacent patches on a surface, easily avoided by using a uniform patch subdivision scheme.

CRACKS Breaks in a material or surface without complete separation. Cracks occur in natural materials, such as rock, when internal stresses build up beyond the strength of intermolecular bonds, producing a pattern of cracks or fissures radiating from a nodal point and separated by about 120°. The crazing in pottery glaze forms a 90° pattern of cracks. Appropriate patterns of cracks rendered in graphics images of rocks, pottery, and similar objects produce realistic effects of aging.

CRANE SHOT A shot taken by a camera mounted on a crane, to view the actors from above or to move up and away from them; a common way of ending a movie. Directors like to have the camera on a boom arm to make it easier to move around actors and objects in a scene. Crane shots are easily simulated in animation scenes.

A crane shot from the film *High Noon*
(www.depauw.edu/acad/ film/Dictionary).

CREPUSCULAR RAYS Shadows cast in the twilight sky after sunset or just before sunrise by clouds or mountains beyond the horizon. The effect of perspective makes them appear to fan out from their point of origin. The image shows crepuscular shadows cast by clouds at sunset.

Gordon Richardson (1999). Shows best in color edition.

Read more about this:
Naylor, John, *Out of the Blue*

CROP To remove parts of a graphics image at its boundaries so that it fits within a frame. This works in much the same way as to mask, except that everything outside the cropped area is deleted, not just masked. See also **CLIP** and **CLIPPING**.

CROP MARKS A notation used to indicate where artwork is to be trimmed; used in printing and film.

CROSS-CUTTING An editing technique used in films to establish continuity. In a cross-cut, the camera cuts away from one action to another action. Because the shots occur rapidly, one after another, cross-cutting suggests simultaneous actions. Cross-cutting can also be used to establish a relationship between actions that do not occur simultaneously. Suspense is built by using cross-cutting. It is built through the expectation that it creates and in the hope that it will be explained with time. Cross-cutting also forms parallels; it illustrates a narrative action that happens in several places at approximately the same time. The length of time between cross-cuts can set the tone of a scene. Increasing the rapidity between two different actions adds tension to a scene. D. W. Griffith's The Birth of a Nation released in 1915 made this technique famous.

CROSS-DISSOLVE A compositing technique in which two images are blended together. Fade-in and fade-out are special instances of cross-dissolve.

Read more about this:
O'Rourke, Michael, *Principles of Three-Dimensional Computer Animation*

CROSS SECTION A plane that intersects a 3D object to reveal internal details, producing a 2D profile curve; or a construction plane used to create 2D cross-sectional curves that determine the shape of an object.

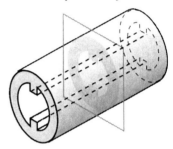

CROWD A group of people, often having a common purpose, such as at a political rally, a sports event, or simply going about their business in an urban setting. Crowd movement is situation-dependent; for example, a crowd marching in a political demonstration moves differently from a crowd scattering from the advances of an enraged bull in a market square. Crowd scenes in animated productions must account for mood and motivation or the dynamics will not be convincing to the viewer.

CSG The acronym for **CONSTRUCTIVE SOLID GEOMETRY**.

CUBE A common geometric primitive in constructive solid geometry (CSG). An instance of a cube is defined by specifying its edge length, location, and orientation. The cube is also one of the five regular polyhedra, having six identical square faces. It has eight vertices, 12 edges, and three faces surround each vertex. The sum of the face angles at each vertex is 270°.

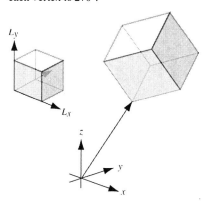

Read more about this:
Mortenson, Michael E., *Geometric Modeling*
_____, *Mathematics for Computer Graphics Applications*

CUBIC POLYNOMIAL An algebraic equation of the third degree; for example,

$$x(u) = au^3 + bu^2 + cu + d$$

Read more about this:
Mortenson, Michael E., *Geometric Modeling*

CUBIC SPLINE A curve that is commonly expressed as a cubic polynomial function of an independent parametric variable.

$$\mathbf{p}(u) = \mathbf{a}u^3 + \mathbf{b}u^2 + \mathbf{c}u + \mathbf{d}$$

where $\mathbf{p}(u)$ is the position vector of any point on the curve and $\mathbf{a}$, $\mathbf{b}$, $\mathbf{c}$, and $\mathbf{d}$ are the vector representatives of the scalar algebraic coefficients. The components of $\mathbf{p}(u)$ correspond to the Cartesian coordinates of a point on the curve.

Read more about this:
Mortenson, Michael E., *Geometric Modeling*

CUCOLORIS In animation and rendering, a device for casting shadows to produce patterned illumination. Cucolorises differ from gobos in that they are placed farther away from the lighting instrument and, therefore, do not need to be as heat resistant. Their shadow edges tend to be softer. Gobos are used when a well-defined edge is needed for a silhouette or projected object

In the image, a cucoloris placed in front of a bright light source casts a pattern of soft shadows.

flickr.com, P. Archer (2009). Shows best in color edition.

See also **GOBOS** and **COOKIES**.

CULLING Eliminating polygonal faces of a model whose normals point away from the camera or viewer. These faces are called *backfacing polygons*. They are eliminated, or culled, from the rendering process because they will not be visible.

Read more about this:
O'Rourke, Michael, *Principles of Three-Dimensional Computer Animation*
Watt, A. and M. Watt, *Advanced Animation and Rendering Techniques*

CURRENT FRAME NUMBER An integer number identifying the currently displayed frame of an animation sequence in play. Frames are numbered sequentially in the order they play. A frame number can be used as a control parameter for various animation elements.

CURVATURE A quantitative property of a curve at any point, $\mathbf{p}_i$, on it. The curvature $1/\rho_i$ at $\mathbf{p}_i$ is

$$\frac{1}{\rho_i} = \frac{\left| \mathbf{p}_i^u \times \mathbf{p}_i^{uu} \right|}{\left| \mathbf{p}_i^u \right|^3}$$

where ρ_i is the *radius of curvature*. We also use κ to denote curvature, where $\kappa = 1/\rho$ and curvature is measured in the osculating plane along the principal normal vector $\mathbf{n}_i$.

CURVE The path of a point moving through space with one degree of freedom. There are many variations on the idea of a curve as a path of one dimension. These kinds of definitions help to impart an intuitive sense of a curve, but they are most valuable if they lead to analytical expressions that are manipulated so that the shape of a curve can be easily changed and analyzed.

In 3D modeling the most useful curves so far are the Hermite, Bézier, B-spline, and NURBS, all of which have natural extensions to surfaces. The NURBS curve is the most general of these, with the B-spline curve a special form and the Bézier and Hermite yet further specializations. All are based on parametric equations that are usually cubic polynomials. Other algebraic forms of representing a curve are intrinsic equations, explicit equations, natural equations, and implicit equations.

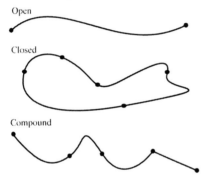

A curve can be open or closed, single or compound. An open curve has two distinct end points, with no break or gap between them along the curve. A closed curve is continuous and without end points. A compound curve is two or more curves joined together at end points to form an open or closed curve.

Read more about this:
Mortenson, Michael E., *Geometric Modeling*
O'Rourke, Michael, *Principles of Three-Dimensional Computer Animation*

CURVES ON SURFACES A surface provides a two-dimensional space suitable for supporting the representation of curves. The two parametric variables defining the surface also serve to supply the coordinate grid on which embedded curves can be defined.

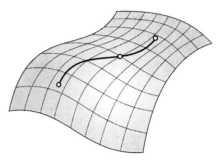

Read more about this:
Mortenson, Michael E., *Geometric Modeling*

CURVILINEAR PERSPECTIVE a graphical projection used to draw 3D objects on 2D surfaces. The system uses curving perspective lines instead of straight converging ones to approximate the image on the retina of the eye, which is itself spherical, more accurately than the traditional linear perspective, which uses straight lines and becomes distorted at the edges of an image.

CUT To divide a curve, surface, or solid into separate segments along an intersection curve or surface; an edited version of a film, as in the *final cut*; a small segment of an animation or film sequence that forms a meaningful part of the whole production; a recorded segment of a work; a stop-action command in the filming or recording of a scene, or an abrupt end to the view from one camera to the view from another camera. When a series of cuts are made over short time intervals a montage of images is produced. A rapid sequence of cuts is often used to communicate action and excitement. *Jump cut, cutaway, cross-cut, match cut,* and *cutting-on-action* are variations on this.

Read more about this:
Giambruno, Mark, *3D Graphics and Animation*

CUT-AWAY SHOT A shot where the camera rapidly, if not instantaneously, switches from one view to another. This rapid transition can be uncomfortably disconcerting for the viewer if not justified by the action or emotional impact sought by the director. The *buffer shot, cross-cut, dissolve* (film-making), *fast cut, jump cut, match cut, shot-reverse-shot, slow cut,* and *flashback* are related techniques.

CUTTING ON ACTION A film editing technique where the editor cuts from one shot to another that matches the first in action and energy. Even though the shots may have been taken hours apart, cutting on action gives a viewer the impression of a continuous action sequence. By having a subject begin an action in one shot and carry it through to completion in the next, the editor creates a visual bridge, distracting the viewer from noticing the cut or noticing any slight continuity error between the two shots.

A variation of this is a cut in which the subject exits the frame in the first shot and then enters the frame in the subsequent shot. The entrance in the second shot should match the screen direction and pace of the exit in the first shot.

In the film *Last Year at Marienbad*, Alain Resnais experiments with this technique, to connect scenes set in different times and places. For example, in this film there is a shot of a large hall in which an actor turns her head, then the editor cuts to the next shot where the same actor finishes her head turn, but now she is seen standing in a completely different room. This sequence creates a sense of blurred space and time. The technique can be used to create similar effects in animation.

CUTTING PLANE A modeling tool for cutting an object into separate parts; a plane whose intersection with a 3D model determines a cross-section view.

CYLINDER A common geometric primitive in constructive solid geometry (CSG): usually a right circular cylinder. An instance of a cylinder is defined by specifying its height, radius, location, and orientation. See also **CYLINDRICAL SURFACE**.

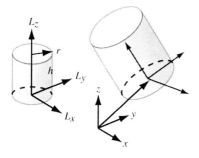

Read more about this:
Mortenson, Michael E., *Geometric Modeling*
_____, *Mathematics for Computer Graphics Applications*
O'Rourke, Michael, *Principles of Three-Dimensional Computer Animation*

CYLINDRICAL COORDINATES A system of coordinates for locating a point in 3D space, consisting of three numbers: a radial distance, r, from the z-axis, an angle θ measured counterclockwise from the x-axis and in the xy-plane, and a distance z.

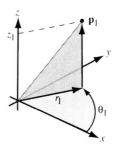

Read more about this:
Giambruno, Mark, *3D Graphics and Animation*
Mortenson, Michael E., *Mathematics for Computer Graphics Applications*

CYLINDRICAL PERSPECTIVE The effect of fisheye and panoramic lenses which project straight horizontal lines above and below the lens axis level as curved while reproducing straight horizontal lines on lens axis level as straight. This is also a common feature of wide-angle anamorphic lenses of less than 40mm focal length in cinematography. The image below is from a high-performance energy-efficiency building façade study, Lawrence Berkeley National Lab.

Lawrence Berkeley National Lab

CYLINDRICAL PROJECTION MAPPING A multi-directional technique for mapping an image or texture onto the surface of an object. A suitably sized cylindrical mapping tool is positioned around the object, and an image on its surface is projected inward and onto the object's surface.

Read more about this:
O'Rourke, Michael, *Principles of Three-Dimensional Computer Animation*
Watt, A. and M. Watt, *Advanced Animation and Rendering Techniques*

CYLINDRICAL SEGMENT A common primitive in constructive solid geometry (CSG) systems; a segment of a circular cylinder. An instance of a cylinder is defined by specifying its height, radius, and wedge angle.

CYLINDRICAL SURFACE A surface generated by moving a straight line (the *generatrix*) parallel to itself along a plane curve (the *directrix*):

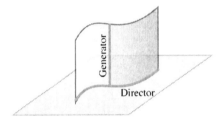

Read more about this:
Mortenson, Michael E., *Geometric Modeling*

D

DAMPING FORCE The reduction over time in the magnitude of the reaction of an object to natural forces. For example, the height of each succeeding bounce of a ball is less than the preceding bounce. Each collision converts some energy into heat, so less is available as kinetic energy for each succeeding rebound. In animation, objects responding to forces in this way appear more realistic. See also **BOUNCE.**

Read more about this:
Mortenson, Michael E., *3D Modeling, Animation, and Rendering*

DANGLING EDGE A curve or line artifact produced by the Boolean combination of 2D or 3D objects. The resulting object is not dimensionally homogeneous. That is, the object consists of parts not all the same dimension. Here a dangling edge is produced by the intersection of two 2D shapes. Such dimensional inhomogeneities can be detected and eliminated in a process called *regularization*.

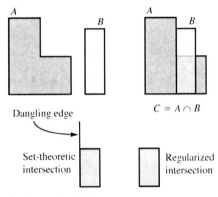

Read more about this:
Mortenson, Michael E., *Mathematics for Computer Graphics Applications*

DAYLIGHT See **OUTDOOR LIGHT**.

DAZZLE To impair vision by intense light, or by less intense light when perceived by dark-adapted eyes; sudden bright light scattered within the eye, making it difficult to see details clearly.

Read more about this:
Naylor, John, *Out of the Blue*

DECAL A localized texture map masked for placement as a top-layer detail on a surface; an image that can be scaled and moved around on the surface of an object independently of any other texture mapping.

Read more about this:
Birn, Jeremy, [digital] *Lighting & Rendering*
Giambruno, Mark, *3D Graphics and Animation*

DECAY See *distance falloff.*

DECORATIVE SYMMETRY Repetitive patterns that occur in two different ways in 2D, the frieze group and the wallpaper group.

Read more about this:
Mortenson, Michael E., *Geometric Transformations*

DEEP FOCUS A filmmaking technique producing a long range of focus, so that all of a scene appears sharp and clear; the foreground, middle ground, and background are all in focus; equivalent to a high *f*-stop number in photography where both near and far objects are in focus. The deep focus shot from Orson Welles' *Citizen Kane* brings all elements of the scene into sharp focus (1941).

Orson Welles' *Citizen Kane* (1941)

Deep focus requires adequate light and small aperture. It is possible to create the illusion of deep focus by compositing two images, where it is the aperture of the physical or virtual camera lens that determines the depth of field. Wide-angle lenses also make a larger portion of the image appear sharp. The aperture of a camera determines how much light enters through the lens.

DEFAULT ACTION A modeling, animating, or rendering operation that is invoked automatically in the absence of specific user instructions.

DEFAULT LIGHTING The startup settings for lighting in a 3D rendering program, allowing the user to begin work on a scene without first having to define a customized lighting scheme.

Read more about this:
Giambruno, Mark, *3D Graphics and Animation*

DEFOCUS A camera effect produced by refocusing the lens to a point nearer or beyond the primary object of attention. Most rendering software can emulate the defocus effect.

farm4.stratic.flickr.com, Kevin (2009)

DEFORMATION GRID A geometric construction used to change the shape of a 3D model in certain constrained ways. Typically, the designer embeds a preliminary geometric model within a flexible 3D grid so that a deformation imposed on the grid is passed on to the model through its control points. See also **LATTICE**.

 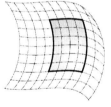

Read more about this:
Giambruno, Mark, *3D Graphics and Animation*
Mortenson, Michael E., *3D Modeling, Animation, and Rendering*
_____, *Geometric Transformations for 3D Modeling*
O'Rourke, Michael, *Principles of Three-Dimensional Computer Animation*
Watt, A. and M. Watt, *Advanced Animation and Rendering Techniques*

DEFORMATION MAP See **DISPLACEMENT MAP**.

DEFORM MODIFIER A technique used to control transformation settings that change the cross-sectional shape of an object as it sweeps along a path.

DEGREE ELEVATION Adding another control point to the definition of a Bézier curve raises its degree by one. Degree elevation allows a designer to increase control of a curve's shape. Usually the extra control point is added in a way that does not initially effect the shape of the curve. Any of the control points can be moved, including the new addition, to alter the curve's shape.

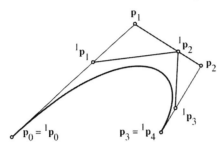

Read more about this:
Mortenson, Michael E., *Geometric Modeling*

DEGREE REDUCTION Removal of a control point on a Bézier curve, reducing its polynomial degree. However, approximations by a reversal of the degree-elevation process are possible under special circumstances. Such a procedure is useful in certain intersection computations and rendering.

Read more about this:
Mortenson, Michael E., *Geometric Modeling*

DEGREES OF FREEDOM (DOF) The number of independent variables needed to describe the positions of all the joints and links of an articulated object or mechanism; the number of independent variables available to describe a geometric shape.

Read more about this:
Mortenson, Michael E., *Geometric Modeling*
O'Rourke, Michael, *Principles of Three-Dimensional Computer Animation*
Watt, A. and M. Watt, *Advanced Animation and Rendering Techniques*

DEMO A non-interactive multimedia presentation or demonstration.. The main goal of a demo is to demonstrate or audition programming, artistic, and musical skills. The key difference between a classical animation and a demo is that the display of a demo is computed in real time, making computing power considerations a big challenge. Demos are mostly composed of 3D anima-

tions mixed with 2D effects and full screen effects.

DEMOSCENE A computer-art subculture that specializes in producing *demos*, which are non-interactive audio-visual presentations that run in real-time on a computer.

DENSITY MAP A mathematical function that assigns a value to each point in 3D space, usually related to the distance of the point from the source of the field, which may be a point or a more complex geometric shape; used in metaball modeling; sometimes called *density field*. A set of points having the same value within a density field defines an isosurface.

Many objects cannot be modeled as surfaces. Examples are clouds and fog. However, they can be modeled using density maps. A density map is a function that gives the density of an object at any point in it. The higher the density at a particular place, the more opaque or solid appearing is the object at that point. Clouds, for example, can be modeled using a fractal density map, with the bulk of the cloud of moderate density and opaque, and the less dense, wispy edges extending out of low-density regions. Fog usually is modeled using a constant density map or one that decreases with height.

Read more about this:
O'Rourke, Michael, *Principles of Three-Dimensional Computer Animation*

DENT A localized shape-changing transformation operating on an object's bounding surface, producing a dent-like concavity.

DEPTH How deep a ray tracing tree proceeds before halting, an index of the level of recursion. For example, if the ray tracer is set to halt after completing a trace depth of two, then it follows the ray through two reflections and refractions and halts. Higher ray trace depths produce a more realistic image but take more time to render it. In most rendering cases, after a few reflections and refractions, the intensity of the rays becomes so low that further ray tracing produces very little effect on the total value. Trace depths of five usually produce realistic pictures. A ray trace depth of zero is the equivalent to ray casting.

DEPTH CUEING A rendering technique used to affect depth perception by dimming scene elements that are farther away from the viewer.

DEPTH CUES Using color, light, and shadows to create an impression of three-dimensionality and enhance the perception of spatial relationships. Warm-colored objects appear closer than cool-colored objects.

DEPTH MAP Also known as *z-depth*.

DEPTH OF FIELD The near- and far-distance limits along the camera's line-of-sight within which objects in the field of view are in focus. The type of lens and the focal-plane settings with respect to the distance of the object from the lens determine the characteristics of the object's image. Light from a point source at the correct distance produces the sharp image of a point on the film or view plane. The image of a point closer or farther away than this distance appears as a disk, whose border is known as the *circle of confusion*. The diameter of this circle increases with distance from the point of focus and can be used as a measure of error.

If a pin-hole-camera model is used, as is common in computer graphics, then the images of all the objects in a scene are rendered in sharp focus on the image plane, independent of their distance from the camera. Depth-of-field computation may be part of the ray tracing process, in which case the lens is treated as another object in the scene and positioned to intercept and affect the rays.

Read more about this:
Giambruno, Mark, *3D Graphics and Animation*
O'Rourke, Michael, *Principles of Three-Dimensional Computer Animation*
Watt, A. and M. Watt, *Advanced Animation and Rendering Techniques*

DEPTH-OF-FIELD BLUR Defocusing of elements in a scene based on their distance from the camera.

DESATURATION Using less saturated colors in a scene to give the impression of darkness without underexposure and loss of action details.

DESIGN IN CONTEXT To design or modify a part within a mechanical assembly of previously modeled parts while that assembly is displayed and can be referenced during the design.

DESIGN TREE A record of a model-building process, listing the geometric elements (primitives) their connectivity, order of construction, and auxiliary constraints and features; used in constructive solid geometry and feature-based modeling.

DETACH A solid modeling command to separate two attached objects, forming two distinct and disjoint objects.

DETAIL SHOT Closer and showing more detail than a close-up shot.

DETERMINANT A square array of elements that reduces to a single value by following a well-defined procedure. Determinants facilitate many vector and matrix operations. However, a matrix must be square to have a determinant, and not every square matrix is associated with a determinant.

For a two-dimensional array,

$$\mathbf{A} = \begin{bmatrix} a_{11} & a_{12} \\ a_{21} & a_{22} \end{bmatrix}, \text{ the determinant is given}$$

by $|\mathbf{A}| = \begin{vmatrix} a_{11} & a_{12} \\ a_{21} & a_{22} \end{vmatrix} = a_{11}a_{22} - a_{12}a_{21}$.

For a three-dimensional array,

$$\mathbf{A} = \begin{bmatrix} a_{11} & a_{12} & a_{13} \\ a_{21} & a_{22} & a_{23} \\ a_{31} & a_{32} & a_{33} \end{bmatrix}, \text{ the determinant is}$$

given by

$$|\mathbf{A}| = a_{11}\begin{vmatrix} a_{22} & a_{23} \\ a_{32} & a_{33} \end{vmatrix}$$

$$-a_{12}\begin{vmatrix} a_{21} & a_{23} \\ a_{31} & a_{33} \end{vmatrix} + a_{13}\begin{vmatrix} a_{21} & a_{22} \\ a_{31} & a_{32} \end{vmatrix}$$

Read more about this:
Mortenson, Michael E., *Mathematics for Computer Graphics Applications*

DIAGONAL MATRIX A square matrix that has zero elements everywhere except on the main diagonal. For example,

$$\mathbf{A} = \begin{bmatrix} a_{11} & 0 & 0 & 0 \\ 0 & a_{22} & 0 & 0 \\ 0 & 0 & a_{33} & 0 \\ 0 & 0 & 0 & a_{44} \end{bmatrix}$$

Thus, $a_{ij} = 0$ if $i \neq j$. If all the a_{ii} are equal, then the diagonal matrix is a *scalar matrix*.

A diagonal matrix that has unit elements on the main diagonal is a *unit matrix* or *identity matrix*:

$$\mathbf{I} = \begin{bmatrix} 1 & 0 & 0 \\ 0 & 1 & 0 \\ 0 & 0 & 1 \end{bmatrix} = \delta_{ij}$$

where δ_{ij} is the *Kronecker delta*.

Read more about this:
Mortenson, Michael E., *Mathematics for Computer Graphics Applications*

DIFFERENCE OPERATOR A Boolean operator in constructive solid geometry (CSG), which subtracts the shape of one object from the shape of another.

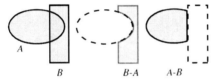

Read more about this:
Giambruno, Mark, *3D Graphics and Animation*
Mortenson, Michael E., *Geometric Modeling*
_____, *Mathematics for Computer Graphics Applications*
O'Rourke, Michael, *Principles of Three-Dimensional Computer Animation*

DIFFERENTIAL SCALING Subjecting a 3D model to different scaling along different axes. A uniform scaling transformation of the cube on the left produces the two central shapes. Nonuniform scaling produces the two rightmost shapes.

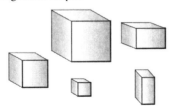

Read more about this:
Mortenson, Michael E., *Geometric Modeling*
_____, *Mathematics for Computer Graphics Applications*

DIFFRACTION The bending of light waves around objects in their path. Waves are modulated when passing the edge of an opaque object, redistributing the energy in the wave front. This phenomenon is often detectable by the presence of extremely narrow light and dark bands at the edge of a shadow. Water waves also exhibit diffraction effects when passing an obstruction. The image shows an intersecting diffraction pattern as waves pass between a promontory and islands.

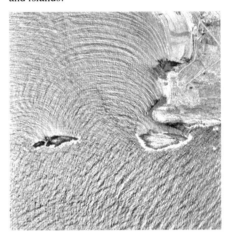

Read more about this:
Naylor, John, *Out of the Blue*

DIFFUSE The scattering of light off a rough surface. Most real surfaces are not perfect reflectors; they are rough and therefore scatter light. The strongest scattering occurs when the surface is perpendicular to the incident light, and a light-to-dark gradient is observed. *Diffuse interreflection* is a phenomenon where light reflects from one object and strikes other objects in the scene, lighting them indirectly. In 3D computer graphics, it is an important component of global illumination. There are a number of ways to model diffuse interreflection when rendering a scene, for example, using radiosity and photon mapping. See also **DIFFUSE SURFACE**.

DIFFUSE COLOR The color of light reflected off a diffuse surface when the object is illuminated by a direct light source.

Read more about this:
Giambruno, Mark, *3D Graphics and Animation*

DIFFUSE MAP A technique used to change an object's previously assigned color into a pattern or image.

Read more about this:
Birn, Jeremy, [digital] *Lighting & Rendering*
Giambruno, Mark, *3D Graphics and Animation*
Watt, A. and M. Watt, *Advanced Animation and Rendering Techniques*

DIFFUSENESS A measure of how much light is reflected off a surface, computed on a scale from zero to one, where zero diffuseness means that none of the light falling on a surface is reflected and the object appears black. See also **REFLECTIVITY**.

Read more about this:
O'Rourke, Michael, *Principles of Three-Dimensional Computer Animation*
Watt, A. and M. Watt, *Advanced Animation and Rendering Techniques*

DIFFUSE SURFACE A surface that reflects light in all directions. A perfectly diffuse surface reflects light equally in all directions, in contrast to a specular surface that is shiny and reflects like a mirror. A diffuse spherical surface is on the left, and a specular spherical surface is on the right.

Read more about this:
Watt, A. and M. Watt, *Advanced Animation and Rendering Techniques*

DIGITAL CINEMA A combination of live action and animation in a digital format, using 3D modeling, digital image processing, and compositing; using digital storage and display instead of film. Digital cinema also refers to the use of digital technology to distribute and project motion pictures. A movie can be distributed via hard drives, optical disks or satellite and projected using a digital projector instead of a conventional film projector.

DIGITAL COMPOSITING Digitally combining several images to make a final image; used for print, motion pictures, animation, and graphics display.

DIGITAL FILM RECORDER A hardware device using a laser beam to expose film to varying intensities of brightness and color to record a computer-generated animation sequence.

DIGITAL IMAGING Also called *computer imaging*.

DIGITIZING The process of recording the surface geometry of a real object in a digital format that modeling, animation, and rendering applications can manipulate. A device scans the object, and determines the relative coordinates of a large set of points on it. Curves and surfaces are then fit to these points. Images of the internal structure of organisms and mechanisms, mechanical drawings, and sound may also be digitized, using somewhat different processes.

DIMENSION A quantitative measure of some geometric feature of an object, such as length or diameter, an integer number describing the geometric or mathematical space of an object or state, a non-integer number describing a property of a fractal object.

DIORAMA A 3D scene using images, pictures, and objects setup in front of a 2D background; a small three-dimensional representation of a scene; a picture (or series of pictures) representing a continuous scene.

DIRECTIONAL LIGHT A light source used in rendering to simulate a distant light source, like the sun, so that its rays are assumed to be parallel and of equal intensity everywhere in a scene. All shadows are cast in the same direction.

Read more about this:
Giambruno, Mark, *3D Graphics and Animation*
O'Rourke, Michael, *Principles of Three-Dimensional Computer Animation*

DIRECTION LINE Also called *control handle*.

DIRECTION POINT Also called *control handle*.

DIRECT LIGHT Light that propagates in a straight line from its source to the surface it illuminates; usually more intense and produces sharper shadows and brighter reflections than indirect light.

DIRECTOR A line or curve along which a generator shape is moved to produce a 3D solid, sometimes called a *directrix*; a person who plans and directs the performance and filming of a motion picture.

DIRECTRIX See **DIRECTOR**.

DIRT A surface detail simulating localized or global effects such as smudges, scratches, stains, wear, the patina of aging, and so forth; a special decal used to add a dirty or used look to the surface of an object.

Read more about this:
Demers, Owen, [digital] *Texture & Painting*

DISJOINT Separate or unconnected, having no common elements. Two disjoint curves are also said to be *discontinuous*.

DISPERSION An effect caused by the change in direction of a beam of light passing through a transparent medium. The most familiar example of dispersion is a rainbow, where dispersion causes the spatial separation of white light into components of different wavelengths or colors. Another example is the rainbow spectrum of light formed by passing it through a glass prism.

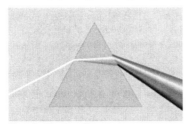

Shows best in color edition.

DISPLACEMENT MAP A grayscale image applied to the surface of an object, whose defining mesh is locally displaced in the direction of the surface normal, changing the appearance of the surface geometry . Lighter grayscale values at a point move the surface outward along the normal and darker values move it inward. This technique is often used to create terrain models.

Displacement mapping is an alternative to bump mapping, normal mapping, and parallax mapping, where the actual geometric position of points over a surface are dis-

placed, according to the value a texture function assigns to at each point on the surface. It gives surfaces a realistic sense of depth and detail, and permits self-occlusion, self-shadowing and silhouettes. However, it has high computation requirements.

Read more about this:
Giambruno, Mark, *3D Graphics and Animation*
O'Rourke, Michael, *Principles of Three-Dimensional Computer Animation*

DISPLAY COORDINATE SYSTEMS A related set of two- and three-dimensional coordinate systems required to compute a displayed image. This set includes the local coordinate system, the global or world coordinate system, the view coordinate system, the picture-plane coordinate system, and the window, viewport, and screen coordinate systems. These systems account for an object's size, shape, location, orientation, and spatial relationships to other objects in a scene.

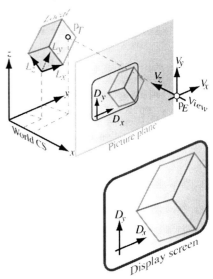

Read more about this:
Mortenson, M. E., *Mathematics for Computer Graphics Applications*

DISPLAY GEOMETRY Addresses such factors as the pixel environment, coordinate system transformations, clipping, and projection transformations.

DISPLAY RESOLUTION The pixel dimensions, for example, 1280x720, of a display device. This does not directly describe the visual resolution of a digital image that is actually displayed, where the resolution is given in pixels per inch. See **DOTS PER INCH**.

DISPLAY VIEW The view shown on the computer graphics monitor, not necessarily the camera view or rendered frame. The display view changes at the direction of the modeler during the course of model construction, as needed, to visualize the model-creation process.

DISSOLVE In film editing, gradual transition from one image to another, using fade-out and fade-in techniques, created by controlled double exposure from frame to frame. Below, the initial image of a circle slowly dissolves and the image of a triangle emerges.

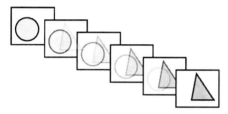

DISTANCE FALLOFF The rate of decrease of light intensity with increasing distance from a light source. In the real world, intensity is inversely proportional to the square of the distance from the source. The light intensity at 10 meters from a light source is four times greater than that at a distance of 20 meters. See also **ATTENUATION AND INTENSITY**.

DISTANCE FOG A technique used in 3D computer graphics to enhance the perception of distance by simulating fog. Using a fog gradient, objects further from the camera are progressively more obscured by haze and by aerial perspective, simulating the effect of light scattering. This also has the effect of reducing the light and color contrast between distant objects.

DISTORTION An effect on an image caused by a camera lens, projector, or projection computations that appears as a deviation from linear and planar features in a scene to curvilinear edges and concave or convex surfaces in the image. The image shows optical distortion caused by a light pattern passing through curved wine glasses. See also **BARREL DISTORTIO**n and **PINCUSHION DISTORTION**.

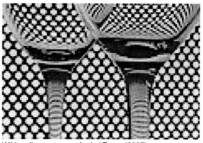
Wikimedia commons, Andrei Toma (2007)

DISTRIBUTE OBJECTS Used by some modeling and illustration applications to place selected objects automatically and uniformly along some specified axis or other geometric reference. See also **DISTRIBUTE SPACING**.

DISTRIBUTE SPACING Used by some modeling and illustration applications to arrange a group of selected objects so that they are automatically and uniformly placed along some line or curve, over some area, or within some region of space. See also **DISTRIBUTE OBJECTS**.

DITHER A way to approximate extra colors within an 8-bit color system by using two colors in adjacent pixels to create the illusion of a third color; a method to reduce high-resolution 2D image data to lower precision, using positional information to preserve as much information as possible. In image processing, dithering is used to reduce multi-level grayscale images to fewer and fewer levels, and ultimately to just black and white, while giving the illusion or appearance of retaining many shades of gray. The objective of dithering is to distribute gray levels uniformly throughout an image matrix, which acts as a filter to select and assign black or white values to pixels.

DIVIDE A Boolean-like operator that partitions overlapping shapes into distinct regions. The divide operation uses a combination of the union and difference operators.

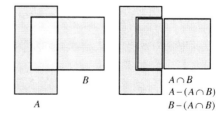

DODECAHEDRON The dodecahedron is one of the five regular polyhedra, having 12 identical pentagonal faces. It has 20 vertices, 30 edges, and three faces surround each vertex. The sum of the face angles at each vertex is 324°.

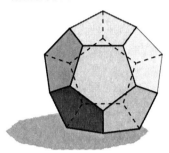

Read more about this:
Mortenson, M. E., *Mathematics for Computer Graphics Applications*

DOLLY A camera motion directly toward (dolly in) or away from (dolly out) the subject; a wheeled platform used in filmmaking on which a camera is mounted, as well as the process of moving the camera around on the dolly during live-action filming. In rendering software, it indicates camera movement toward, away from, or around a subject as though the camera is mounted on a dolly.

Dolly is not the same as zoom. Zoom-in and zoom-out are photographic effects of lens adjustments to magnify the image and can result in distorted perspective, which may or may not be desirable.

Read more about this:
Mortenson, Michael E., *3D Modeling, Animation, and Rendering*

DOLLY SHOT Any shot from a camera mounted on a wheeled support; a moving shot that uses a camera mounted on a wheeled platform known as a dolly; any shot taken while the camera moves through space. Dolly shots are usually smoother than a hand-held shot.

There are several types of dolly shots:

1. Character dolly: used to focus attention on a character in a scene.

2. Pull-back reveal: used to show the complete scene.

3. Depth dolly: used to emphasize the depth of a scene as characters move toward or away from the camera.

4. Expand dolly: used to follow a character moving away, with the camera moving more slowly.

5. Contract dolly: used for dramatic effect, with the camera and character moving toward each other.

Read more about this:
Mortenson, Michael E., *3D Modeling, Animation, and Rendering*

DOLLY ZOOM An in-camera special effect that attempts to unsettle normal visual perception. This effect is created by adjusting the field of view of a zoom lens while the camera moves toward or away from the subject, in a way that keeps the subject the same size within the frame. In its classic form, the camera is pulled away from a subject while the lens zooms in, or vice-versa, creating a continuous perspective distortion. The most apparent visual effect is that the background appears to change size relative to the subject.

Read more about this:
Mortenson, Michael E., *3D Modeling, Animation, and Rendering*

DOMINANT CONTRAST The difference between the lightest and darkest parts of a scene.

DOT PITCH The diagonal distance between phosphor dots on a computer graphics monitor measured in millimeters (mm). It is an important characteristic, where a smaller dot pitch indicates a higher-quality image. For a color monitor, dot pitch ranges from about 0.15 mm to 0.30 mm. It is sometimes referred to as *phosphor pitch.*

DOTS PER INCH Or *dpi*, quantifies the resolution of an image; equivalently, pixels per inch; the smallest individual element of controllable phosphor on a computer graphics monitor; the smallest element of ink deposited by a printer.

DOUBLED SHADOW Improperly compositing the effect of overlapping shadows from the same light sources. Instead of a uniform shadow effect, the overlap area appears darker.

DOUBLE EXPOSURE Two images exposed on the same frame of film, producing of superposition; also called DX. Below is a NASA image of an Apollo 8 Saturn launch double exposed, or superimposed, on the image of a crescent moon, which was neither visible nor in that phase during the launch (1968).

NASA (1968)

DOWNSAMPLE To decrease the overall pixel dimensions of an image; related to *resample up* and *resampling*. This reduces the amount of information in an image, producing lower resolution.

DPI See **DOTS PER INCH**.

DROP-OFF The variation in light intensity with distance from the central beam of a directed light source; related to **DISTANCE FALLOFF**.

DUCTS Highly constrained shapes used in solid modeling in mechanical CAD; hollow thin-walled tubes of rectangular or circular cross section.

DUST A modeling and rendering element, simulating dust particles suspended in the atmosphere or deposited on surfaces.

Read more about this:
Demers, Owen, [digital] *Texture & Painting*

DUTCH ANGLE A camera orientation to a scene used to portray the psychological uneasiness or tension in the subject being filmed. A Dutch angle is achieved by tilting the camera so that the shot is composed with the horizon at an angle to the bottom of the frame. The 1949 film *The Third Man* makes extensive use of Dutch angle shots, to emphasize the main character's alienation in a foreign environment.

A Dutch angle shot from *The Third Man* (1949)

DYNAMICS The analysis of an object's motion resulting from forces applied to it.

E

EASE–IN, EASE–OUT Keyframe parameters that control the rate of change (acceleration or deceleration) of an animation element as it is successively imaged between keyframes. Spline curves can be shaped to provide the desired control and interpolations. Here is a simple example.

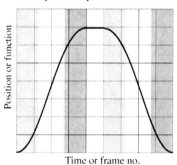

Ease in: speeding up
Ease out: slowing down

An exterior elevator rises up the side of a high-rise hotel. At first it slowly gains speed (accelerates), rises at a constant rate, and then slows down (decelerates) and stops. It is stationary while passengers enter and leave. Then it begins its descent to the ground floor, slowly gaining speed until it reaches a constant rate, and then slowing to a stop. The curve in the image below represents this process.

Read more about this:
Giambruno, Mark, *3D Graphics and Animation*
O'Rourke, Michael, *Principles of Three-Dimensional Computer Animation*

EASES Also known as *ease–in* and/or *ease-out*.

ECCENTRIC DENSITY FIELD A mathematical function used to produce nonspherical iso-surfaces in metaball models; a special kind of *density field*.

EDGE A line segment joining two vertices of a polygon or polyhedron.

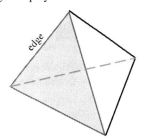

EDGE-BASED RENDERING Model geometry and rendering based on polygon edges, rather than the polygons themselves, where polygon surface information and direction are obtained from the edge data. This method of geometry database construction and rendering is transparent to the user.

Read more about this:
Watt, A. and M. Watt, *Advanced Animation and Rendering Techniques*

EDIT GROUP A command that allows the user to alter all members of a pre-selected group in the same way; for example, to translate all objects in a group the same distance and direction.

EDIT POINT A type of control point used to alter the shape of a curve; for NURBS curves called a *knot*.. See also **NON-UNIFORM RATIONAL B-SPLINE CURVE**.

EDITING The process of selecting and sequentially assembling the scenes created and rendered during production, joining them into a cohesive whole. Film editing is the process of selecting and joining together shots, connecting the resulting sequences,

and ultimately creating a finished motion picture.

Read more about this:
Giambruno, Mark, *3D Graphics and Animation*
O'Rourke, Michael, *Principles of Three-Dimensional Computer Animation*

EFFECTS PASS One of several separate rendering passes whose purpose is to achieve a visual or mask effect. See also **RENDERING IN PASSES**.

EFFICIENCY A measure of computation speed and memory usage, achieving a cost effective balance between maximum speed and minimum memory. For example, in ray tracing, speed depends on efficient computation, using techniques such as Bounding Volume Hierarchy (BVH) and other effective data structures.

ELASTIC DEFORMATION A temporary shape change to an object that is self-reversing after a deforming force is removed, so that the object returns to its original shape. See also **ELASTICITY**.

Read more about this:
Mortenson, Michael E., *3D Modeling, Animation, and Rendering*

ELASTICITY A physical property of a material object that determines how easily it is deformed by stretching, bending, or compressing and still returns to its original shape. A ball with high elasticity bounces higher than one with lower elasticity. A bouncing ball or any colliding objects undergo what is called *elastic deformations*, temporary shape changes that are self-reversing after the deforming forces are removed. Accounting for this in animating collision events enhances the reality of the scene. See also **PLASTIC DEFORMATIONS**.

ELLIPSE A closed conic curve; the locus of points each of whose combined distance from two given fixed points (foci) is constant.

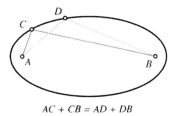

$$AC + CB = AD + DB$$

ELLIPSOID An ellipsoid is the three-dimensional equivalent of an ellipse. Just as an ellipse looks like a squashed circle, an ellipsoid looks like a squashed sphere. An ellipsoid is a quadric; its equation in the standard form when centered at the origin is

$$\frac{x^2}{a^2} + \frac{y^2}{b^2} + \frac{z^2}{c^2} = 1$$

The quantities a, b and c may be thought of as "radii" of the ellipsoid along the x, y, and z axes. A sphere is a special case of an ellipsoid with $a = b = c$ = radius.

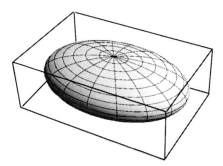

EMBEDDED CURVE See **CURVES ON SURFACES**.

EMBOSS A rendering technique applied to text or 2D objects, creating a raised effect by using edge shadows and highlights. Each pixel of an image is replaced either by a highlight or a shadow, depending on light and dark boundaries on the original image. A gray background replaces low contrast areas.

EMITTER A simple polygonal shape that acts as a source of particles in a particle system.

Read more about this:
Mortenson, Michael E., *3D Modeling, Animation, and Rendering*
O'Rourke, Michael, *Principles of Three-Dimensional Computer Animation*

END EFFECTOR The free end of the last, or driving, link in a mechanism. When the mechanism or animated object is controlled by inverse kinematics, all other links and joints are moved via geometric transformations (translation and rotation) to accommodate the motions applied to the free end. In robotics, an end effector is the device at the end of a robotic arm, designed to interact with the environment. The exact nature of this device depends on the application of the robot. See also **ROOT**.

Read more about this:
O'Rourke, Michael, *Principles of Three-Dimensional Computer Animation*
Watt, A. and M. Watt, *Advanced Animation and Rendering Techniques*

ENVIRONMENTAL PRIMITIVE Standard environmental elements such as clouds, fire, fog, and smoke. Each environmental primitive has a unique set of properties and controls.

ENVIRONMENTAL REFLECTION MAPPING A specialized technique for efficiently representing an object's surroundings such that from it an image can be produced and mapped onto the object's surface to make it shiny and highly reflective, such as a mirror, glass, or water, and to give the appearance of reflecting the scene surrounding it. This technique is not as accurate as ray tracing, but is much faster. The object is temporarily placed "inside" a mapping cube or sphere on whose surfaces a simplified rendition of the object's general environment has been created, which is then projected onto the object's surface.

Read more about this:
Watt, A. and M. Watt, *Advanced Animation and Rendering Techniques*

EPS Acronym for *encapsulated postscript* file, a common graphics image format. This image format produces high-resolution graphics when printed.

ESTABLISHING SHOT A wide shot, relative to those immediately following, introducing the audience to the surrounding elements and background of a scene; for example, a shot framing a group of racing sailboats tacking around a buoy, preceding a series of medium and close-up shots of deck activity on a specific sailboat. See also **SHOT SIZE**

EULER ANGLES A system developed by the eighteenth century Swiss mathematician Leonhard Euler to describe the rotational relationship between two three-dimensional Cartesian coordinate systems. Let one coordinate system be the reference frame, and the other the rotated frame. The two systems share the same origin, and the intersection of the xy and XY planes define the line of nodes N. α is the angle between the x-axis and the line of nodes. β is the angle between the z-axis and the Z-axis. γ is the angle between the line of nodes and the X-axis.

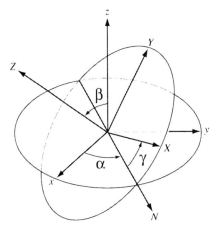

Euler angles are one of several ways of specifying the relative orientation of two such coordinate systems. Moreover, different authors may use different sets of angles to describe these orientations, or different names for the same angles, leading to different conventions.

Read more about this:
Mortenson, Michael E., *3D Modeling, Animation, and Rendering*
_____, *Geometric Transformations for 3D Modeling*

EULER'S FORMULA States a mathematical relationship between the number of vertices, edges, and faces of a polyhedron. For any simple polyhedron, this law states $V - E + F = 2$. To apply Euler's formula, certain conditions must be met:

1. A single ring of edges must bound each face, with no holes in the faces.

2. The polyhedron must have no holes through it.

3. Each edge is shared by exactly two faces and is terminated by a vertex at each end.

4. At least three edges must meet at each vertex.

An extended version of the formula includes terms defining topological connectivity, accounting for holes or "handles." It is expressed as $V - E + F = 2 - N$, where N is the so-called *genus* of the polyhedra. For example, $N = 0$ for a sphere, $N = 2$ for a torus, and $N = 4$ for a solid figure eight.

Read more about this:
Mortenson, Michael E., *Geometric Modeling*
— — —, *Mathematics for Computer Graphics Applications*

EXAGGERATION The amplification of motion or emotion in an animated scene. The degree of exaggeration is largely an artistic judgment call. Too much exaggeration becomes unintentionally comedic, too little may cause a scene to fall far short of its potential impact.

EXCLUDE Setting up lighting that affects only specified objects by excluding the few that are to be left unaffected; the opposite of an include control that is used when only a few are affected by the controlled light setting; also, the complement of the Boolean operator intersect.

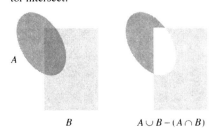

Read more about this:
Mortenson, Michael E., *3D Modeling, Animation, and Rendering*

EXCLUSIVE LIGHTS Also called *light linking*.

EXCLUSIVITY Also called *color exclusivity*.

EXPLICIT EQUATION OF A CURVE An algebraic form for representing a curve, whose general expression is $y = f(x)$. In this form there is only one y value for each x value. Consequently, it cannot represent closed or multiple-valued curves. This limitation is avoided by using an implicit equation.

Read more about this:
Mortenson, M. E., *Geometric Modeling*

EXPLODED VIEW A view of an assembly of parts shown disassembled in an organized way that preserves some geometric constraints, such as collinearity; used to highlight some feature of an assembly not otherwise readily apparent.

EXPLOSION MODEL A simulation created and rendered using particle system methods.

Read more about this:
O'Rourke, Michael, *Principles of Three-Dimensional Computer Animation*

EXPOSURE The amount of time a camera's shutter allows light to reach the film, directly effecting the brightness and contrast of a shot; effects the quality of motion captured; an effect simulated by graphics programs in rendering 3D scenes. When the shutter is open too long or not long enough **OVEREXPOSURE** or **UNDEREXPOSURE** is the result.

Read more about this:
Birn, Jeremy, [digital] *Lighting & Rendering*

EXPOSURE LATITUDE The acceptable range of brightness for a specific photographic film, may be simulated in digital animation rendering.

EXPOSURE SHEET A chart or graph of timing and frame-count relationships, used in traditional animation and some computer animation applications.

EXTREME CLOSE-UP A shot that fills a frame with extremely fine detail of the subject, such as just the eyes of a character, or dew drops on a rose petal. See also **SHOT SIZE**.

EXTREME LONG SHOT A wide-angle shot taken from a long distance, often used as an establishing shot.

EXTRUDE A highly constrained solid modeling operation defined by translating a fixed or variable cross section along a straight line, producing what is called an *extrusion*.

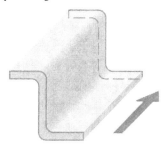

Note that the cross section does not change its rotational orientation along the path, while the cross section of a sweep may change its orientation, remaining in a plane perpendicular to the sweep path. Moving a fixed 2D shape along a straight line to create a 3D volume forms the simplest kind of extrusion.

If the path is a curve twisting through space instead of a straight line, then something like a sweep or swept solid is produced. The 2D shape, or cross-section, itself may vary in some predetermined way along the length of the path. The extruded object can be combined with other objects to form even more complex forms.

Read more about this:
O'Rourke, Michael, *Principles of Three-Dimensional Computer Animation*

EYE COORDINATE SYSTEM Also called *view coordinate system*.

EYE-LEVEL SHOT A camera position set at eye level.

EYE POINT Location of the viewer's eye or the virtual camera within a 3D scene, in the world coordinate system; the camera position or view reference point.

Read more about this:
O'Rourke, Michael, *Principles of Three-Dimensional Computer Animation*
Watt, A. and M. Watt, *Advanced Animation and Rendering Techniques*

EYE POSITION Framing a shot so that the subject's eyes are given priority; also *eyeroom*. Good composition frames the eyes in a position about one third of the way down from the top of the frame and almost never allows them to be framed below the centerline.

F

FACE The plane area enclosed by a circuit of edges of a polygon.

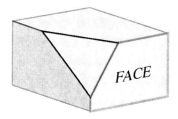

FACE EXTRACTION To copy a selected face from a polygon-based model.

FACE EXTRUSION To sweep a selected polyhedron face to modify the shape of the underlying model.

Read more about this:
Giambruno, Mark, *3D Graphics and Animation*
O'Rourke, Michael, *Principles of Three-Dimensional Computer Animation*

FACE MAPPING To apply a texture to faces of a polygon-based 3D model.

Read more about this:
Giambruno, Mark, *3D Graphics and Animation*

FADE A camera and rendering action that causes an image to fade to a blank screen. See also **DISSOLVE**, **FADE-IN**, and **FADE-OUT**.

FADE-IN, FADE-OUT Special forms of a cross-dissolve: a fade-in is a cross-dissolve from a black screen to the next sequence of images; a fade-out is a cross-dissolve from an animation sequence to a blank screen. See also **FADE**.

FALLOFF The decrease in light intensity with increasing distance from the light source. Lighting systems with ellipsoidal lenses do not lose as much intensity as other types of lenses with increasing distance from the source. Most of their radiation remains parallel and tends to cast hard shadows. This kind of light is said to have *throw*. See also **DECAY** and **DISTANCE FALLOFF**.

FALSE-COLOR LIGHTS Used to analyze and differentiate the individual effect of multiple light sources lighting a subject or scene, where each light source, in turn, is temporarily assigned a different bold, easy to identify color.

FAST CUTTING A film editing technique that refers to several consecutive shots of a brief duration (about 3 seconds). Fast cutting is used to convey information very quickly, or to indicate energy or chaos. Its opposite is **SLOW CUTTING**.

FAST MOTION An effect produced when film runs through a camera at slower than normal speed; also called accelerated motion; the opposite of slow motion. When the film is projected at the standard rate, action on the screen appears more rapid than it would in actual life. In time-lapse photography each film frame is captured at a rate much slower than it will be played back. When replayed at normal speed, time appears to be moving faster and thus lapsing. Time-lapse photography can be considered to be the opposite of high-speed photography. Time-lapse is the extreme version of the cinematography technique of undercranking, and can be confused with stop motion animation.

FEATHERING To delicately merge two differently colored areas across a common border; a technique used in computer graphics to smooth or blur the edges of a feature. The term is inherited from a technique of fine retouching using fine feathers.

FEATHERSTONE'S ALGORITHM A technique used to compute the effect of forces applied to a system of joints and links, such as a skeleton used in ragdoll physics.

FEATURE-BASED MODELING To create a 3D model of an object using standard mechanical shapes and geometric characteristics, such as plain holes, threaded holes, slots, bosses, and fillets.

FEATURE-BASED SOLIDS See **FEATURE-BASED MODELING**.

FIELD OF VIEW (FOV) Everything that can be seen through a camera lens (real or virtual), similar to the cone of vision of the human eye, given as an angle measured in degrees; the area defined by the camera's angle of view at a given distance from its lens. When we look at some object or group of objects, we cannot see other objects that are too far to the right or left, or too far above or below our focus of attention. These objects are outside our cone of vision or outside our field of view.

The screen of a computer graphics display monitor or cinema screen is normally rectangular, its field of view is the frustum of a pyramid. The angle subtended by the top and bottom edges of the screen with the presumed position of a viewer's eye is the field-of-view angle. A large angle produces a distorted perspective of the image, and a small angle produces a flattened image. A sophisticated rendering program allows the user to adjust this angle to achieve a desired effect. Other factors affecting the field –of-view include *clipping* algorithms, the *clipping plane*, the *offscreen space*, and the *view volume*.

The image shows the angle of view of a camera, including horizontal, diagonal, and vertical.

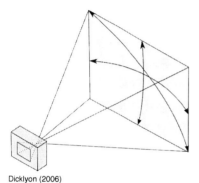

Dicklyon (2006)

Read more about this:
Giambruno, Mark, *3D Graphics and Animation*
O'Rourke, Michael, *Principles of Three-Dimensional Computer Animation*

FIF The acronym for **FRACTAL IMAGE FORMAT.**

FILL A texture or color inside a closed two-dimensional curve or path; to paint the area within a closed boundary with color or texture. If a boundary curve is open, a straight-line boundary is assumed between its end points.

FILLET SURFACE A curved transition surface between two plane surfaces that is specified by its radius of curvature.

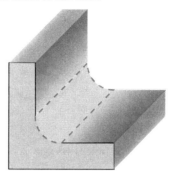

FILL LIGHT Also called *rim light*, a light source used to fill in dark areas of a scene, usually dimmer than the key light; minimizes or eliminates the effect of shadows cast by the key light source, and reduces contrast.

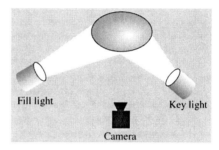

Fill light is usually softer and, by definition, less intense than the key light. The ratio between light and shadow depends on the desired effect. For example, a fill light that is a small fraction of the power of the key light will produce very high-contrast or low-key lighting, while filling with half or more of the key light power will produce a high key, low-contrast tone.

An alternative to using a direct light source as a fill is to re-direct or "bounce" the key light towards the subject by using a reflector.

Read more about this:
Birn, Jeremy, [digital] *Lighting & Rendering*
Giambruno, Mark, *3D Graphics and Animation*

FILTER A gel or other transparent or translucent material used to alter the color of light to achieve color balance or other effects.

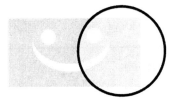

Read more about this:
Demers, Owen, [digital] *Texture & Painting*

FINAL CUT The final edited version of a movie as approved by the director and producer. See **OUTTAKES**.

FINITE ELEMENT ANALYSIS A computational method that subdivides an object into very small but finite-size elements, called the finite element model. Each element is assigned a set of characteristic equations (describing mechanical and other properties, boundary conditions, and imposed forces), which are then solved as a set of simultaneous equations to predict the behavior of the object. Smaller (and consequently more) finite elements produce a more accurate results. This technique is most often used for structural analysis, but is also broadly applicable to other types of analysis, including, hydrodynamic analysis, thermodynamic analysis, and computational fluid dynamics.

FINITE-ELEMENT MODEL (FEM) A specialized model specifically constructed for the purpose of *finite element analysis*.

FIRE PRIMITIVE A standard environmental primitive, fire modeling may include controls for the following characteristics: number of flames, size, base color, tip color, opacity, pattern, and edge appearance. There is great variation in the behavior of fire and in the way it is modeled. Texture and particle systems are two of the ways this can be done. Applying a fire-simulating texture to a model is fast and less computationally demanding than a particle system representation, which is more realistic but also more computationally demanding.

Read more about this:
O'Rourke, Michael, *Principles of Three-Dimensional Computer Animation*

FIRST VERTEX The reference vertex used for orientation of a shape during skinning operations.

FIX To shoot a scene without camera motion.

FLASH To desaturate color and reduce levels of black by exposing certain elements on film to more light; to add a small amount of an averaged color of a background plate to a foreground object to blend and unify tone over a scene.

FLASH ANIMATION An animated film created using Adobe Flash animation software and often distributed in the .swf file format. It can be created in Flash or with other programs capable of writing .swf files.

FLASHBACK A shot showing action that took place prior to the film's present.

FLASHFORWARD A shot showing action that takes place in the future of the film's present.

FLAT AREA LIGHT An area light source with a flat or planar shape, such as a rectangle or circular disc, simulating light from a ceiling or wall panel, for example. See also **LINEAR LIGHTS** and **SPHERICAL AREA LIGHT**.

FLAT PATTERN The surface of a 3D object laid out in a plane. Only some surfaces may be developed and represented this way. A rectangular box and a cone are examples. However, a sphere has no flat pattern equivalent.

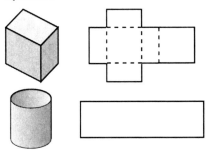

FLAT SHADING A rendering method that produces a uniform color over each polygon face, producing a faceted appearance, because colors are not blended (shaded) across the common edge between adjacent faces where each may be slightly different because of lighting and shading effects. This produces flat, unrealistic pictures with no gradation in tone across a polygonal surface. This method is fast and often used in computer-aided design applications where photorealism is not a necessary factor. The flat-shaded polygonal bunny shows these effects.

B. Cutler, Rensselaer Polytechnic Institute (no date.).

Read more about this:
Giambruno, Mark, *3D Graphics and Animation*

FLEX A shape-changing transformation acting on an object's geometric model through an embedding deformation grid that produces bending-type deformations.

FLOCKING An animation function used to simulate the patterns of movement of large groups of animals, where functions and controls include collision avoidance, velocity matching, and flock centering. The term *flocking* applies specifically to birds. Other animals exhibit analogous behavior, with its own terminology: insects swarm, fish shoal or school, cattle herd or stampede, and so forth.

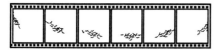

Read more about this:
O'Rourke, Michael, *Principles of Three-Dimensional Computer Animation*
Watt, A. and M. Watt, *Advanced Animation and Rendering Techniques*

FLOODLIGHT A light source giving uniform illumination over a large area.

FLUID FLOW EFFECTS Animation techniques used to simulate streamline flow, eddies, and turbulence, and based on computational fluid dynamics.

FOCAL BLUR A ray tracing method used to model camera lens effects in which objects in focus are sharp but those out of focus are blurred.

Wikipedia, Gilles Tran (2006). Shows best in color edition.

Focal blur at a pixel is modeled by distributing rays over the area of the lens (placed in front of the camera), tracing the rays after refraction through the lens, and averaging the intensities obtained. It is simulated in the computer-generated image of glasses and dice in the image below.

FOCAL LENGTH The distance from the center of a lens to its image plane (or focal plane), which is perpendicular to the axis of the lens. In photography a longer focal length, or lower optical power, is associated with a larger image magnification of distant objects, or a narrower angle of view. Conversely a shorter focal length, or higher optical power, is associated with a wider angle of view.

Read more about this:
Giambruno, Mark, *3D Graphics and Animation*

FOCOLTONE A custom color space consisting of 763 CMYK colors, designed to minimize prepress trapping and registration problems when printing color illustrations.

FOG An atmospheric effect that mutes color and blurs the image of a distant object, available in a variety of special effects; for example, z-depth fog and horizontal fog. Vertical or layered fog is used to obscure the images of objects relative to their location in the y-direction, or height; for example, obscuring the tops of mountains more than their lower slopes. Volumetric fog is used to obscure the images of objects within a geometrically confined beam of light, including randomizing fog density. The image is an example of atmospheric rendering that includes the effect of distance and density variation in a foggy scene.

Jeffwofford.com (2008). Shows best in color edition.

Read more about this:
Giambruno, Mark, *3D Graphics and Animation*
Naylor, John, *Out of the Blue*
O'Rourke, Michael, *Principles of Three-Dimensional Computer Animation*

FOG BOW An almost colorless rainbow formed when sunlight illuminates a patch of fog; often seen as an arc of dense fog along the edge of a fog bank; sometimes called a *white rainbow*.

National Science Foundation, P. West (no date)
Shows best in color edition.

The diameter of the water droplets making up the fog is too small for refraction effects to produce the complete and precise spectrum of colors in an ordinary rainbow. Instead light scattered by the small droplets produces weak overlapping colors, resulting in a hazy white bow rather than the more colorful rainbow. Mist bows and clouds bows are also colorless and produced by the effect of sunlight shining on very small water droplets.

Read more about this:
Naylor, John, *Out of the Blue*

FOG PRIMITIVE A standard environmental primitive, fog modeling may include controls for the following characteristics: dispersion or patchiness, color, opacity, and edge appearance.

FOLEY ARTIST A specialist who creates the synchronized sound effects for an animation sequence.

Read more about this:
Giambruno, Mark, *3D Graphics and Animation*
O'Rourke, Michael, *Principles of Three-Dimensional Computer Animation*

FOLLOW SHOT A filming technique where the camera moves with the subject.

FOLLOW THROUGH Ending an action and establishing its relationship to the next action; also known as *overlapping action*.

FOREGROUND The nearest objects in the current display of a 3D-modeling scene or rendering relative to the viewer or camera.

FORESHORTENING To distort the geometric elements of a 3D model that are not parallel to the picture plane to convey the illusion of three-dimensional perspective; the apparent reduction in size of surfaces in linear perspective. Those parts of an object that are closer to a viewer look proportionately larger.

Google Images (no date).

The cartoon sketch shows a figure leaping toward the camera or viewer. The hands appear much larger than normal and the feet much smaller because the animator is using exaggerated perspective or foreshortening.

FORGING A highly constrained shape-defining technique used in CAD/CAM solid modeling, based on and to implement a manufacturing process of the same name.

FORWARD KINEMATICS A method for controlling the movements of an articulated object (that is, an object comprised of several interconnected movable parts: joints and links), in which the movement of one part affects all of the links and joints along the chain between it and the end effector, the free end of the last link; sometimes called *keyframe animation*.

The end effector's motion is the accumulation of all the motions of the upstream links. For example, in a model of the arm, a rotation of the upper arm about the shoulder joint propagates down through the forearm and wrist to the fingertips; and the animator must define all these joint motions. As the number of links increases, the complications of their interaction and control may swiftly exceed the ability of an animator to orchestrate them. In animation this difficulty is in part offset by the added degrees of freedom available to express the character's attitude and personality. **INVERSE KINEMATICS** propagates motions in the opposite direction along a chain of links.

Read more about this:
Giambruno, Mark, *3D Graphics and Animation*
Mortenson, Michael E., *3D Modeling, Animation, and Rendering*
O'Rourke, Michael, *Principles of Three-Dimensional Computer Animation*
Watt, A. and M. Watt, *Advanced Animation and Rendering Techniques*

FOUR-UP VIEW Side-by-side display of four versions of a graphics rendering or sequence of animation frames. The *two-up view* is another way to display and review the results of animation sequences and rendering passes. Here are four different renderings of an explosion.

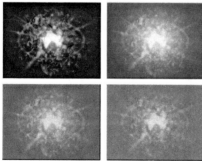

Shows best in color edition.

FRACTAL A mathematical and geometric form based on the principal of self-similarity at all scales; fractal surfaces are most successfully used to model certain land and plant forms, as well as water, waves, and turbulence, because they capture both form and texture whether viewed from a distance or close up. Here the first steps in the construction of a fractal shape.

Benoit Mandelbrot was the first to use the term, naming both the class of formal mathematical objects he was instrumental in discovering, and the identification of these forms in nature. Here is an example: a fractal landscape.

Copyright K. Musgrave (1998). Shows best in color edition.
Read more about this:
Barnsley, Michael, *Fractals Everywhere*
Mandelbrot, Benoit B., *The Fractal Geometry of Nature*
O'Rourke, Michael, *Principles of Three-Dimensional Computer Animation*
Watt, A. and M. Watt, *Advanced Animation and Rendering Techniques*

FRACTAL CURVE A curve or curve segment generated by an iterative process of subdivision and repetition of self-similar segments. This example uses an equilateral triangle.

Read more about this:
Barnsley, Michael, *Fractals Everywhere*
Mandelbrot, Benoit B., *The Fractal Geometry of Nature*

FRACTAL IMAGE FORMAT (FIF) A commercial graphics file format, using fractal geometry to compress images.

FRAME In filmmaking or computer animation, any single still image that is part of a sequence of images; a *cel*; also, the visible portion of a scene that is viewed through a camera or viewport.

Read more about this:
Mortenson, Michael E., *3D Modeling, Animation, and Rendering*
O'Rourke, Michael, *Principles of Three-Dimensional Computer Animation*

FRAME RATE The speed at which film, video, or animated image frames are advanced and displayed, and measured as frames per second.

Read more about this:
Birn, Jeremy, [digital] *Lighting & Rendering*

FRAMING The art of positioning subjects within the borders of an image, creating and taking advantage of *positive* and *negative space*, graphic emphasis (called *graphic weight*), and long-standing rules-of-thumb, such as the *rule of thirds*. Positive space includes that part of the image filled by the main subject or objects. Negative space is the area filled by the background and minor objects. An image showing a character looking to the left may have more negative space to that side, a situation called *look space* or *nose space*.

The graphic weight of an object or character is a somewhat subjective measure of how much it dominates a scene and attracts a viewer's attention. The rule of thirds suggests imagining the image frame divided by lines into thirds both horizontally and vertically, and then positioning the principle subject or area of focus along one of these lines. The *aspect ratio* determines the overall framing format. For framing formats, see also **ASPECT RATIO**.

Read more about this:
Birn, Jeremy, [digital] *Lighting & Rendering*

FRAMING FOR TELEVISION Adapting widescreen images with aspect ratios of 1.85 or 2.35 to the standard video format whose aspect ratio is 1.33, requiring some form of the letterbox technique. The original full-size film or digital image is displayed, as well as a black area above and below to fill in the television screen format.

FREE FORM DEFORMATION (FFD) A shape-changing technique based on deforming a three-dimensional lattice or grid constructed and positioned to contain the geometric model of the object whose shape is to be changed. The image shows the deformation of a cone embedded in a three-dimensional lattice, which transfers its deformation to the cone.

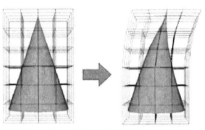

Digital Human Research Center (no date)

A model's shape-defining control points are locked into the lattice so that deformations of the lattice are automatically passed on to the model, producing bumps, dents, bends, twists, or other complex modifications of the model's shape. The modeler must consider the size and shape of the region to be deformed, the shape of the transition boundary between the deformed region and the original adjacent surface, as well as the position of the deformed region on the surface.

Lattices are used to create and confine deformations to a limited region of the model or to deform the entire model, distinguished as local or global deformations, respectively. An animator or modeler can produce global free-form deformations by embedding a model in a 3D parametric space whose deformations are passed on to the model. The advantage of these FFDs is a greatly simplified way of changing the shape of a model without resorting to direct manipulation of its many control points. See also **SOFT OBJECT ANIMATION**.

Read more about this:
Watt, A. and M. Watt, *Advanced Animation and Rendering Techniques*

FREE FORM SURFACE A surface whose shape is not constrained by classical analytical forms (such as conic surfaces), and which is defined by a set of control points (as with Bézier, B-spline, and NURBS surfaces).

Read more about this:
Mortenson, M. E., *Geometric Modeling*

FREEZE A command used during animation modeling or editing, allowing a selected object in a scene to remain visible but temporarily not editable; also called *ghost*. Some applications dim an object's image to indicate it is frozen. This makes it easier to work with other objects in a crowded scene.

FREEZE FRAME SHOT Used when a single shot is repeated over a sequence of frames, creating the illusion of a still photograph.

FREQUENCY The number of cycles per second of alteration of a light wave's amplitude; the number of waves contained within the distance light travels in one second. Frequency is the speed of light divided by the wavelength, that is: $f = c/\lambda$.

FRESNEL EFFECT The variation with viewing angle in the amount of light seen reflecting off a surface; for example, the view of a calm pond of water from directly above may reveal details on the bottom that are otherwise obscured by specularity and other reflections when seen at shallow viewing angles: pronounced "fre-nel", the "s" is silent.

Read more about this:
Watt, A. and M. Watt, *Advanced Animation and Rendering Techniques*

FRESNEL LIGHT A focusable spotlight used in film, television and theater settings.

FRESNEL SHADER A shading renderer that accounts for the viewing angle of a surface. See **FRESNEL EFFECT**

FRICTION EFFECTS In natural force behavior, the resistance of a surface to the relative motion between it and another surface; for instance, the sliding or rolling of a object moving along a given surface or through some medium, such as air or water. The energy lost is in the form of heat. Static friction prevents objects at rest from sliding down an inclined plane, unless the inclination angle is increased beyond a critical value, which in turn depends on the properties of the two contact surfaces. Kinetic

friction causes a moving object to stop its slide across a surface, taking more or less time depending on the surface properties.

Read more about this:
Mortenson, M. E., *3D Modeling, Animation, and Rendering*

FRIEZE A repeating decorative pattern lying in a band or strip on a plane or cylindrical surface; examples are found in architecture and industrial and decorative design, and illustration borders. There are only seven mathematically distinct frieze patterns. Here examples of each of these patterns.

F	F	F	F	F	F	F	F

⅃F	⅃F	⅃F	⅃F	⅃F	⅃F	⅃F	⅃F

Ⴀ	Ⴀ	Ⴀ	Ⴀ	Ⴀ	Ⴀ	Ⴀ	Ⴀ
F	F	F	F	F	F	F	F

⅃Ⴀ	⅃Ⴀ	⅃Ⴀ	⅃Ⴀ	⅃Ⴀ	⅃Ⴀ	⅃Ⴀ	⅃Ⴀ
⅂F	⅂F	⅂F	⅂F	⅂F	⅂F	⅂F	⅂F

⅂F	⅂F	⅂F	⅂F	⅂F	⅂F	⅂F	⅂F

⅂F	⅃Ⴀ	⅂F	⅃Ⴀ	⅂F	⅃Ⴀ	⅂F	⅃Ⴀ

	Ⴀ		Ⴀ		Ⴀ		Ⴀ
F		F		F		F	

Frieze patterns form what mathematicians call a symmetry group, meaning that they are not changed when subjected to a sequence of geometric transformations along the strip

Read more about this:
Mortenson, M. E., *Geometric Transformations*

FRINGING Refers to *blue spill*.

FRUSTUM A 3D volume, either a truncated cone conical or pyramid, used to define a view volume.

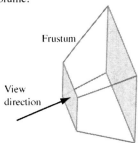

Frustum

View
direction

Read more about this:
Mortenson, Michael E., *3D Modeling, Animation, and Rendering*

F–STOP Indicates the aperture size of a camera, which controls exposure and depth of field: the higher the $f-$ stop, the smaller the size of the aperture and the greater the depth of field. Some 3D modeling and rendering applications simulate the effects of $f-$ stop control.

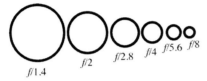

Read more about this:
O'Rourke, Michael, *Principles of Three-Dimensional Computer Animation*

FULL SHOT A shot whose subject fills the screen.

FUNCTION A mathematical expression whose value depends on the values assigned to its dependent variables. For example, $2x+1$ is a function of x. If $x=3$, then $2x+1=7$. The symbol $f(x)$ is a shorthand way to write the function of an independent variable x, so that if $f(x)=2x+1$, then

$$f(3)=7.$$

Read more about this:
Mortenson, Michael E., *Geometric Transformations*
———, *Mathematics for Computer Graphics Applications*

FUNCTION CURVE A graph of time-dependent transformations of a model or other time-dependent animation parameters; the graph of a function. Bézier curves are frequently used to control the rate of motion transformation or other scene elements between keyframes.

Read more about this:
Giambruno, Mark, *3D Graphics and Animation*
Mortenson, Michael E., *Geometric Transformations for 3D Modeling*

FUSE To collect a selected group of vertices together into a single vertex at a new location, locally changing the shape of the polyhedron mesh. Sometimes known as a *weld operation*.

FUSION The process of combining two overlapping metaballs to form a single shape. The final shape depends on how much fu-sion is specified. For example, two overlapping spheres may be fused into something like a 3D hourglass, or into something more like a capsule or lozenge.

Read more about this:
O'Rourke, Michael, *Principles of Three-Dimensional Computer Animation*

G

GAIN A video camera exposure control amplifying the imaging signal, affecting graininess and resolution.

GAME PHYSICS The introduction of the laws of physics into a simulation or game animation software, particularly in 3D computer graphics, adding to its realism. Usually it is only an approximation to real physics. Usually part of the standard software imposes the laws of Newtonian physics on the forces and motions of moving objects. Another part solves collision detection problems. Related methods include **PARTICLE SYSTEMS** and **RAGDOLL PHYSICS.**

GAMMA A monitor calibration parameter controlling the brightness of midtone values, defining a value halfway between black and white. Gamma adjustment compensates for the nonlinear tonal reproduction of output devices, defining the rate of change from light to dark tones.

GAMMA CORRECTION Adjustment of the brightness, contrast or color balance by assigning new values to the gray or color tones. Gamma correction can be either linear or nonlinear. Linear changes affect all tones, non-linear changes affect only areas tone by tone, like highlights, shadows, or mid-tones.

GAMUT The range of displayable colors for a particular graphics monitor (device gamut); the range of colors in an image. See also **COLOR SPACE**.

Read more about this:
Giambruno, Mark, *3D Graphics and Animation*

GAMUT MAPPING Adjusting the image gamut to lie within the device gamut.

GEL A transparent filter or substance placed between a light source and the illuminated object to create different shades or patterns when the scene and object are rendered, simulating the effects in movie making caused by celluloid filters placed over spotlights to change their color during filming. See also **COLOR GEL**.

GENERATOR An open or closed curve or 2D shape whose movement along some director curve or axis sweeps out a solid. In 3D modeling, if an open curve is used, then some thickness is specified for the resulting swept surface so that a solid object is produced.

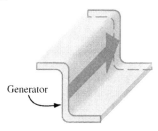

Generator

Read more about this:
Mortenson, Michael E., *3D Modeling, Animation, and Rendering*
O'Rourke, Michael, *Principles of Three-Dimensional Computer Animation*

GENERATRIX See *generator*.

GEOGRAPHIC INFORMATION SYSTEM (GIS) A computer graphics application that includes images, text, and quantitative information for applications in mapping, land use and planning, demographics, and civil engineering.

GEOMETRIC AREA LIGHT An area light whose shape is a specially created 3D model, such as that simulating a neon light bent into the shape of a letter of the alphabet. Specific effects include **FLAT AREA LIGH***t*, **LINEAR AREA LIGH***t*, and **SPHERICAL AREA LIGHT**.

GEOMETRIC CONTINUITY The degree of smoothness throughout a curve or surface or across a point joining two curves or across a curve common to two surfaces. Geometric continuity is defined in terms of the intrinsic differential properties of a curve or surface, such as the unit tangent vector and curvature. These properties are independent of the parameterization. Parametric continuity absorbs more degrees of freedom than geometric continuity. If the conditions producing parametric continuity are relaxed while maintaining geometric continuity, then ad-

ditional degrees of freedom become available to control the shape of a curve or surface, for example, beta-splines.

A curve or surface can be described as having G^n continuity, n being the increasing measure of smoothness. So with respect to conditions at a point between two curve segments:

If the segments just touch at their common point, then G^0 continuity is present.

If the segments touch and share a common tangent direction at the point, then G^1 continuity is present.

If, in addition to the two conditions above, the segments also share a common center of curvature, then G^2 continuity is present.

Surprisingly, to produce smooth reflections on a car body or other surface with similar aesthetic requirements, G^2 continuity is necessary. Structural and mechanical shapes may require G^1 and G^2 continuity to minimize stresses. Thus, the presence of various degrees of geometric continuity may be part of the design criteria for an object. See also **PARAMETRIC CONTINUITY**.

Read more about this:
Mortenson, Michael E., *Geometric Modeling*

GEOMETRIC ELEMENT A simple geometric construct, such as a point, line, plane, polygon, polyhedron, curve, surface, or sphere.

GEOMETRIC MODELING The mathematical representation of the curves, surfaces and other geometric elements that make up a 3D model. The geometric model includes the numerical data describing each element and the connectivity between elements of a 3D model. Its analytic form enables quantitative geometric properties and relationships to be computed. 3D modeling includes geometric modeling, with the addition of interactive graphics solid-model construction tools, as well as tools controlling model presentation and rendering.

Read more about this:
Mortenson, Michael E., *Geometric Modeling*

GEOMETRIC PRIMITIVE Also called **PRIMITIVE**.

GEOMETRIC RELATIONSHIP Quantitative or qualitative geometric information about two or more objects that answers the following types of questions: How far apart are two objects? Does object *A* fit inside object *B*? Can an object be moved through a group of other objects without interference? What point on object *A* is closest to object *B*?

Read more about this:
Mortenson, Michael E., *3D Modeling, Animation, and Rendering*
_____, *Geometric Modeling*
_____, *Mathematics for Computer Graphics Applications*

GEOMETRIC SOURCE LIGHTING An area light whose shape is a specially created 3D model, such as in simulating a neon light bent into the shape of a letter of the alphabet. See also **FLAT AREA LIGHT, LINEAR LIGHTS**, and **SPHERICAL AREA LIGHT**.

Read more about this:
Mortenson, Michael E., *3D Modeling, Animation, and Rendering*

GHOST See *freeze*.

GIF Acronym for Graphic Image Format, a common pixel-based image format used on the web using a 256-color palette (8-bit color) and features such as single-color transparency, interlacing, and animation capability. A GIF image incorporates the LZW lossless data compression method. Although the number of colors available for a GIF image is severely limited, this can be an advantage because it makes high data compression ratios possible.

Read more about this:
Giambruno, Mark, *3D Graphics and Animation*
O'Rourke, Michael, *Principles of Three-Dimensional Computer Animation*

GIS Acronym for **GEOGRAPHIC INFORMATION SYSTEM**.

GLOBAL COORDINATE SYSTEM Also known as the **WORLD COORDINATE SYSTEM**.

GLOBAL ILLUMINATION MODEL A rendering algorithm used to produce more realistic object and light interactions in a scene, including diffuse and specular effects. In a purely diffuse lighting situation, radiosity computation is the method of choice. In a purely specular lighting environment, ray tracing is the most effective method. Most scenes representing realistic settings contain aspects of both diffuse and specular lighting.

Read more about this:
Birn, Jeremy, [digital] *Lighting & Rendering*
Watt, A. and M. Watt, *Advanced Animation and Rendering Techniques*

GLOBAL REFLECTION MODEL A rendering process used to approximate the reflections seen on the surface of a shiny object of its surrounding environment. This process is faster and computationally cheaper than performing a long and complex ray tracing analysis.

Read more about this:
Giambruno, Mark, *3D Graphics and Animation*

GLOSS A quantitative reflection property of a surface (sometimes called the *gloss factor*),determining the proportion and directions of diffuse and specular reflections. For a perfect mirror the gloss factor equals one, and for a perfect diffusing surface, the gloss factor equals zero.

Five types of glossiness have been defined: specular, sheen, contrast, directness of image, and absence of bloom. Specular glossiness is the brightness of a highlight measured as the ratio of reflected to incident light intensity, ϕ_r/ϕ_i , measured at $60°$ from the normal to the surface for both incident and reflected light. Sheen is the brightness of a highlight measured at a glancing angle, $85°$ from the normal, or again ϕ_r/ϕ_i . Contrast gloss is also a measure of the relative brightness of a highlight at a glancing angle, $85°$ from the normal, but in this case given by ϕ_r/ϕ_n . Directness of image measures the sharpness of a highlight's edges. Absence of bloom measures the haziness around a highlight.

GLOSSY REFLECTION Reflected light mostly concentrated in one direction, with some surrounding diffuse reflection.

GLOW Lighting and rendering effects that create a soft halo of light around selected objects in a scene; a soft, diffuse light that emanates from an object. It may be directly associated with a light source, as with a candle's glow or a glowing ember. Intensity, spread, and shape are common control parameters for this effect.

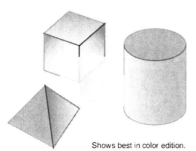

Shows best in color edition.

Read more about this:
Giambruno, Mark, *3D Graphics and Animation*
O'Rourke, Michael, *Principles of Three-Dimensional Computer Animation*

GLUING OPERATION A constructive solid geometry operation that joins two solids along a common surface. See also **ATTACH**.

GOBOS Short for *go betweens*; specially shaped opaque or translucent panels placed between a light source and subject in order to cast a complex shadow pattern or to re-shape the light beam; similar to texture mapping. See also **THROW** and **COOKIES**.

Read more about this:
Birn, Jeremy, [digital] *Lighting & Rendering*
Giambruno, Mark, *3D Graphics and Animation*

GOURAUD SHADING MODEL A surface-shading technique that eliminates most of the faceted appearance of flat shading. Gouraud shading produces smoothly blended surfaces that are more realistic looking than flat shading. The Gouraud technique computes an average normal vector at each vertex of the polyhedron formed by the polygonal approximation of a surface, using the normals to the polygons surrounding that vertex. A color is then computed at each vertex, using the average normal. Finally, the color shading within each polygon is determined by interpolating the color and intensity values of the sur-rounding vertices.

Gouraud shading is faster than the Phong shading technique, but can produce flat edges when seen from certain angles, which may become more visible as subtle linear discontinuities in color or shading near bright highlights. Furthermore, if a surface highlight is entirely within a polygon and does not extend to a vertex, then Gouraud shading misses it. Phong shading does not produce these effects. The left image is a low polygon count Gouraud-shaded sphere.

On the right is the same sphere rendered with a high polygon count.

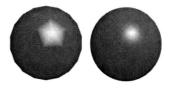

Read more about this:
Giambruno, Mark, *3D Graphics and Animation*
O'Rourke, Michael, *Principles of Three-Dimensional Computer Animation*
Watt, A. and M. Watt, *Advanced Animation and Rendering Techniques*

GRADIENT A controlled shading of color in-tensity or hue; the simplest are linear and radial gradients.

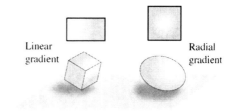

Linear gradient

Radial gradient

GRAININESS An image that appears to be made up of small particles.

GRAMMAR-BASED MODEL A high-level, top-down model-building technique using text-based statements that conform to a pre-programmed modeling grammar and syntax.

GRAPH-BASED MODEL A geometric model that based on topological structure, with data pointers linking an object's faces, edges, and vertices. It represents a solid ob-ject as a list of its faces and their respective surface equations; it lists the edges of these faces as curve equations, with pointers to their endpoint vertices and adjoining faces; and it lists the vertices as coordinates, with pointers to the edges meeting at each vertex.

The model contains two kinds of informa-tion: 1. Pointers defining the topology or connectivity between vertices, edges, and faces, and 2. Numerical data defining curve and surface equations and vertex coordi-nates.

Later modeling operations may alter the pointers, the numerical data, or both. Po-lygonal models have the simplest graphs, because their surfaces are planes bounded by straight-lines. See **TREE DATA STRUCTURE**.

GRAPHICAL USER INTERFACE (GUI) A computer graphics interface, displaying icons to represent onscreen desktop objects, such as documents and programs, and that can be accessed and manipulated through these icons with a pointing device, such as a mouse, trackball, or touch pen. Computer applications also use this kind of interface as a way for the user to control their function.

GRAPHICS Computer systems and applications used to create and display images on a computer monitor; an image, model, or rendering produced by these systems. Graphics hardware includes computers, graphics display monitors or screens, and a variety of input and output devices. Graphics applications include 3D modeling, animation, rendering, paint, illustration, and CAD/CAM programs. See **COMPUTER GRAPHICS**.

GRAPHICS CHIP A computer chip designed to help render the images of objects in a computer graphics scene; also called *graphics accelerator*. For example, a graphics chip may be designed to create a mesh framework of an object whose faces are composed of triangles or other simple polygons. The chip then computes the color and texture of each face, rendering the complete image of an object for display. Graphics chips are extremely fast and efficient because their functions are severely limited to only a few specialized tasks. Other functions may include transformations, special lighting effects, bump mapping, and environmental reflection mapping.

GRAPHICS FILE FORMATS A standardized format for organizing and storing digital images. Image files are composed of either pixel or vector (geometric) data that are rasterized to pixels when displayed in a vector graphic display. The pixels that constitute an image are ordered as a grid (columns and rows); each pixel consists of numbers representing magnitudes of brightness and color.

GRAPHICS PIPELINE Describes the sequence of special groups of computations required to render a 3D model, including position and orientation transformations, lighting effects, viewing transformations, clipping, texture, and display transformations.

GRAPHIC WEIGHT A qualitative measure of relative perceptual dominance of different parts of a scene; a quality that attracts attention or is eye-catching. All elements of a scene have graphic weight, some much more than others. Large objects with bold colors and high contrast have higher graphic weight than smaller ones with dull colors and low contrast; motion also confers graphic weight.

Read more about this:
Birn, Jeremy, [digital] *Lighting & Rendering*

GRAVITY A force acting on an object that accelerates it toward the center of the earth, affecting its motion path. The gravitational force between two objects is proportional to their masses and to how far apart they are. Imaginary worlds can be modeled whose gravitational forces are different from that of the earth, and the motion path and natural force behavior of an object in such a world is also different.

Read more about this:
Mortenson, Michael El, *3D Modeling, Animation, and Rendering*
O'Rourke, Michael, *Principles of Three-Dimensional Computer Animation*

GRAYSCALE A color model using mixtures of white and black.

GRAYSCALE IMAGE An image whose colors are a mixture of black, white, and shades of gray, and sometimes with another color added to affect its saturation or value (brightness). The image is a grayscale Rubik's cube.

productwiki.com (no date)

GRAYSCALING The process of converting a continuous-tone color image into a gray-scale image, unlike dithering that simulates shades of gray by altering the density pattern of black and white dots within the pixel matrix.

GREEKING Replacing a line of type or characters too small to be displayed with a gray bar as a placeholder.

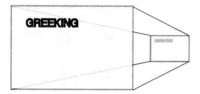

GREEN FLASH A flash of green light appearing at the point on the horizon where the sun has just set; an effect of atmospheric refraction, which may be enhanced by temperature inversion. The shape of the flash is a horizontal band, usually somewhat smaller than the apparent width of the setting sun.

Read more about this:
Naylor, John, *Out of the Blue*

GRID A network of two or three mutually perpendicular families of uniformly spaced parallel lines, providing a frame of reference for the scale and position of an object and its relationship to other objects, as in a coordinate system grid; also, a special 3D grid set up to implement deformation transformations (a lattice). See also **RULER**.

GROUP A model-organizing process used to put together a selected set of objects that must preserve their spatial relationships to each other. Individual objects may be grouped together, and also groups themselves may be grouped together to form a group of groups, creating a hierarchical series of objects and groups. In addition, groups may be grouped with individual objects or to several other objects. Transformations and other operations may then be applied to a group as a whole.

The term *group* also refers to a special mathematical structure, consisting of a set of elements and an operator that combines elements two at a time. It is an important concept in geometric transformations.

Read more about this:
Giambruno, Mark, *3D Graphics and Animation*
Mortenson, Michael E., *Geometric Transformations for 3D Modeling*

GUI Acronym for **GRAPHICAL USER INTERFACE**.

GUIDE A modeling aid not part of the model itself, such as construction lines and planes.

H

HAIDINGER'S BRUSH A visual effect of polarized light; a faint, yellow, narrow elliptical patch about 2° or 3° wide that appears in the center of the field of vision and that is seen when looking at a wide expanse of polarized light.

Shows best in color edition.

Read more about this:
Naylor, John, *Out of the Blue*

HALATION The blurring of an image near highlights or around bright objects, similar to a halo.

HALF ANGLE The angle of spread of a cone of light from its central ray, produced by a spotlight.

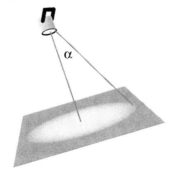

HALF-SPACE A mathematical function expressed as an inequality and interpreted geometrically as dividing a 2D or 3D space into two separate and distinct regions, where the function describes the boundary between the two regions. Constructive solid geometry uses Boolean combinations of half-spaces to construct primitives that are then used to construct more complex 3D solids.

In geometry, a half-space is either of the two parts into which a plane divides three-dimensional space. More generally, a surface may divide a plane into two half-spaces.

A half-space can be classified as open or closed. An open half-space is either of the two open sets produced by subtracting the points of the plane or surface from the space. A closed half-space is the union of an open half-space and the plane or surface that defines it.

If the space is two-dimensional, then a half-space is called a half-plane (open or closed). A half-space in a one-dimensional space is called a *ray*.

Read more about this:
Mortenson, Michael E., *Mathematics for Computer Graphics Applications*

HALF-SPACE MODEL The Boolean intersection of an appropriate set of half-spaces forming a closed three-dimensional solid., a primitive solid used in constructive solid geometry. Truncating a cylindrical surface half-space with two planar half-spaces produces a solid cylindrical model.

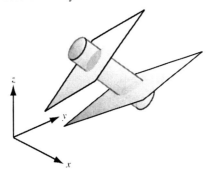

A primitive is a Boolean combination of directed surfaces or half spaces forming a simple closed three-dimensional solid. A directed surface is a surface whose normal at

any point determines the inside and outside of the primitive solid. What distinguishes a primitive from any general shape formed in this way is its geometric regularity, which is defined by a very few parameters. Thus, a rectangular solid primitive is defined by length, width, and height.

Read more about this:
Mortenson, Michael E., *3D Modeling, Animation, and Rendering*
_____, *Geometric Modeling*
_____, *Mathematics for Computer Graphics Applications*

HALFTONE A printing process that uses dithering techniques to create black-and-white copy of a continuous-tone color original, such as a photograph, a reprographic technique that simulates a continuous tone image by using an array of dots, varying either in size or in spacing. Color printing is possible by repeating the halftone process for each of a set of subtractive colors, usually using the CMYK color model. The semi-opaque property of ink allows halftone dots of different colors to create the optical effect that yields full-color imagery. In the upper figure are halftone dots. In the lower figure is how the eye sees this from a sufficient distance.

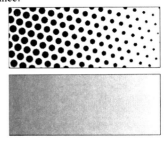

HAPTIC INTERFACE DEVICE A wearable sensing device, usually an electronic glove, that allows the user to create, manipulate, or experience objects in a computer graphics scene through the sense of touch. Haptic means related to or based on the sense of touch.

HARD LIGHT Bright, crisply focused light, casting hard, high contrast shadows, and producing small but bright highlights. Hard light is used to simulate direct sunlight, light from a bare light bulb, or other small similarly compact light source, and sunlit space scenes where there is no atmosphere to diffuse the light.

photoshopessentials.com. Shows best in color edition.

HAZE A brightening of the sky when sunlight is scattered by a high concentration of aerosols.

Read more about this:
Naylor, John, *Out of the Blue*

HDRI Acronym for **HIGH DYNAMIC RANGE IMAGING**.

HEAD-ON SHOT A shot where the action comes directly toward the camera.

HEIGHT FIELD A height field is a structure usually used for modeling terrain. It is described as a grid of points at user-specified heights above a reference plane. A renderer displays a height field by tessellating the grid into a mesh of triangles or polygons and rendering these. Height fields are useful for modeling landforms, jagged structures etc.

HEILIGENSCHEIN A German word that means *holy glow*; for example, the halo of light that appears as a faint sheen or increased brightness around the shadow of your head cast on a damp lawn at sunset or sunrise. (When you look at your shadow you are looking toward the antisolar point.) This is explained as follows: individual blades of grass near the edge of the shadow of your head look brighter than more distant blades because they are near your antisolar point and hide their own shadows and thus reflect more light toward you. A similar effect is apparent around the shadow of an

airplane about to take off or land when the pilot or a passenger looks toward the antisolar point. Heiligenschein is seen around the shadow of a balloon on a farm field.

Wikipedia, N. Thomas (2006). Shows best in color edition.

Read more about this:
Naylor, John, *Out of the Blue*

HELICAL SWEEP A swept solid whose cross section follows a 3D spiral curve. A circular cross section swept along a circular spiral produces a coiled spring.

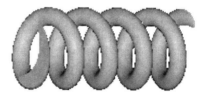

Read more about this:
Giambruno, Mark, *3D Graphics and Animation*

HERMITE CURVE A special form of parametric curve based on parametric cubic equations, with the curve's shape controlled by its endpoint positions and tangent vectors at those endpoints. This curve is not invariant under affine transformations. Changing the tangent vector changes the curve shape:

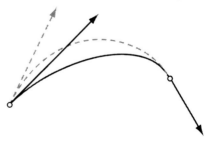

Read more about this:
Mortenson, M. E., *Geometric Modeling*

HERMITE SURFACE A bicubic patch defined by its four corner points, tangent vectors of the four boundary curves, and the so-called twist vectors at the corner points. Composite arrays of these patches may be assembled to represent complex surfaces. This surface representation exhibits advantages similar to those for the Hermite curves.

Read more about this:
Mortenson, M. E., *Geometric Modeling*

HIDDEN LINE An occluded edge of an object; a computer graphics display or rendering method that draws the edges of an object as in a wireframe display, omitting lines and parts of lines not visible from the current viewpoint; an edge of a 3D object obscured from view by the object itself, often displayed as a dashed line to indicate it is obscured.

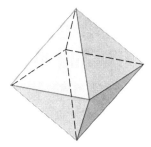

Read more about this:
Mortenson, Michael E., *3D Modeling, Animation, and Rendering*

HIDDEN SURFACE Any surface on the far side of an object, opposite the current viewpoint; not visible from the camera's viewpoint. Surfaces D, E, and F of the cube are hidden by surfaces A, B, and C.

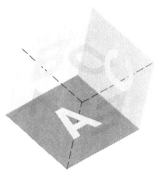

Read more about this:
Mortenson, Michael E., *3D Modeling, Animation, and Rendering*
Watt, A. and M. Watt, *Advanced Animation and Rendering Techniques*

HIERARCHICAL ANIMATION Grouping animated elements and their action transformations according to an organized scheme of assemblies and subassemblies.

Read more about this:
Watt, A. and M. Watt, *Advanced Animation and Rendering Techniques*

HIERARCHICAL ASSEMBLY The construction, organization, and spatial relationships between individual parts, groups of parts, and their final assembly.

HIERARCHICAL MODEL A model whose parts are organized in a series of increasingly complex subassemblies, based on connectivity and spatial proximity. For example, in a human model, fingers are connected to a hand, the hand to an arm, and the arm to the torso, to the complete body structure.

Read more about this:
O'Rourke, Michael, *Principles of Three-Dimensional Computer Animation*
Watt, A. and M. Watt, *Advanced Animation and Rendering Techniques*

HIERARCHY A tree structure representing relationships between objects, processes, or characteristics. A data hierarchy has a tree-like structure. There is a root node, which links to child nodes, and child nodes that link to "grandchild" nodes and so on. Data hierarchies are encountered in graphics applications, especially in ray tracing and in space subdivision methods.

HIGH-ANGLE SHOT The view from a camera positioned higher than the subject. High angle shots tend to make the subject appear smaller. See also **LOW ANGLE SHO***t*.

HIGH CONTRAST A condition in which the difference between light and dark tones or values are extreme; used to achieve a dramatic effect, focusing a viewer's attention on those parts of an image that have high contrast. The following image emphasizes the light on the water and break in the horizon clouds, while deemphasizing the foreground detail. This technique also applies to animation rendering. See also **CONTRAST**.

sheepynic.info/ireland/ (photographer and date unknown)

Read more about this:
Birn, Jeremy, [digital] *Lighting & Rendering*

HIGH DYNAMIC RANGE IMAGING A set of techniques that allows a greater range of intensity between light and dark areas of a scene than normal digital imaging techniques. The intention of HDRI is to accurately represent the wide range of intensity levels found in real scenes ranging from direct sunlight to shadows. The photo below is an excellent example of HDRI technique.

Paulo Barcellos, Jr. (2006)

HIGH-KEY LIGHTING Indicates a brightly lit scene with low contrast, producing a low key-to-fill ratio.

©Harold Davis www.photoblog2.com

HIGHLIGHT The area of most intense light reflecting off the surface of an object and directly into the camera or viewer's eye.

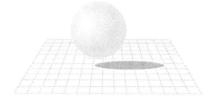

The geometry of a reflected highlight varies, depending on the surface, from a focused, unscattered reflection, to some light scattered around a strong specular reflection or glossy reflection, to a completely diffuse reflection, or to a mixture of glossy and diffuse. See also **SHININESS**.

Read more about this:
Birn, Jeremy, [digital] *Lighting & Rendering*
Mortenson, Michael E., *3D Modeling, Animation, and Rendering*
O'Rourke, Michael, *Principles of Three-Dimensional Computer Animation*

HIGHLIGHT PASS Isolates and renders specular highlights of objects in a scene, ignoring other reflection and shading effects. This allows more creative control over highlights. See also **RENDERING IN PASSES** and **SPECULAR REFLECTION**.

Read more about this:
Birn, Jeremy, [digital] *Lighting & Rendering*

HISTOGRAM A graphic representation of an image's color information; a graph of the frequency distribution of some property, where the vertical axis indicates the frequency of occurrence of value intervals, and fixed intervals along the horizontal axis represent the values; in lighting and rendering for 3D modeling, a graph of tone or brightness distribution frequency taken over all pixels in a displayed rendering of an image, with the horizontal scale ranging from black to white (left to right); a graphic aid in the analysis of lighting exposure in a scene. A histogram is an aid to identifying lighting and rendering problems of low contrast, high contrast, underexposure, overexposure, banding, and clipping.

The leftmost graphic shown here is underexposed, and the histogram below it shows that dark tones are more frequent than middle and light tones. The rightmost graphic is overexposed and its histogram shows that only light or bright tones are present in the image.

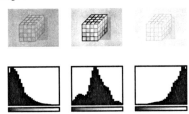

Read more about this:
Birn, Jeremy, [digital] *Lighting & Rendering*

HITCHCOCK ZOOM Adjusting the field of view with a zoom lens while the camera moves toward or away from the subject so that the subject is the same size in each frame of the scene, also called dolly zoom.

HOMOGENEOUS COORDINATES A reference frame and mathematical scheme that makes calculations possible in projective space just as Cartesian coordinates do in Euclidean space. Homogeneous coordinates have a range of applications, including to computer graphics where they allow affine transformations and, in general, projective transformations to be easily represented by a matrix. Here is an example of homogeneous coordinates used to perform a translation transformation:

$$[\,x'\ y'\ z'\ 1\,] = \begin{bmatrix} 1 & 0 & 0 & t_x \\ 0 & 1 & 0 & t_y \\ 0 & 0 & 1 & t_z \\ 0 & 0 & 0 & 1 \end{bmatrix} [\,x\ y\ z\ 1\,]$$

HORIZONTAL FOG An atmospheric effect, also called *radiation fog*. This atmospheric effect forms at ground level during the night under clear skies, and varies in thickness from just a meter or so to 300 meters.

NOAA image (no date)

Read more about this:
O'Rourke, Michael, *Principles of Three-Dimensional Computer Animation*

HOT POINT A point in 3D space locating the center of rotation of an object, light, or camera, at the geometric center of the object's bounding box unless specified otherwise.

HOT SPOT That segment or range of the spectrum of a light source that is set at full intensity.

HSB COLOR MODEL A color model based on human perception of color; a selection-and-control interface used in computer graphics to adjust hue (color components), saturation (intensity), and brightness, producing more accurate color and allowing finer tuning of color than the RGB system, which is simpler and uses three discrete mixing colors; sometimes called the *HSV color model*, for hue, saturation, and value.

Consider the following experiment with color to more fully understand the HSB concept: Add one drop of red dye to a glass of water. Red is the hue of the mixture. Adding another drop of red does not change the hue, but it increases the color saturation of the mixture. Adding a third drop of red dye increases the saturation even more. If a drop of pure white dye is added, the mixture is brighter, giving the color a higher value. Adding even more white, increases its value again, and the color of the mixture is still brighter yet. On the other hand, adding gray or black lowers the value, darkening the color. However, throughout this experiment, the hue has not changed.

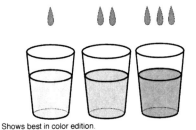

Shows best in color edition.

Read more about this:
Demers, Owen, [digital] *Texture & Painting*
O'Rourke, Michael, *Principles of Three-Dimensional Computer Animation*

HUE The property of light that defines a color as a combination of its color-model components; for example, in the RGB model hue is determined by a mixture of red, green, and blue components, and limited to the total RGB color spectrum available. A specific hue is selected for an object's surface along with the color's saturation and value. See also **HSB COLOR MODEL.**

Read more about this:
Demers, Owen, [digital] *Texture & Painting*
O'Rourke, Michael, *Principles of Three-Dimensional Computer Animation*

HULL SURFACE The model of a ship's external shape from the rails to the keel. See also *convex hull.*

HUMAN MODEL The mathematical and geometric description of the shape of a human body, usually only the external surface, but sometimes including the internal musculature, skeleton, and organs.

Read more about this:
O'Rourke, Michael, *Principles of Three-Dimensional Computer Animation*
Ratner, Peter, *3-D Human Modeling and Animation*

HYDRODYNAMICS The study of forces acting on an object moving through water or other liquid; necessary for engineering analysis of a ship's motion through the water and for model-related natural force behavior.

I

ICC COLOR PROFILE A cross-platform (device-independent) standard color profile developed by the International Color Consortium. A color profile includes a description of the color gamut capabilities of a specified device. When a digital image is sent to a proofing device with the profile of a printing press, the proofing device uses the press's ICC profile to transform the image color to the press's color gamut and automatically makes the necessary adjustments to the proofing device so that this image is as accurate as possible.

ICOSAHEDRON One of the five regular polyhedra, having twenty identical equilateral triangle faces. It has 12 vertices, 30 edges, and five faces surround each vertex. The sum of the face angles at each vertex is $300°$.

Read more about this:
Coexeter, H. S. M., *Regular Polytopes*
Mortenson, M. E., *Mathematics for Computer Graphics Applications*

IDENTITY MATRIX A diagonal matrix that has unit elements on the main diagonal; also called a *unit matrix.*

$$\mathbf{I} = \begin{bmatrix} 1 & 0 & 0 \\ 0 & 1 & 0 \\ 0 & 0 & 1 \end{bmatrix} = \delta_{ij}$$

where, again, δ_{ij} is the *Kronecker delta.*

IGES Acronym for *Initial Graphics Exchange Specification.*

IK Acronym for *inverse kinematics.*

ILLUMINANCE The amount of light per unit area lighting a surface.

IMAGE PLANE The background of an animation sequence displayed to analyze and adjust its alignment with the animated objects, also called *rotoscope background.*

IMAGE RESOLUTION Measured in pixels per inch (ppi), a high-resolution image has more and smaller pixels (a higher ppi) than a low-resolution image. Hi-res images show finer details and subtler color effects than lo-res images.

IMMERSIVE THEATER A computer and computer graphics-driven multi-media entertainment or educational setting, combining passive and interactive sensory devices to enhance a participant's sense of realism. See also **VIRTUAL REALITY.**

IMPLICIT EQUATION OF A CURVE An algebraic form for representing a curve, whose general expression is $f(x,y) = 0$. This form is useful as an adjunct to a larger, parameter-based, modeling system. It is an effective form when computing intersections or determining point containment (point classification). However, the implicit form requires the solution of nonlinear equations to trace out points on a curve, while the parametric form does not.

Read more about this:
Mortenson, M. E., *Geometric Modeling*

IMPLICITIZATION Mathematical conversion of a geometric element or model defined by parametric equations into its equivalent defined by implicit equations. This is done to expedite computing intersections or point classification.

Read more about this:
Mortenson, M. E., *Geometric Modeling*

INBETWEENING Creating the sequence of frames between two keyframes; sometimes called *tweening*, to give the appearance that the image in the first keyframe evolves smoothly into the image in the second keyframe.

Michael D. Smith, Brigham Young University (2003).

Read more about this:
Giambruno, Mark, *3D Graphics and Animation*
Mortenson, Michael E., *3D Modeling, Animation, and Rendering*
O'Rourke, Michael, *Principles of Three-Dimensional Computer Animation*
Watt, A. and M. Watt, *Advanced Animation and Rendering Techniques*

IN-CAMERA EFFECT Any special visual effect that is produced solely by manipulating the camera. A Hitchcock zoom or a simple pan motion is an in-camera effect.

INCANDESCENCE A measure of the brightness of a light-emitting surface; a high incandescence value makes a surface appear brighter than a low value; the emission of light from a hot object.

Read more about this:
O'Rourke, Michael, *Principles of Three-Dimensional Computer Animation*

INCANDESCENCE MAPPING See **LUMINOSITY MAPPING**.

INCANDESCENT LIGHT Produced when a material object is hot enough to glow, like an ordinary light bulb, a candle flame, or a hot branding iron.

INCIDENT LIGHT The amount and type of light reaching a subject.

INCLUDE See **EXCLUDE**.

INDEX OF REFRACTION A number indicating the speed of light in a specific medium as either the ratio of the speed of light in a vacuum to that in the given medium (the absolute index of refraction), or the ratio of the speed of light in a specified medium to that in a reference medium (relative index of refraction); a number used to compute how much a light ray bends at the boundary between two different types of light-transmitting materials. This number varies depending upon the specific materials. See also **REFRACTION**.

Read more about this:
Watt, A. and M. Watt, *Advanced Animation and Rendering Techniques*

INDIRECT LIGHT Light reaching a surface not directly from a light source, but after **REFLECTING** off one or more other surfaces in a scene or by atmospheric scattering. See also **DIRECT LIGHT**.

INEQUALITY A mathematical relationship indicating a difference between two functions, statements, or objects.

INFERENCING GEOMETRY Automatic determination of unspecified dimensions or features from existing model data.

INFRARED Electromagnetic radiation not visible to the eye but perceptible as warming of the skin. The sun emits about half its radiant energy as infrared and the other half as visible light.

INITIAL GRAPHICS EXCHANGE SPECIFICATION (IGES) A standardized CAD data format developed by the National Bureau of Standards to make it easier to exchange 3D model data between different CAD software systems. A CAD file in IGES may be exported to another CAD system. The imported model can be added to, but the

original imported features cannot be altered.
IGES is used by companies operating two
different CAD modeling systems that need
to exchange data, by manufacturers that
must transmit model design data to subcon-
tractors, and by rapid prototyping service
bureaus that prefer IGES files rather than
STL files.

INSERT SHOT A close-up or extreme close-
up shot, intercut within a scene to explain
the action, emphasize a point, or improve
continuity; a close-up of some detail in the
scene. An insert shot may consist of a close-
up shot of a letter, a hand holding a gun, or
an airline departure schedule, for example.

INSIDE FILLET A transitional curved surface,
usually cylindrical, between two intersecting
plane surfaces, used in the design of mechanical parts to minimize stresses or for
aesthetic reasons.

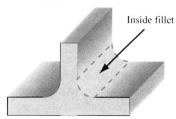
Inside fillet

INSIDE/OUTSIDE A spatial relationship between geometric objects. For any solid an
arbitrary point is either inside, outside, or on
the boundary of it.

INSTANCE A fully specified 3D model of a
class of geometric objects, used in constructive solid geometry and elsewhere. A sphere
with radius 31.87 cm whose world coordinate center is at the point
$(16.57, 27.09, -9.28)$ is an instance of the
primitive unit sphere positioned at the origin
of its own local coordinate system.
Read more about this:
Giambruno, Mark, *3D Graphics and Animation*
O'Rourke, Michael, *Principles of Three-Dimensional
Computer Animation*

INTENSITY A relative measure of the strength
or brightness of a light source or the saturation of a color. Increasing the brightness of a
color is perceived as an increase in the intensity of the incident light.

Read more about this:
Watt, A. and M. Watt, *Advanced Animation and
Rendering Techniques*

INTERCUT See **CROSS-CUTTING**.

INTERFERENCE The process in which two
light waves simultaneously passing through
the same volume of space reinforce or diminish their combined effect. Waves arriv-
ing at a point in step combine construc-
tively, and if they meet out of step they
combine destructively.

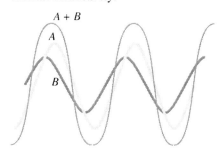

INTERFERENCE CHECKING In mechanical
assemblies, mechanisms, and scenes containing moving objects, the process of determining if and where two or more objects
intersect or collide. See also **COLLISION
DETECTION** and **KINEMATICS**.

INTERLACING An image-scanning technique
used in television to reduce the flickering effect of a one-pass top-to-bottom scan. In
constructing an interlaced image, the television electron beam first scans the odd-
numbered horizontal lines onto the screen
and then the even-numbered lines.

INTERPOLATE To calculate an intermediate
value between two given values: position,
speed, brightness, color, and so forth. In
animation, the position of a moving object
between keyframes is found by proportionally interpolating between them. If the object is moving with a constant speed, then a
linear interpolation scheme is used. If the
object is accelerating, then a spline interpolation method is used.

Read more about this:
O'Rourke, Michael, *Principles of Three-Dimensional
Computer Animation*
Watt, A. and M. Watt, *Advanced Animation and
Rendering Techniques*

INTERPOLATING SPLINE A spline curve that
passes directly through each of its control
points. The advantage of being able to pre-
cisely locate the curve at these points must
be weighed against the difficulty of producing a smooth curve, that is one without

local bumps at some control points. (Mathematically, the bumps are regions of rapidly changing curvature.) Contrast this spline with the approximating spline.

Read more about this:
Mortenson, M. E., *Geometric Modeling*
O'Rourke, Michael, *Principles of Three-Dimensional Computer Animation*
Watt, A. and M. Watt, *Advanced Animation and Rendering Techniques*

INTERSECTION A part that is common to two objects. A geometrical intersection of two objects is a point or points common to both objects. In constructive solid geometry, the intersection of two solid objects produces a third solid object. In ray tracing, ray-object intersections determine visibility. Intersection computations are also used in clipping algorithms. The line of intersection between a plane and a surface is shown in red, in the illustration.

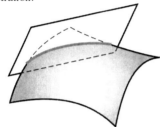

Read more about this:
Mortenson, Michael E., *3D Modeling, Animation, and Rendering*
_____, *Geometric Modeling*
_____, *Mathematics for Computer Graphics Applications*

INTERSECTION OPERATOR A Boolean operator in constructive solid geometry that combines two solids to produce a new solid defined by their common solid space.

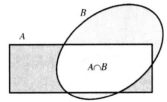

Read more about this:
Mortenson, M. E., *Geometric Modeling*
_____, *Mathematics for Computer Graphics Applications*
O'Rourke, Michael, *Principles of Three-Dimensional Computer Animation*

INTRINSIC EQUATION OF A CURVE An algebraic form for representing a curve. An intrinsic property is one that depends on only the shape of the curve, and not its relation to a coordinate system or other external frame of reference. For example, the fact that a rectangle has four equal angles is intrinsic to the rectangle, but the fact that a particular rectangle has two vertical sides is not, because an external frame of reference is required to determine which direction is vertical. A curve requires two intrinsic equations, one expressing its curvature $1/\rho$ and one its torsion τ, each as functions of its arc length s: $1/\rho = f(s)$ and $\tau = g(s)$. Torsion is a measure of how much a space curve deviates from a plane curve, and arc length is measured along the curve. It is instructive to distinguish between intrinsic equations and the so-called *natural equations*.

Read more about this:
Mortenson, M. E., *Geometric Modeling*

INVERSE KINEMATICS Also known as *IK*; goal-directed motion; a method of controlling the motions of an articulated object (that is, an object comprised of many hierarchically-related, joined movable parts or links), in which the position of the free end of a chain of links, or end effector, is specified and its motion affects the position and orientation of one or more links upstream along the chain. For example, in a model of the arm, any specified motion of a fingertip is propagated up through the finger joints, hand, wrist, and forearm. It is also quite possible that some motions of the fingertip do not necessarily require much propagation upstream to be physically realizable.

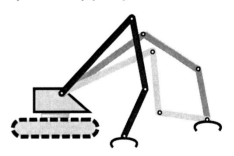

The animator specifies the motion of the end effector from which motions of the other links are computed by an inverse kinematics program.

As the number of links increases, the total assembly becomes under-defined, permitting many possible solutions for the positions and orientations of the intermediate links. This, in turn, allows the animator to specify additional constraints, such as those related to natural force behavior (the effects of friction, inertia, and various forms of energy conservation). Also, as the number of links increases, the process becomes more computationally expensive. See also **FORWARD KINEMATICS** in which motions propagate in the opposite direction along the chain of articulated parts.

Read more about this:
Giambruno, Mark, *3D Graphics and Animation*
O'Rourke, Michael, *Principles of Three-Dimensional Computer Animation*
Watt, A. and M. Watt, *Advanced Animation and Rendering Techniques*

INVERSION A special form of reflection; reflection through a point. However, inversion in a point is a true reflection only in odd-dimension spaces. In even-dimension spaces, the transformation produces a half-turn, or rotation through 180°. Inversion does not change distances. Inverting an object in 3D space reverses its orientation. Notice that inversion is not physically realizable in a 3D solid.

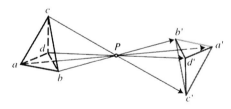

Read more about this:
Mortenson, Michael E., *Geometric Transformations for 3D Modeling*
O'Rourke, Michael, *Principles of Three-Dimensional Computer Animation*

INVERT COLOR A process that creates the color negative of a selected color, for example the negative or inverse of the color given by hue = 191°, saturation = 75%, and brightness = 82% is H = 11°, S = 77%, and B = 80%. These particular HSB color values apply to the upper and lower example of the word *color* shown here. The HSB values of the word *invert* are also mutually inverse.

Shows best in color edition.

INVERTED LIGHT In rendering, a negative or dark lighting effect that moderates or cancels the effect of other light sources by reducing the total illumination of a target object.

INVERTED MATTE Transforms all color values in a matte to their opposite values. See also **INVERT COLOR**.

IRIDESCENCE A play of lustrous colors similar to those of the rainbow. The two soap bubbles shown here exhibit the phenomenon of iridescence.

Wikipedia, DBD (2003). Shows best in color edition.

Read more about this:
Demers, Owen, [digital] *Texture & Painting*

IRRADIATION Light is scattered within the retina and so light from a bright source may stimulate retinal cells that lie outside the immediate area within which the source's image is focused. The result is that the image of the object appears larger than it really is. Irradiation also occurs in photographs.

ISOCONTOUR, ISOSURFACE A special curve or surface, representing a constant value of some variable; for example, a contour map showing curves of equal altitude. They are used in GIS systems, scientific visualization, engineering design and analysis, as well as general graphic design. The isocontour curve shown on the ellipsoidal solid is a constant distance above the plane.

In metaball modeling, an isosurface is defined by a constant value within a single density field or the combined effect of overlapping density fields.

Isocontour

Isosurfaces

Shows best in color edition.

Read more about this:
O'Rourke, Michael, *Principles of Three-Dimensional Computer Animation*

ISOMETRIC DRAWING A 2D projection of a 3D object whose horizontal edges are usually drawn at a 30° angle and all vertical edges are drawn perpendicular to a horizontal reference base, with all edges drawn to scale.

ISOPARAMETRIC CURVE A curve of constant parametric value on a surface or in a solid.

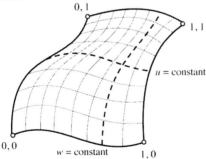

Read more about this:
Mortenson, Michael E., *Geometric Modeling*

ITERATE To repeat a computation using as input results of the previous computation, usually until some terminating criterion is produced.

J

JAGGIES The zigzag effect on straight lines of a computer graphics monitor's rectangular array of pixels See also **ALIASING** and **ANTI-ALIASING**.

Read more about this:
Giambruno, Mark, *3D Graphics and Animation*
O'Rourke, Michael, *Principles of Three-Dimensional Computer Animation*

JITTER An animation technique used with anti-aliasing and stochastic sampling, a small random offset added to a quantity. Ray tracer algorithms make scenes more natural looking by adding a jitter value to the direction vector of the eye rays. This ensures that any sharp pattern captured by the rays is randomly broken up to give a dithered or antialiased appearance. This applies to shadow rays as well.

Read more about this:
O'Rourke, Michael, *Principles of Three-Dimensional Computer Animation*

JOIN A connection between two surfaces that includes a transition surface along their intersection.

JOINT A connection between two rigid links in animated or mechanical design that allows some constrained motion between the links; for example, a ball joint socket, permitting a high degree of rotational freedom between the links.

JOINT CONSTRAINTS Rotational constraints on the joints of an articulated system, used in an inverse kinematics chain in 3D animation or robotics. Joint constraints are implemented in a number of ways, the most common is to limit rotation about the x-, y- and z-axis independently.

JPEG The acronym for Joint Photographic Experts Group image format; a common, pixel-based image format used on the Web, and having 24-bit color capability. It compresses image data using a lossy data compression method, and the user can preselect the amount of compression.

Read more about this:
Giambruno, Mark, *3D Graphics and Animation*
O'Rourke, Michael, *Principles of Three-Dimensional Computer Animation*

JUMP CUT An immediate shift from one scene to another; a cut made in the middle of a continuous shot rather than between shots, creating discontinuity in time and drawing attention to the film itself instead of its content; an intentional editing mismatch between scenes or within a shot, creating a visual disturbance when replayed. A jump cut occurs between two consecutive frames when a subject common to both frames appears to "jump" to a different position within the frame.

K

KALMAN FILTER A mathematical technique used in computer graphics to interpret real-world sensing input.

KEYFRAME A small subset of nonadjacent frames in an animation sequence that control the content of the inbetween frames. A keyframe contains the entire image, instead of only changes from the previous frame. Subsequent frames are constructed by modifying the keyframe image according to the modeler's instructions, until the next keyframe is reached, where a new image and instructions continue the process.

The keyframing process is an iterative one. The animator adjusts trajectories and other motions and effects, and then plays back these motions. The cycle is repeated until the animator is satisfied with the result.

The term originally identified a series of master frames or keyframes manually created by an animation artist. Less skilled animators created the inbetween frames.

Read more about this:
Giambruno, Mark, *3D Graphics and Animation*
O'Rourke, Michael, *Principles of Three-Dimensional Computer Animation*

KEYFRAME ANIMATION See **FORWARD KINEMATICS**.

KEYFRAME CONTROL PARAMETERS Includes location and orientation of characters and scene background objects, scale, kinematic joint angles, shape deformations, textures, camera motions and effects, lighting, and other parameters related to rendering during this phase of the graphics pipeline. The animator must attend to how velocity depends on the interpolation style.

KEYFRAME INTERPOLATION Mathematical techniques governing keyframe control parameters. Two major categories of interpolation are linear and spline based, related to time and position.

KEYFRAME WEIGHTING Animation controls, allowing control-of-motion transformations between keyframes by using function curves, TCB weighting, ease in and ease out (or *ease from* and *ease to*).

KEYFRAMING Defining keyframes for animation.

Read more about this:
Watt, A. and M. Watt, *Advanced Animation and Rendering Techniques*

KEY LIGHT The main source of illumination in a scene, and casting the most apparent shadows, the brightest light source. See also **HIGH KEY**, **LOW KEY** and **LIGHT PLACEMENT**.

Read more about this:
Birn, Jeremy, [digital] *Lighting & Rendering*
Giambruno, Mark, *3D Graphics and Animation*

KEY-TO-FILL RATIO A measure of the contrast in the lighting of a scene; the ratio of the brightness of key light to fill light.

Read more about this:
Birn, Jeremy, [digital] *Lighting & Rendering*

KINEMATICS The physics of moving mechanical systems without regard to forces causing motion or to forces dampening it. In kinematics attention is focused on the position, velocity, and acceleration of the various joints and links of a mechanical system; the geometric and time-dependent properties of motion, including determining the paths of joints, the geometric envelopes swept out by combinations of joint and link motions, and interference studies. See also **INVERSE** and **FORWARD KINEMATICS**, **PHYSICS-BASED ANIMATION**, and **DYNAMICS**.

Read more about this:
Giambruno, Mark, *3D Graphics and Animation*
Mortenson, Michael E., *3D Modeling, Animation, and Rendering*
O'Rourke, Michael, *Principles of Three-Dimensional Computer Animation*

KINEMATIC TRANSFORMATION Mathematically described motion of linked mechanical parts or animated objects.

Mortenson, Michael E., *3D Modeling, Animation, and Rendering*
_____, *Geometric Transformations for 3D Modeling*

KINETIC FRICTION A force opposing the motion of two surfaces in contact and sliding past one another; a special friction effect in natural force behavior. In the absence of other forces kinetic friction decelerates and eventually brings to a stop an object sliding on a surface. The kinetic energy of motion is dissipated as heat.

Read more about this:
O'Rourke, Michael, *Principles of Three-Dimensional Computer Animation*

KNOT A type of control point used to alter the shape of a NURBS curve; also called an *edit point*.

Read more about this:
O'Rourke, Michael, *Principles of Three-Dimensional Computer Animation*

L

LABEL MAP See *decal*.

LANDSCAPE VIEW An image whose horizontal dimension is greater than its vertical dimension, and whose content has greater visual impact when displayed this way.

LATH A thin, narrow strip of wood, metal, or plastic flexible enough to be used as a guide to draw smooth curves through a series of fixed points in a manual drafting environment..

LATHE TOOL A special CAD modeling procedure for creating lathed, or turned, 3D shapes.

LATHING A procedure that creates a solid model by rotating a closed two-dimensional shape (the generator or profile) around an axis, sweeping out a 3D solid. This is the rotational equivalent of extruding a solid by moving a two-dimensional shape along a straight line. However, in contrast to extrusions and sweeps, the plane of the cross section remains perpendicular to the circular arc of the rotation, and, thus, always contains the axis of rotation.

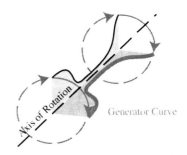

Axis of Rotation

Generator Curve

A partial lathe is one in which the rotation is less than 360°. Some 3D modeling systems also allow a closed curve or a curve whose end points lie on the axis of rotation to be generators. *Lathe* is also the name of a machine tool that is used to produce turned shapes in wood or metal. For example, a block of hickory wood is rapidly turned past a cutting blade on a woodworking lathe to carve out the shape of a baseball bat.

Read more about this:
Giambruno, Mark, *3D Graphics and Animation*
Mortenson, Michael E., *3D Modeling, Animation, and Rendering*
_____, *Geometric Modeling*

LATTICE A 3D framework of points and lines used to change the shape of an object embedded in it; usually a three-dimensional array of control points and interconnecting lines whose deformation alters the shape of an embedded model by transmitting its deformation to the model's polygonal mesh; used to simplify shape deformation of the model; also called a *squishy box*. Using the lattice technique significantly reduces the number of control points that otherwise must be manipulated.

LATTICE ANIMATION Animation of lattice control points in order to animate deformations of an embedded model.

Read more about this:
O'Rourke, Michael, *Principles of Three-Dimensional Computer Animation*

LAYER Part of a scene created separately, to be rendered and assembled later with other layers to form the final scene; for example, scene background may comprise one layer, and each foreground object may be created in its own separate layer. See also **RENDERING IN LAYERS** and **PASS**.

Read more about this:
Birn, Jeremy, [digital] *Lighting & Rendering*

LAYERED FOG An atmospheric effect that mutes color and blurs the image of an object. Vertical or layered fog is used to obscure the images of objects relative to their location in the *y*-direction, or height; for example, the tops of mountains may be more obscured than their lower slopes.

Flikr.com, D. Geoghegan (2006)

Read more about this:
O'Rourke, Michael, *Principles of Three-Dimensional Computer Animation*

LAYERED SHADER Combines and renders two complete shaders.

L CUT Also known as a *split edit*, an edit transition from one shot to another in film or video, where the picture transition does not occur coincidentally with the audio transition. This may be done to enhance the aesthetics or flow of the film. For example, a conversation between two people can feel like a tennis match without L cuts. L cuts allow the audience to see the reactionary impulse to speak, or the aftermath of speaking rather than simply the act of speaking.

LEAD ROOM The space in front of and in the direction of the moving or stationary principal subject. Good composition leaves space in the direction the subject is moving or looking. See also **NOSE ROOM**.

LEAF NODE The end node of a path through a tree data structure. All paths through a binary tree begin at the root node and end at a leaf node, which has no further branches or descendants.

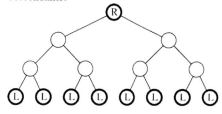

LENS A specially curved glass piece used to focus the light entering a camera to form a sharp image. Any transparent material with a curved surface may act as a lens, however imperfect, to redirect and partially focus light passing through it. A convex lens causes light rays to converge, usually at a focal point. A concave lens causes light rays to diverge.

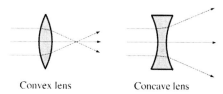

Convex lens   Concave lens

LENS FLARE A pattern of bright circles and rays produced when a camera is aimed at or near a bright light. Rendering allows control of a variety of lens-flare modes, including central ring color and size, and star filter enhancements.

NASA

In the NASA photo, above, of the lunar lander, the sun behind the lander produces an example of lens flare.

Read more about this:
Giambruno, Mark, *3D Graphics and Animation*
O'Rourke, Michael, *Principles of Three-Dimensional Computer Animation*

LETTERBOX Adapting wide-screen images to the standard video format; transforming widescreen film to video format while preserving the original aspect ratio. The conversion to new format necessarily includes added areas both above and below the original wide-screen picture area, referred to as black bars and resembling a letterbox slot. These added areas adjust the aspect ratio of the wide-screen format to match that of the video format. See also **FRAMING FOR TELEVISION**.

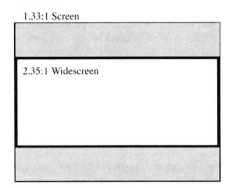

1.33:1 Screen

2.35:1 Widescreen

LEVEL-OF-DETAIL (LOD) The capability to vary the amount of detail displayed in a computer graphics scene to improve performance. Faraway objects in a scene may be displayed in a simpler, less detailed manner than nearby ones. When a viewer zooms in for a closer look a more detailed representation is produced.

LIGHT A fast-moving stream of particles, called *photons*, traveling through space with coordinated wave-like properties. We see objects because photons of light bounce (reflect) off the surfaces of objects and into our eyes. Actually, the process is somewhat more complicated than this, because there is almost always absorption of some of the photons, some of which are re-emitted with a different wavelength.

Light is described by its wavelength: the distance between adjacent peaks of its intensity, or its frequency, the number of peaks passing a given point in one second. Wavelength is measured in centimeters or meters, and frequency is measured in cycles per second or hertz. The entire range of possible wavelengths of light defines the electromagnetic spectrum. Rendering is concerned with the effects of light whose wavelength is in the visible portion of the electromagnetic spectrum but may include other segments like infrared, ultraviolet, and x-rays, depending on the display objectives and effects desired.

The so-called visible part of the spectrum, the part to which our eyes are sensitive, is very narrow, ranging from the longest visible wavelengths, the deep reds, of about 7.5×10^{-7} meters, to the shortest, extreme violet, of about 3.9×10^{-7} meters. What we identify as blue-green light has a wavelength of 5×10^{-7} meters, or 20 millionths of an inch.

Read more about this:
Mortenson, Michael E., *3D Modeling, Animation, and Rendering*

LIGHT ANIMATION Varying through time the position, direction, and intensity of light sources in an animated scene.

Read more about this:
Mortenson, Michael E., *3D Modeling, Animation, and Rendering*

LIGHT ASSOCIATION See **LIGHT LINKING**.

LIGHTING EFFECTS The way a scene is lighted affects its informational and emotional impact. Controlling light characteristics such as intensity, color, falloff, throw, softness, and motion or light animation does this.

Read more about this:
Birn, Jeremy, [digital] *Lighting & Rendering*

LIGHTING MODEL A geometric and mathematical representation of illumination of a scene or object. The lighting model is a key part of scene composition and rendering, and encompasses such elements and characteristics as natural light, artificial light (key light, fill light, point source or omnidirectional, directional, spotlight, floodlight, geometric light source), atmospherics, glows, motion blur, and so forth. Lighting models include ambient, diffuse, and specular components.

Read more about this:
Giambruno, Mark, *3D Graphics and Animation*
O'Rourke, Michael, *Principles of Three-Dimensional Computer Animation*

LIGHTING PASS Separate rendering of the effects of one or more light sources, allowing for more creativity in manipulating lighting effects during compositing. See also **RENDERING IN PASSES**.

Read more about this:
Birn, Jeremy, [digital] *Lighting & Rendering*

LIGHTING RATIO The comparison of key light (the main source of light from which shadows fall) to the fill light (the light that fills in the shadow areas). The higher the lighting ratio, the higher the contrast of the image; the lower the ratio, the lower the contrast.

LIGHT INTENSITY A measure of the brightness of a light source, which is determined by the number of photons being emitted per second and their energy. Intensity of light is inversely proportional to the square of the distance from its source. See also **DISTANCE FALLOFF.**

LIGHT LINKING A special lighting-effects technique that associates a light source with only specific objects in a scene and not the entire scene. Also known as *light association*, *exclusive lights*, or *selective lights*.
Read more about this:
O'Rourke, Michael, *Principles of Three-Dimensional Computer Animation*

LIGHT PLACEMENT Locating light sources to produce an effectively lighted image. The figure shows some of the important lighting setups relative to camera and subject.

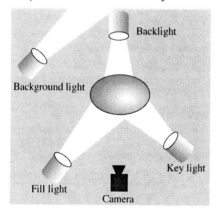

LIGHT PROBE A passive object with specific reflective properties that is used to test lighting conditions and establish the color and position of lights in a real-world scene that is to be photographed as a background plate for a digital scene; also called a *reference ball*. Two commonly used probes are the *matte ball* and the *mirror ball*. The matte ball acts as a measurable reference for incident color at a specific location, which allows color correction and matching to digital objects added to the scene. A mirror ball helps determine the angular relationships of light sources and objects, the relative

brightness of light sources, and the effects of highlights and reflections.

Read more about this:
Birn, Jeremy, [digital] *Lighting & Rendering*

LIGHT SOURCE(S) An object that emits light. Natural and artificial light sources are simulated in 3D modeling, animation, and rendering applications. Light effects mood, impact, and understanding of objects within a scene , as well as the entire scene.

Natural light includes light effects encountered in the real world whose sources include the sun, moon, stars, firelight, and their reflected light. Natural light may enter through windows and doors and affect an interior scene. If a scene is set outdoors, then the natural light is called outdoor light, which is a combination of light colors: direct sunlight, blue sky, scattered clouds, and general overcast conditions. This is also called *daylight*, which has a color temperature ranging from 5000°K to 7500°K.

Artificial light encompasses a variety of lighting effects for a scene, including key light, fill light, point light source, directional light, spotlight, floodlight, and geometric source lighting.

Ambient light is the cumulative effect of all the light bouncing off all the objects in a scene. It is treated as a global value that illuminates all objects in a rendered scene equally. Therefore, it produces no shadows or surface shading, and it has no distinct source. In the absence of any other type of lighting, objects in a scene lighted only by ambient light appear flat or two-dimensional. Use ambient light with great care, and rarely as the only source of light. Ambient light is also called *ambience* and *global lighting*.

LIGHT-OBJECT INTERACTION The alteration of light in direction or color when it strikes, reflects, or passes through a material object or some translucent medium. a variety of optical effects are produced by these interactions, and a modeling and rendering application must take these into account, including absorption, diffraction, interference, reflection, refraction, and transmission of light.

LIMIT Restriction on the range of a model's motions or shape transformations; restriction on the range of motion of a link or joint of an inverse kinematic chain. Limits apply to translations, rotations, and scaling (in the case of shape transformations). A limit is selected that produces the desired animation effects. Limits may simulate natural restraints, such as anatomical limits of joint movements for animal models. Or, limits may support the actual construction of the model, such as position limiting planes in mechanical part assemblies.

LINE A straight line is the next simplest geometric object after a point. All physical examples of a straight line are finite line segments with well-defined endpoints and length. However, the mathematical or geometric line may be unbounded or infinite, or it may be a semi-infinite half-line or ray.

Read more about this:
Mortenson, M. E., *Mathematics for Computer Graphics Applications*
O'Rourke, Michael, *Principles of Three-Dimensional Computer Animation*

LINEAR ATTENUATION See **ATTENUATION**.

LINEAR GRADIENT A continuous variation of fill color or shading along a straight-line direction or along a curve. See also **GRADIENT**.

LINEAR INTERPOLATION A method for determining the value of some property between two adjacent boundary values, directly proportional to its relative position on a straight line drawn between them. See also **SPLINE INTERPOLATION** and **TCB CONTROLLER**.

LINEAR LIGHTS An area light similar to a straight fluorescent tube light, where length is the only geometric variable. See also **FLAT AREA LIGHT**s and **SPHERICAL AREA LIGHT**s.

LINE ART Graphics images consisting entirely of lines, without any shading.

LINEAR VECTOR SPACE An abstract space whose points are defined by vectors whose origin is at a common point, and that combines any two vectors according to the parallelogram law of addition. Vectors must be subjected to the following two operations to qualify as members of a linear vector space:

1. Addition of any two vectors must produce a third vector, identified as their sum
$$\mathbf{a} + \mathbf{b} = \mathbf{c}$$

2. Multiplication of a vector $\mathbf{a}$ by a scalar k must produce another vector $k\mathbf{a}$ as the product.

The set of all vectors is *closed* with respect to these two operations, which means that both the sum of two vectors and the product of a vector and a scalar are themselves vectors. These two operations have the following properties:

1. Commutativity: $\mathbf{a} + \mathbf{b} = \mathbf{b} + \mathbf{a}$

2. Associativity: $(\mathbf{a} + \mathbf{b}) + \mathbf{c} = \mathbf{a} + (\mathbf{b} + \mathbf{c})$

3. Identity element: $\mathbf{a} + 0 = \mathbf{a}$

4. Inverse: $\mathbf{a} - \mathbf{a} = 0$

5. Identity under scalar multiplication: , when $k = 1$

6. $c(d\mathbf{a}) = (cd)\mathbf{a}$

7. $(c + d)\mathbf{a} = c\mathbf{a} + d\mathbf{a}$

8. $k(\mathbf{a} + \mathbf{b}) = k\mathbf{a} + k\mathbf{b}$

A set of vectors that can be subjected to the two operations with these eight properties forms a linear vector space.

Read more about this:
Mortenson, Michael E., *Geometric Transformations for 3D Modeling*

LINEAR WEIGHTING An animation control method used in the generation of inbetween frames. It governs frame-to-frame changes in the position of objects or other time-varying effects in a uniform continuous manner, without accelerated rates of change.

LINE CLIPPING In a model or database with many line segments, only those within the computer-graphics display-screen window are displayed. This means that a test is needed to decide if a line segment is entirely inside, partially inside, or entirely outside the window area. A line segment is completely within the window area if, and only if, all the following inequalities are true: $W_L \le x_0, x_1 \le W_R$ and $W_B \le y_0, y_1 \le W_T$. Otherwise, the line is partially inside the window or entirely outside it. In the first case, the line is clipped at its point of intersection with the window boundary; in the second, it is omitted (not displayed).

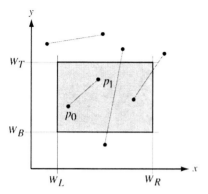

Read more about this:
Mortenson, Michael E., *3D Modeling, Animation, and Rendering*
_____, *Mathematics for Computer Graphics Applications*

LINE OF ACTION The line along which the principal objects or characters in a scene are looking, moving, or interacting. All camera angles and positions should be shot from the same side of the line of action. It also governs the arrangement and kind of lighting.

LINK A rigid segment of a mechanism or animated object connected to another link through a joint that allows relative movement between them; sometimes denotes a model-building command that creates an edge between two vertices of a polygonal mesh where none existed before.

LINKS AND CONSTRAINTS Hierarchical connections between parts of an articulated object that specify the kind and limits of allowed relative motions between adjacent parts, for example the joints in an animated object or a robotic mechanism.

LOCAL COORDINATE SYSTEM The coordinate system in which an object is initially defined. It is permanently associated with the object in the model database, and is independent of the world coordinate system in which the object is placed with other objects to form a scene. An object is created within its local coordinate system in a geometrically and computationally convenient way: for example, the center of a sphere is located at the origin of its local system, while a cube may have its edges aligned with the principal axes of its local coordinate system, with one of its vertices at the origin. The data defining the object in the local system be-

comes part of the object database. Complex objects made-up of more than one primitive object may require a hierarchy of local coordinate systems.

Read more about this:
Mortenson, M. E., *3D Modeling, Animation, and Rendering*
_____, *Mathematics for Computer Graphics Applications*
O'Rourke, Michael, *Principles of Three-Dimensional Computer Animation*

LOCAL ILLUMINATION The condition in which selected light sources illuminate only a single subject, without affecting any other objects in a scene.

Read more about this:
Birn, Jeremy, [digital] *Lighting & Rendering*

LOCUS OF POINTS A set of points satisfying a rule of construction or mathematical function. For example, in 3D the locus of all points equally distant from a given point is a sphere whose radius is equal to the given distance.

LOFTED SURFACE A surface fit smoothly to a series of parallel 2D cross sections; also, a form of skinning.

Lofting was used in the design and construction of airplane wings. The airfoil shapes define the wing surface in the figure.

Read more about this:
Giambruno, Mark, *3D Graphics and Animation*
O'Rourke, Michael, *Principles of Three-Dimensional Computer Animation*

LONG TAKE An uninterrupted shot in a film which lasts much longer than the conventional editing pace either of the film itself or of films in general, usually lasting several minutes. It can be used for dramatic and narrative effect if done properly, and in moving shots is often accomplished through the use of a dolly or *Steadicam*.

LOOMING A mirage in which distant objects below the horizon seem to be raised above their true positions. See **ATMOSPHERIC REFRACTIO**n.

Read more about this:
Naylor, John, *Out of the Blue*

LOSSLESS DATA COMPRESSION A technique that reduces the amount of data needed to record, store, and transmit a graphics image. It allows the reconstruction of an image without loss of original detail. Most pixel-based image data formats allow lossless data compression; for example, GIF, JPEG, and PNG.

Read more about this:
Giambruno, Mark, *3D Graphics and Animation*

LOSSY DATA COMPRESSION A technique that reduces the amount of data needed to record, store, and transmit a graphics image. Unlike the lossless method, it does not allow reconstruction of the image in its original detail. The JPEG format allows the user to set the amount of data compression used.

Read more about this:
Giambruno, Mark, *3D Graphics and Animation*

LOW-ANGLE SHOT The view from a camera positioned below the subject. Low-angle shots tend to make the subject appear larger, a shot from a camera positioned low on the vertical axis, often at knee height, looking up. See also **HIGH-ANGLE SHOT**.

Tower Bridge , A. Leroux (2006).

LOW CONTRAST A condition in which there is little difference between the lightest and darkest tones or values; used to create a subdued or somber image, to produce a neutral background for foreground title text or special effects, or to simulate a foggy, dusty or snowy image. See also **CONTRAST**.

Formatt.com.uk (date unknown).

LOW-KEY LIGHTING Indicates a dark scene with low light levels, and thus a high key-to-fill ratio. The low-key lighting image of a shadowy Humphrey Bogart is from *The Big Sleep*.

The Big Sleep, Howard Hawks, Warner Bros. (1946)

LUMINANCE The brightness of a color. See also *value*.

Read more about this:
O'Rourke, Michael, *Principles of Three-Dimensional Computer Animation*

LUMINOSITY The total amount of electromagnetic energy (usually the visible light part of the spectrum) emitted per second by a radiating source such as the sun, a star, or artificial light; radiant or reflected light from an object.

Read more about this:
Naylor, John, *Out of the Blue*

LUMINOSITY MAPPING Using a textured map to simulate self-illumination of an object; also referred to as *incandescence*, *ambience*, or *constant mapping*.

Read more about this:
Birn, Jeremy, [digital] *Lighting & Rendering*
Giambruno, Mark, *3D Graphics and Animation*

LUSTROUS A soft shininess, glowing as from an internal or backlight.

LZW Acronym for Lempell-Ziv-Welch image data compression algorithm. See also **LOSSLESS DATA COMPRESSION**.

M

MACHINED PART An object whose shape is designed to satisfy a particular function and the constraints of manufacturing methods; shapes used in CAD/CAM solid modeling.

MACRO A shortcut modeling (or other) procedure; a small program written to permit the user to do a repetitive task with a minimum of interactions that would ordinarily require many.

MAGNET TOOL An interactive modeling tool designed to make 3D shape changes by attracting or repelling vertices when its on-screen icon is brought close to a polygonal mesh. See also **WELD** and **FUSE**.

Read more about this:
Giambruno, Mark, *3D Graphics and Animation*

MAPPING Applying two-dimensional images or textures to a surface. See **TEXTURE MAPPING**.

Read more about this:
Giambruno, Mark, *3D Graphics and Animation*

MAPPING COORDINATES A set of coordinates that specify the location, orientation, and scale of any textures applied to an object.

MAQUETTE A reduced scale model or sculpture of a character, often highly detailed, used to develop and study the effects of position, lighting, shadow, and relation to scene background and surrounding characters.

Read more about this:
Giambruno, Mark, *3D Graphics and Animation*

MASK A 2D shape or silhouette used to block out areas of an image with a uniform and neutral color, such as blue, black, or gray-scale, and subsequently fill in with a different image, allowing superimposing images from different sources and types; a filter excluding selected colors or values. Still and animated masks allow superimposing images.

MASS A physical property of real objects, used to compute natural force behavior. The total mass of an object depends on both the size and material of which it is made. Given two balls of the same size, one made of steel is more massive than one made of wood. Their motion dynamics is different as a result of their mass difference.

MATCH CUT In filmmaking and animation, a cut in which elements of two camera shots suggest continuity of an idea across two different actions or locations Here are two match-cut frames from Stanley Kubrick's 2001: *A Space Odyssey*.

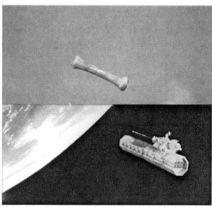

Stanley Kubrick, 2001: *A Space Odyssey*.

MATCH MOVING Setting up a digital scene and camera to smoothly blend live action, animated components, and background.

MATING RELATIONSHIPS Specifies how parts are fit together to form an assembly; used to control spatial relationships between parts of an assembly.

MATRIX set of numbers or other mathematical elements arranged in a rectangular array of rows and columns. In the example shown here, the lowercase subscripted letters are the elements of the matrix. The double subscript gives the position of each element in the array by row and column, respectively. Thus, a_{ij} represent a matrix element in the ith row and jth column. If there are more than nine rows and columns, then the subscripts are separated by a comma.

$$\begin{bmatrix} a_{11} & a_{12} & a_{13} \\ a_{21} & a_{22} & a_{23} \\ a_{31} & a_{32} & a_{33} \end{bmatrix}$$

The structure of a matrix makes it easy to assemble and work with certain kinds of mathematical data. The coefficients of a set of simultaneous linear equations or the coordinates of a point can be written as a matrix.

MATTE A dull finish on a surface, with low reflectivity and no specular effects; also, a mask used to block out or hide a specific region on a frame of film or animation.

MATTE BALL See **LIGHT PROBE**.

MATTING A compositing technique for combining or superimposing images: for example, adding a new foreground image and a background image. See also **MASK**

Read more about this:
O'Rourke, Michael, *Principles of Three-Dimensional Computer Animation*

MCAD The acronym for *Mechanical Computer-Aided Design*.

MECHANICAL COMPUTER-AIDED DESIGN (MCAD) A solid modeling computer application used in mechanical design engineering.

MECHANICAL MODEL A 3D model of an object with moving parts, incorporating links and joints, constraints, kinematic transformations, motion envelops, configuration space, and tolerance effects.

MEDIUM CLOSE-UP A shot somewhere between a medium shot and a close-up; for example, a shot framing the forelegs and hooves of a horse trampling a rattlesnake. See also **SHOT SIZE**.

MEDIUM SHOT A general, all-purpose shot, often used for dialogue sequences; a shot framing most of a character or object, including the most active portion if animated;

for example, the ball, racket and upper torso of a tennis player in the act of serving. See also **SHOT SIZE** and **WIDE SHOT**.

MESH A grid-like polygonal subdivision of the surface of a geometric model. See also **POLYGONIZATION**.

Read more about this:
Giambruno, Mark, *3D Graphics and Animation*
Mortenson, Michael E., *3D Modeling, Animation, and Rendering*
O'Rourke, Michael, *Principles of Three-Dimensional Computer Animation*

MESH FORM MODELER Used to create 3D objects by directly manipulating vertices, edges, and face polygons of a polygonal model.

MESH GENERATION The process of generating a polygonal or polyhedral mesh that approximates a surface.

MESHING A process for subdividing the surface of a geometric model into a grid-like mesh of polygons, creating an appropriate form for subsequent finite-element analysis, rendering or similar processes. See also **POLYGONIZATION**.

MESH OPTIMIZATION A procedure to reduce the density of a mesh by combining closely aligned (that is, nearly coplanar) adjacent faces.

Read more about this:
Giambruno, Mark, *3D Graphics and Animation*

METABALLS A 3D modeling technique that blends and transforms an assembly of spheres into a complex shape; most suitable for animal and other organic forms. A metaball is defined by a so-called three-dimensional variable density field, radiating from a given center point. The value of the field can vary linearly with distance from the center, or in any way expressed by a mathematical formula. A field can have a negative density distribution, or even an eccentric distribution.

A point on a metaball surface is constructed at all points in the field that have the same density value. This value is given by the modeler or derived from the modeling context. The figure shows the affect of two (positive) metaballs on each other.

ClydeG, (2007). Shows best in color edition.

If two or more metaballs are constructed in close proximity to one another so that they overlap, they coalesce and their fields are added in a process called *fusion* to produce a composite field, which is then evaluated to produce a composite surface. Metaball fields can be transformed in a variety of ways to produce organic shapes necessary to represent, for example, the human form. Metaball surfaces are rendered as polygons.

Read more about this:
Giambruno, Mark, *3D Graphics and Animation*
O'Rourke, Michael, *Principles of Three-Dimensional Computer Animation*

METACHROMATIC Susceptible to a change of color; for example, the variation of the color of an object with variation in its temperature.

METANURBS A lattice deformation technique for shaping underlying NURBS surfaces.

METRIC A mathematical function used to determine the distance s between any two points P_1 and P_2 in a coordinate space, where each type of space has its own unique metric. In Euclidean space the Pythagorean theorem gives the metric:

$$s = \sqrt{\left(x_2 - x_1\right)^2 + \left(y_2 - y_1\right)^2 + \left(z_2 - z_1\right)^2}$$

where $P_1 = \left(x_1, y_1, z_1\right)$ and $P_2 = \left(x_2, y_2, z_2\right)$. Differential geometry provides for the more general case of distances on arbitrary curved surfaces and spaces.

MICROFACET SURFACE ROUGHNESS A reflection model that treats a surface as consisting of very small mirror-like faces, whose orientation is statistically perturbed to simulate the desired degree of roughness. In the aggregate, this causes specular reflection to spread out about the mirror direction.

MICROGEOMETRY Surface characteristics too small to be modeled directly, such as roughness and texture. Instead, the underlying geometric model may be stochastically perturbed at each rendered location to create a height field affecting reflection and shading. Alternatively, texture mapping may be used to represent microgeometry.

MINIATURE EFFECT A special effect produced by using scale models. Scale models are often filmed with high-speed photography so that gravitational and other physics effects appear natural. This is not a problem with animation, where size, frame rate, and natural force behaviors are accounted for from the beginning. Not just objects or characters are scaled, but also natural phenomena that are too difficult or too expensive to produce life size; for example, fires, floods, and explosions.

MINMAX BOX See *bounding box* and *bounding volume*.

MIPMAP Also called *MIP mapping*; in 3D computer graphics texture filtering, precalculated, optimized collections of images that accompany a main texture, used to increase rendering speed and reduce aliasing artifacts. It is used in 3D computer games, flight simulators and other 3D imaging systems.

MIRAGE An effect of atmospheric refraction. There are two kinds of mirage: inferior and superior. An inferior mirage looks like a shimmering pool of water in the distance and occurs on a hot day when a thin layer of hot air has formed at ground level, commonly seen in the desert or over the asphalt surface of a road or highway. The image of an object, like a tree at the distance and direction of the mirage, may be reflected within the mirage, adding to the perception that the mirage is a real a pool of water. Under some conditions of geography and atmospheric conditions, an inferior image of the sun is formed just as it is setting.

Read more about this:
Naylor, John, *Out of the Blue*

MIRROR BALL See *light probe*.

MIRROR DIRECTION Refers to the direction in which light is reflected off a shiny surface. The angle of incidence of a light ray striking a shiny surface is reflected at an equal angle relative to the local normal to the surface.

MIRROR, MIRRORING A modeling transformation that creates the mirror image of an object.

MISE EN SCENE A French phrase meaning, literally, "to put into the scene," or "setting the scene;" an approach to film-making that advocates long takes and frequent camera moves in preference to chopping up a scene through editing; referring to everything appearing before the camera, including sets, props, actors, costumes, camera movements and performances; pronounced *mee-zahn-sen*.

MIXED REALITY A scene or animation sequence blending real life and virtual reality, using direct views, stereoscopic graphics, and video. See also **AUGMENTED REALITY**.

MOCAP Short for *motion capture*.

MODEL The mathematical or physical representation of an object. Physicists use mathematical models of real-world phenomena. Computers use models of data structures and relationships. Models may be static or procedural. In most cases, they are simple, manageable and analyzable versions of the originals. Geometric models used in computer graphics are mathematical descriptions, supporting data, and algorithms defining their interpretation.

MODELING The process of describing objects and scenes in a way that can be analyzed and from which an image can be created.

MOIRÉ A visual effect having a wave-like appearance caused by the superposition of small and repetitive patterns within an image that periodically overlap and reinforce and cancel each other. These patterns may be an intentional part of a rendering or an unintended and undesirable artifact of some combination of the image's characteristics, the output device, and the rendering process.

Read more about this:
Demers, Owen, [digital] *Texture & Painting*
Giambruno, Mark, *3D Graphics and Animation*

MOLDED PART A highly constrained shape used in CAD/CAM solid modeling.

MOLECULAR GRAPHICS Modeling the geometric arrangement and reactions of atoms in a molecule or system of molecules.

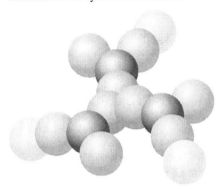

MONITOR RESOLUTION Also *display resolution*; the highest number of pixels per inch (ppi) a computer graphics monitor is capable of displaying.

MONOCHROME An image rendered in different shades of a single color.

Read more about this:
Demers, Owen, [digital] *Texture & Painting*

MONTAGE A filmmaking and animation editing technique, consisting of a series of short shots that are combined into a coherent sequence, used to suggest the passage of time, rather than to create symbolic meaning.

MONTAGE SEQUENCE A segment of a film summarizing a topic or compressing the passing of time into brief images. Some familiar examples are whirling newspaper headlines, gangster gunfire dissolving in and out, pages flying off a calendar, clock hands dissolving to different positions, and seasons changing.

MONTE CARLO METHOD A random sampling technique used in performing certain kinds of computations. The use of jitter in antialiasing is a Monte Carlo method, since it introduces random variations within the grid restriction. A method of global illumination, because of its implicit dependence on random sampling, has almost monopolized the use of the word "Monte Carlo" to describe itself. This method is an alternative to radiosity, and models multiple interdiffuse reflections by sending out rays in random scattering directions from a surface point and averaging the intensities obtained.

MORPHING A modeling and animation technique that smoothly transforms the shape of one object into the shape of the another; a special effect in traditional motion pictures and animation that changes (or morphs) one image into another through a seamless transition.

Most often it is used to depict one person turning into another through technological means or as part of a fantasy or surreal sequence. Such a depiction could be achieved through cross-fading techniques on film. However, since the early 1990s, this has been replaced by computer software to create more realistic transitions. Here a car morphs into a tiger. See also **MORPH TARGET ANIMATION**, and **TWEENING**.

Madison Area Technical College, W. Phillips, (no date)

Read more about this:
Giambruno, Mark, *3D Graphics and Animation*

MORPH TARGET ANIMATION A method of 3D computer animation used as an alternative to skeletal animation. Movements are stored as a series of changing vertex positions. In each keyframe of the animation, the vertices are moved to a different position.

The advantage to using morph target animation over skeletal animation is that the artist has more control over movement by defining positions of individual vertices within a keyframe, avoiding constraints imposed by skeletons. This is useful for animating cloth, skin, and facial expressions because these are difficult motions to achieve using skeletal animation.

One disadvantage is that vertex animation computations are more time-consuming than skeletal animation, because every vertex position has to be calculated. Another disadvantage is that when vertices move from position to position between frames, a distortion may be created that doesn't happen using skeletal animation. This is described as *looking shaky*. Or, the distortion may be part of the desired look.

MOSAICING Assembling a set of smaller, partially overlapping spatial volumes into a single larger volume without overlapping spaces or information, where the volumes represent graphic data, such as 3D CAT, MRI, or ultrasound scans.

MOTION BLUR Intentional slight smearing of the image when the subject or camera is in motion, enhancing the illusion of motion; image blurring occurring when the film exposure time is long relative to the motion of the subject.
Read more about this:
Demers, Owen, [digital] *Texture & Painting*
O'Rourke, Michael, *Principles of Three-Dimensional Computer Animation*

MOTION CAPTURE The process of capturing and recording movement and translating that movement onto a digital model; using a sequence of time-lapse photos, film, or video recording to derive realistic motions (usually human or animal) for subsequent computer graphics animation. It is used in military, entertainment, sports, and medical applications. In filmmaking it refers to recording actions of human actors, and using that information to animate digital character models in 3D animation. When it includes face, fingers and captures subtle expressions, it is often referred to as *performance capture* or also *mo cap*.
Read more about this:
Giambruno, Mark, *3D Graphics and Animation*
O'Rourke, Michael, *Principles of Three-Dimensional Computer Animation*

MOTION CONTROL PHOTOGRAPHY A special effects technique creating the illusion of normal size from a small model by moving a small camera by the model at very slow speed. Motion control photography was effectively used in *Star Wars* to produce stunningly realistic scenes using small models.

MOTION DYNAMICS The physical effects of motion upon an animated model, an important part of animation and modeling natural force behavior. See also **DYNAMICS**.

Read more about this:
Mortenson, Michael E., *3D Modeling, Animation, and Rendering*
O'Rourke, Michael, *Principles of Three-Dimensional Computer Animation*

MOTION ENVELOPE A curve, surface, or solid swept out by the end effector or intermediate joints of a mechanical part or animated object, representing the locus of possible positions; useful for range and interference studies. A rectangle moving through space generates a motion envelope, consisting of four curved surfaces bounding a volume.

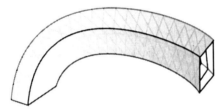

MOTION PATH A mathematical and geometric representation of the path of an object, which may be modified to make adjustments to the animation. An object may be constrained to follow a curved path and maintain a specified orientation with respect to that path. Straight lines, spline curves, or combinations of these or other types of curves may represent motion paths. The rate of progress along a motion path is controlled by a timing curve.

Read more about this:
Giambruno, Mark, *3D Graphics and Animation*
Mortenson, Michael E., *3D Modeling, Animation, and Rendering*

MULTI-PASS RENDERING See **COMPOSITING**, **PASS**, and **RENDERING**.

N

NATURAL EQUATION OF A CURVE An equation connecting the curvature $1/\rho$, torsion τ, and arc length, s, of a curve: $f(1/\rho,\tau,s) = 0$. This equation imposes a condition on the curve, so that it has certain special properties, but many curves may also have these properties. For example, $\tau = 0$ is a natural equation characterizing all plane curves, and $1/\rho = 0$ is also a natural equation characterizing all straight lines. An additional independent natural equation $g(1/\rho,\tau,s) = 0$ of the curve determines the curve still more. Solving the two natural equations $f(1/\rho,\tau,s) = 0$ and $g(1/\rho,\tau,s) = 0$ simultaneously for $1/\rho$ and τ as functions of s produces intrinsic equations. Two natural equations determine a curve uniquely, except for its position.

NATURAL FORCE BEHAVIOR Actions of animated objects that conform to the laws of physics, including motion, shape-deforming forces of acceleration and gravity, collisions (elastic and plastic deformations), bounce and rebound, friction effects, centrifugal deformations, fluid flow effects, and others.

Read more about this:
Mortenson, Michael E., *3D Modeling, Animation, and Rendering*

NATURALISTIC MODEL Incorporating true-to-life organic forms into a scene, such as plants, animals, water, and atmospheric phenomena such as rain, snow, fire, and smoke. Fractals, particle systems, and metaballs are common underlying techniques used to simulate these effects.

NATURAL LIGHT Light effects encountered in the real world whose sources include the sun, moon, stars, and fire light, and their reflected light.

NECKER CUBE A two-dimensional wireframe drawing of a cube, giving the illusion of depth in the absence of depth cues. The cube's orientation may seem to alternate, depending on the particular point of focus of the viewer. This is one of the undesirable effects of purely wireframe models.

The cube can be seen as tilting up or down.

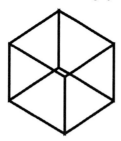

NEGATIVE DENSITY FIELD A density field whose points all have negative values; used to produce a concave surface in a metaball model.

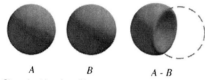

A   *B*   *A - B*

Shows best in color edition.

Read more about this:
O'Rourke, Michael, *Principles of Three-Dimensional Computer Animation*

NEGATIVE IMAGE Reversing light and dark in an image.

NEGATIVE SPACE The space around and between the subjects of an image. See **FRAMING**.

NOISE A random number generator used to produce effects of scattering, roughness or turbulence.

NONLINEAR FINITE-ELEMENT ANALYSIS A structural analysis technique used when materials, geometries, loads, or boundary conditions deviate from linear behavior. Linear behavior is described by first-degree polynomials or differential equations, and nonlinear behavior is described by second-degree or higher polynomials or differential equations. For linear behavior, doubling the input driving a behavior doubles the response. And it is possible to compute a unique input for a given output. However, with nonlinear behavior, doubling the input may produce an eight-fold increase in the response for a third-degree (cubic) driving function, In this case, computing the input from a given output requires extracting a cubic root, for which there may be three distinct solutions.

NONORGANIC FORMS Models of nonliving objects from the natural world, including rocks, mountains, water, clouds, smoke, rain, snow, and fire.

NON-UNIFORM RATIONAL B-SPLINE CURVE (NURBS) One of the most versatile curve-modeling techniques. The NURBS curve, as it is popularly called, has become so widely used that it is almost an industry standard. Non-uniform and rational refer to specific mathematical properties of the curve equations. This curve is based on the ratio of two nonrational B-spline basis functions, making it a vector-valued piecewise rational polynomial. NURBS curves are invariant under translation, rotation, scaling, shear, and parallel and perspective projection. They can be used to produce an exact representation of a conic curve. The shape of a NURBS curve can be changed over a small segment of it. This is known as local control and is done by moving one or more edit points (sometimes called *knots*), which lie exactly on the curve. B-splines do not necessarily interpolate their end points. However, the nonuniform B-spline basis functions allow this.

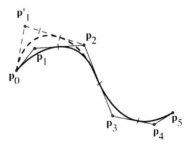

Read more about this:
Giambruno, Mark, *3D Graphics and Animation*
Mortenson, M. E., *Geometric Modeling*
O'Rourke, Michael, *Principles of Three-Dimensional Computer Animation*
Watt, A. and M. Watt, *Advanced Animation and Rendering Techniques*

NORMAL A straight line or vector perpendicular to some point on a curve or surface. The normal varies from point to point on a curved surface. The unit normal is indispensable in CAD/CAM surface modeling. For example, the convention is for the normal to point outward from the surface of a solid model. Computing silhouette curves, hidden surfaces, shadows, and shading effects requires surface normal information.

Given two noncollinear tangent vectors **s** and **t** to any point on a surface, then the unit normal at that point is $\hat{\mathbf{n}} = \dfrac{\mathbf{s} \times \mathbf{t}}{|\mathbf{s} \times \mathbf{t}|}$.

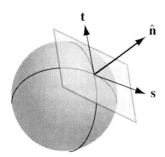

Read more about this:
Mortenson, M. E., *Geometric Modeling*
_____, *Mathematics for Computer Graphics Applications*

NORMAL MAPPING A method for representing bumps and dents in a surface to be rendered. It enhances the appearance of surface detail in a relatively low polygon-count model by producing a normal map from a higher polygon count version of the same model.

NULL An object that does not render, so it can be used as an invisible component of a model; also called a *dummy object*.

Read more about this:
Giambruno, Mark, *3D Graphics and Animation*

NUMERICAL CONTROL PROGRAMMING A method of creating the instructions to drive numerically controlled (NC) machine tools; also called *computer-numerically-controlled* or *CNC*. The geometry for the instructions is obtained from a CAD solid model.

NURBS The acronym for the *non-uniform rational b-spline*.

O

OBJECT DATABASE The data defining a 3D model in its local coordinate system, including its geometry, topology (or connectivity), and surface and physical properties.

OBJECT-ORIENTED GRAPHICS The mathematical representation of geometric and graphic objects, as opposed to using a bitmap image. See also **VECTOR GRAPHICS**.

OBLIQUE ANGLE SHOT A shot taken with the camera tilted so that the final image itself looks tilted; also called a *tilt shot*. The photo of the Eiffel Tower is an example of how effective an extreme oblique angle shot can be. See also **DUTCH ANGLE**.

Flickr.com, Doubletee (2007).

OBLIQUE COORDINATE SYSTEM One in which the principal axes are not mutually perpendicular. here is an oblique coordinate system of the most general sort

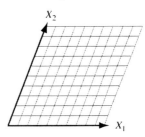

In the following illustration, the vectors $\mathbf{e}_1$ and $\mathbf{e}_2$ define an oblique coordinate system in the *xy* plane. Every point in the plane has a position vector given by

$\mathbf{p} = \alpha \mathbf{e}_1 + \beta \mathbf{e}_2$, where the oblique coordinates of a point are (α, β) and the magnitudes of $\mathbf{e}_1$ and $\mathbf{e}_2$ establish the scaling along the two axes.

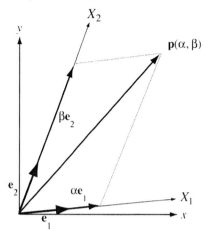

Read more about this:
Mortenson, Michael E., *3D Modeling, Animation, and Rendering*

OCCLUDING CONTOUR The silhouette outline of an object blocking the view of another object or part of a scene; to occlude means to block from view. See also **SILHOUETTE**.

OCCLUSION CULLING Hidden surface determination in 3D modeling.

OCTAHEDRON The octahedron is one of the five regular polyhedra, having eight identical equilateral-triangle faces. It has six vertices, 12 edges, and four faces surround each vertex. The sum of the face angles at each vertex is $240°$.

Read more about this:
Coexeter, H. S. M., *Regular Polytopes*
Mortenson, M. E., *Mathematics for Computer Graphics Applications*

OFFSCREEN SPACE The actual or implied continuation of a scene beyond the field of view by visual clues within the scene; for example, shadows cast by objects outside the field of view.

Read more about this:
Birn, Jeremy, *[digital] Lighting & Rendering*

OFFSET A 3D modeling technique used to create an offset surface.

OFFSET SURFACE A new or derivative surface, the points on which are perpendicularly offset an equal distance from corresponding points on the original surface.

OMNIDIRECTIONAL LIGHT See **POINT LIGHT**.

ONION SKINNING In computer graphics animation an editing technique that displays several frames at once, allowing the animator to manipulate and review the effect of changes. Here a sequence of frames of a galloping cartoon horse superimposes leg motions.

Wikipedia, J-E Nyström (2006).

ON ONES, ON TWOS Rendering and recording thirty frames for each second of animation is called *recording on ones*; producing only fifteen frames for each second is called *recording on twos*. The later requires half the rendering effort, but produces acceptable results only under special conditions.

OPACITY A measure of how much light is prevented from passing through an object. Opacity defines the same property as transparency, but from the opposite end of the scale. An opaque object does not transmit any light.

Read more about this:
Giambruno, Mark, *3D Graphics and Animation*

OPACITY MAP A grayscale image that makes an object's surface appear to vary from opaque to transparent.

Read more about this:
Giambruno, Mark, *3D Graphics and Animation*

OPACITY WEIGHTING A method to control and vary the opacity within a solid object; used in volume rendering in scientific visualization applications.

OPALESCENCE, OPALESCENT Showing a shimmering play of colors like that of an opal; having a milky iridescence.

Shows best in color edition.

Read more about this:
Demers, Owen, [digital] *Texture & Painting*

OPAQUE A physical property of an object that prevents all light from passing through it; the opposite of transparent.

OPEN GL A software standard adopted by the graphics industry for 3D video hardware communication.

OPEN ML A standard cross-platform environment that supports creation and display of digital media, including audio, video, and graphics.

OPEN SET Also called *open interval*; a line segment defined by the set of points X on it, $a < X < b$, where a and b are limiting points of the segment (and set). It is an open set because the points a and b are not included in it. The open circles at a and b in the figure symbolize this.

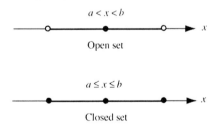

$$a < x < b$$

Open set

$$a \leq x \leq b$$

Closed set

A closed set means that these points are included in the line segment (and set), and the solid circles indicate that. The closure of an open set is the union of the set with the set of all its limit points. These concepts naturally extend to two- and three- dimensional spaces and point sets, and are used in the Boolean algebra of constructive solid geometry.

The *boundary* of a closed set is the set of all its limit points. Conversely, the *interior* of a closed set is the set of all points of a set not on its boundary. Thus, $X = bX \cup iX$, where bX denotes the set of boundary points and iX denotes the interior points.

Read more about this:
Mortenson, Michael E., *Mathematics for Computer Graphics Applications*

OPERAND In constructive solid geometry, either of the two shapes being combined by a Boolean operator. For example, in the Boolean equation $C = A \cup B$, the operands are A and B, and the operator is $\cup$.

Read more about this:
Giambruno, Mark, *3D Graphics and Animation*
Mortenson, M. E., *Geometric Modeling*
_____, *Mathematics for Computer Graphics Applications*

OPTICAL EFFECTS Phenomena originating in a camera's lens or film, such as lens flare or overexposure. Other examples are film titles, fades, dissolves, wipes, blow-ups, skip frames, bluescreen, compositing, double exposures, zooms and pans, and other special effects using light and shadow. Optical effects are usually rendered as a separate pass.

OPTICS A branch of physical science that deals with the properties of light and its transmission through lenses and transparent media, including cameras, prisms, fiber optics, microscopes, and telescopes.

ORBIT A motion that rotates the camera about an axis through a fixed aim point. A more general orbit motion for a camera is along any closed or open curve more or less encircling the aim point.

Read more about this:
Mortenson, M. E., *Mathematics for Computer Graphics Applications*
O'Rourke, Michael, *Principles of Three-Dimensional Computer Animation*

ORGANIC FORMS Representations of the shapes and textures of real or imaginary living things.

Read more about this:
Giambruno, Mark, *3D Graphics and Animation*

ORIENTATION The directional placement of an object in 3D space, that is, where it's face or a specific feature is pointing. Also, orientation is a topological property of certain shapes, characterized by terms such as clockwise or counterclockwise, right handed or left handed; for example, in a plane a triangle and its reflection have opposite orientations.

Read more about this:
Mortenson, Michael E., *3D Modeling, Animation, and Rendering*
_____, *Geometric Transformations for 3D Modeling*
Watt, A. and M. Watt, *Advanced Animation and Rendering Techniques*

ORIGIN The zero-valued reference point for quantifying position in a coordinate system; the point of intersection of the principal axes of a coordinate system.

ORTHOGRAPHIC DRAWING A standard engineering drawing consisting of 2D projections from three mutually perpendicular directions, creating the so-called three principal views of a 3D object.

ORTHOGRAPHIC PROJECTION A method of representing an object by a line drawing on a projection plane that is perpendicular to parallel projectors; one of several important projection transformations that produce two-dimensional images of three-dimensional objects.

Read more about this:
Giambruno, Mark, *3D Graphics and Animation*
Mortenson, M. E., *Mathematics for Computer Graphics Applications*

OUTDOOR LIGHT A combination of light colors: direct sunlight, blue sky, scattered clouds, and general overcast conditions; also called *daylight*; a color temperature ranging from 5000°K to 7500°K.

OUTTAKES Shots that are not included in the final cut of a film.

OVER-DEFINED MODEL A condition of conflicting or redundant constraints or dimensions used to define a 3D model.

OVEREXPOSURE The presence of only light tones, with little or no contrast, caused by too much light and too many light sources. A histogram reveals an overexposed condition when all the highest-frequency-of-occurrence tones are concentrated at the light end of the graph. Common ways to correct for overexposure include ensuring that shadows are fully rendered, restricting the angular falloff of lights, deleting some lights, eliminating global illumination, limiting ambient light, and reducing the number of light sources used in a scene. See also **EXPOSURE** and **UNDEREXPOSURE**

The photograph below was intentionally overexposed to produce an artistic effect. Similar effects can be obtained with proper rendering techniques.

R. Lestrade (2008). Shows best in color edition.

Read more about this:
Birn, Jeremy, [digital] *Lighting & Rendering*

OVERSCANNING Projecting a slightly larger-scale image than the actual size of a video screen, producing minor cropping; originally designed into early television sets to crop out variation in picture size caused by current and signal fluctuations.

Read more about this:
Birn, Jeremy, [digital] *Lighting & Rendering*

OVERSHOOTING An undesirable side effect that may occur during spline interpolations used to determine actions between keyframes. Certain arrangements of control points intended to control the shape of a spline interpolation curve over several keyframes may produce inflections in the curve, which in turn may produce reversals of motion or positions exceeding planned limits for the objects they are controlling. Such conditions are easily corrected by careful analysis of the interpolation curve's behavior, which often may be done simply by looking at its graph.

Read more about this:
O'Rourke, Michael, *Principles of Three-Dimensional Computer Animation*

OVER-THE-SHOULDER SHOT See **SHOT/COUNTER-SHOT**.

P

PAINT To fill the bounded surface of a 3D object with a color or texture. Computer graphics paint applications simulate the tools of traditional art: oils, watercolors, pencil, and charcoal.

PAINTER'S ALGORITHM A rendering technique that presorts objects by depth (distance from the camera or viewer) so that objects rendered last are the closest ones; analogous to the way an artist might paint the background scenery first and the foreground subjects last. This approach makes heavy computational demands that slow down the rendering process, because not only does each object have to be presorted by depth, but also every polygon making up each object must be similarly presorted.

Read more about this:
O'Rourke, Michael, *Principles of Three-Dimensional Computer Animation*

PAINTING MAP A texture map created using a paint program.

PALETTE An interactive list showing tools available within 3D modeling, paint, and illustration programs, where specific tools are often context sensitive; a set of colors or fill patterns available to the illustrator or renderer.

PAN The rotation of a camera around its vertical axis to keep a moving object in view or to record a panoramic view of a scene. The camera location remains fixed while the aim point moves parallel to the horizon.

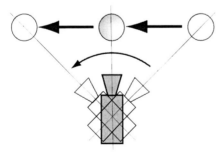

The illustration above shows a camera panning a sphere moving horizontally through a scene, viewed from above, and looking down along the camera's axis of rotation. See also **CAMERA MOVES**.

Read more about this:
Giambruno, Mark, *3D Graphics and Animation*
O'Rourke, Michael, *Principles of Three-Dimensional Computer Animation*

PAN AND SCAN A technique used to adapt wide-screen film image frames to standard television proportions by cropping left and right sides of each frame; an active pan across the full width of a frame that is then transformed into video format.

PANEL One of a set of sketches and images making up the storyboard for an animation sequence.

Read more about this:
O'Rourke, Michael, *Principles of Three-Dimensional Computer Animation*

PARALLAX The apparent displacement of an object against a distant background when the viewing point is moved.

PARAMETER The independent variable in Hermite, Bézier and NURBS equations; a free variable determining specific instances of a more general form.

PARAMETERIZED TEXTURE MAPPING A rendering technique for adding 2D images, patterns, or the appearance of texture to the surface of a 3D object. Typically, the image is created in the unit interval, $0 \leq u, v \leq 1$, in a 2D planar coordinate system, called a 2D *parametric space* whose principle axes are u and v (analogous to the x and y axes). This image is then mapped onto parametric surfaces defining a 3D object's boundary (such as, Bézier, b-spline, or NURBS surfaces). Any of these surfaces, in the 3D space of the object or the 2D parametric space of the image or pattern, may be reparameterized to achieve the desired effect.

Read more about this:
O'Rourke, Michael, *Principles of Three-Dimensional Computer Animation*

PARAMETRIC CONTINUITY Applies to parametric curves, such as B-spline and Bézier curves, describing the smoothness of the parameter's value along a curve or surface.

For example, a curve has C^n continuity if $d^n \mathbf{p}(u) / du^n$ is continuous throughout its length. Joining two curve segments at a common point so that their first n parametric derivatives are equal at that point creates a condition of continuity called nth -order *parametric continuity*, denoted as C^n. A less restrictive form of nth order continuity is nth-order *geometric continuity*, denoted as G^n. See also **GEOMETRIC CONTINUITY**.

Read more about this:
Mortenson, Michael E., *Geometric Modeling*

PARAMETRIC CURVE An algebraic form for representing a curve, whose general expression for a 3D curve is $x = f(u)$, $y = g(u)$, and $z = h(u)$, where u is the parametric variable, and also the independent variable. Each value of u defines a point in space. Because it is not meaningful or practical to allow values of the parametric variable to range from $-\infty$ to $+\infty$, an interval is chosen that has some significance to 3D modeling as well as computational advantages, and that interval is $0 \leq u \leq 1$. This interval establishes the curve's two end points and creates a curve segment between them, for example, for the following set of linear parametric equations: $x = a + du$, $y = b + eu$, and $z = c + fu$, where a, b, c and d, e, f are constants. Assigning numerical values to these constants produces a specific curve, in this case a straight line starting at point (a, b, c) and ending at point $(a+d, \ b+e, \ c+f)$, where $u = 0$ and $u = 1$, respectively.

Parametric equations have many advantages over other forms of representation:

1. They allow separation of the dependent variables, producing greater flexibility in controlling their shape.

2. They allow direct computation of the coordinates of points on the curve.

3. They can be written as vector or matrix equations.

4. All dependent variables are treated alike.

5. They offer more degrees of freedom to control the shape of a curve than other forms do.

6. Transformations are performed directly on the equations if the curve is defined by control points.

7. They accommodate all slopes without computational breakdown.

8. Extension or reduction into higher or lower dimensions is direct.

9. They are inherently bounded when the parameter is constrained to a finite interval.

10. The same curve can be represented by many different parameterizations.

11. It is possible to trace out the shape of a curve directly, which is not possible for curves represented by implicit equations.

12. The implicit form of representation requires the solution of nonlinear equations to trace out points on a curve.

The Hermite, Bézier, B-spline, and NURBS curves are all based on parametric equations. Many 3D modelers use all of these curves, converting between representations via a basis-function transformation.

Read more about this:
Mortenson, M. E., *Geometric Modeling*
Watt, A. and M. Watt, *Advanced Animation and Rendering Techniques*

PARAMETRIC EQUATION In geometric modeling, the coordinates of points defining curves and surfaces are given by equations in terms of a common independent variable, called a *parametric variable*.

Read more about this:
Mortenson, M. E., *Geometric Modeling*

PARAMETRIC MODELING A 3D modeling system using standard shapes, each of which is modeled by assigning values to its key dimensions, or parameters.

Read more about this:
Mortenson, Michael E., *Geometric Modeling*

PARAMETRICS A capability of some modeling systems allowing the user to define certain interdependent dimensions and constraints to which the model must conform. Any change in one of these parameters is automatically adjusted in the related parameters. Usually parametrics works in only one direction; that is, altering object A affects object B, and not vice-versa. However, most systems now allow the changes to operate in either direction. See also **VARIATIONAL GEOMETRY**.

PARAMETRIC SPACE A mathematical space whose coordinate system is based on the parametric variables that are linked to the curves, surfaces, or other geometric elements defining an object in ordinary 3D

space; used to define curves on surfaces, irregular boundaries of surfaces, holes in surfaces, and images or textures mapped onto
surfaces. It works with any parametrically
defined curves or surfaces (Bézier, B-spline,
or NURBS).

Read more about this:
Mortenson, Michael E., *Geometric Modeling*

PARAMETRIC SURFACE An algebraic form
for representing a surface patch, whose general expression is $x = f(u,w)$, $y = g(u,w)$,
and $z = h(u,w)$, where u and w are the parametric variables, and where $0 \le u \le 1$ and
$0 \le w \le 1$. The shape of a patch is revealed
by an intersecting network of parametric
curves for a series of constant values of the
parametric variables, u and w. The characteristics and advantages of parametric equations associated with curves by simple extension.

Read more about this:
Mortenson, M. E., *Geometric Modeling*
Watt, A. and M. Watt, *Advanced Animation and
Rendering Techniques*

PARENT NODE In a hierarchical chain of
linked objects, given two adjacent objects or
nodes in a graph, the object that is closest to
the root or base of the hierarchy is called the
parent node, the other is called the *child
node*; used in graph-based modeling systems, animation, robotics, and mechanism
design.

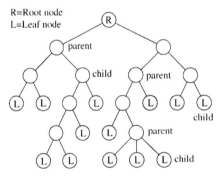

Read more about this:
Mortenson, Michael E., *Mathematics for Computer
Graphics Applications*
O'Rourke, Michael, *Principles of Three-Dimensional
Computer Animation*

PART A generic term indicating a manufactured object, one element of an assembly of

elements, or the 3D CAD/CAM model of an
object to be manufactured.

PARTIAL LATHE A lathe operation in which
the cross-sectional shape is not revolved a
full 360°.

Read more about this:
Giambruno, Mark, *3D Graphics and Animation*

PARTICLE SYSTEM A special effects modeling application that can simulate a great variety of natural phenomena not easily done
by other means. It enables a modeler to generate and control the behavior of a large
number of particles, simulating fire, sparks,
smoke, fog, rain, snow, explosions, and
similar phenomena. Here a particle system
simulates a fire.

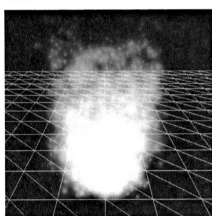

Wikipedia, Jtsiomb (2007). Shows best in color edition.

In particle system animation, the software
introduces a set of particles into a scene by
an emitter. Each new particle is assigned
special individual characteristics depending
on the nature of the simulated phenomenon;
particles are extinguished when they reach
their predetermined life expectancy based
on deterministic or random functions; particles are moved, again, according to deterministic or random functions and usually

conforming to natural force behavior; finally, particles are rendered frame-by-frame, where over the time of the animation sequence particle size, shape, color, transparency, and so forth, may also vary.

Read more about this:
Giambruno, Mark, *3D Graphics and Animation*
O'Rourke, Michael, *Principles of Three-Dimensional Computer Animation*
Watt, A. and M. Watt, *Advanced Animation and Rendering Techniques*

PASS Rendering an attribute of a scene. Different attributes are rendered separately, in a process called rendering in passes, where the rendering order is important. The most common passes are beauty pass, highlight pass, reflection pass, shadow pass, lighting pass, effects pass, and depth maps.

The term *pass* is originally from the motion-control filmmaking technique, where a camera repeats a controlled sequence of motions through a scene under a variety of lighting, physical arrangements, film type, and camera settings. Finally all the passes are optically merged and printed on a single film-strip.

Read more about this:
Birn, Jeremy, [digital] *Lighting & Rendering*

PASSIVE BODY Objects that do not react when they collide. See also *active body*.

PATCH A mathematically defined surface derived from differential geometry and applied to geometric modeling through Bézier, B-spline, and NURBS methods. A patch is limited or local in that parametric curves bound it. See also **SURFACE PATCH**.

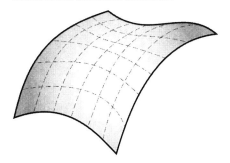

Read more about this:
Mortenson, M. E., *Geometric Modeling*

PATCH MODELER A 3D surface modeling system that uses a grid of control points to define and modify the shape of a patch.

Read more about this:
Giambruno, Mark, *3D Graphics and Animation*

PATH A curve, either single or compound, designed to control the movement of an object or virtual camera. An open path has two distinct end points, while a closed path is a continuous loop without a break.

PATH DEFORMATION Changing the shape of a path to control the movement, orientation, or other animation elements of an object, which are dependent on the object's position along the path and its local geometry.

Read more about this:
O'Rourke, Michael, *Principles of Three-Dimensional Computer Animation*

PATINA An irregular film or encrustation that forms on the surfaces of objects exposed to weathering or corrosive environments; a weathering or aging of a surface finish. A surface patina develops over time, the rate depending on the surface's material properties and atmospheric conditions. Patina-like rendering effects enhance the realistic appearance of an object, indicating aging or the passage of time in an animated sequence.

PATTERN MAP A grid temporarily projected onto the surface of an object to serve as a guide for applying texture. Grid cells may be numbered or colored to assist in the identification of their position on the surface.

PEN PLOTTER A machine that draws lines on paper, or other flat medium, by moving one or more pens across the surface of the paper; a multi-pen drawing head allows multiple colors to be used.

PENUMBRA Soft shadow edges produced by extended light sources, where light from the source of illumination is only partially blocked by an opaque body casting a shadow. An observer standing behind an object casting a shadow is in the penumbra region if only part of the light source is visible. If it is not visible, then the observer is in the umbra. A point-like light source has no penumbra.

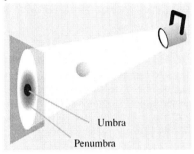

Umbra

Penumbra

Read more about this:
Naylor, John, *Out of the Blue*
Watt, A. and M. Watt, *Advanced Animation and Rendering Techniques*

PERCEPTUAL RENDERING INTENT To emphasize preserving the colors to which the human eye is sensitive when transforming from one color space to another.

PER-PIXEL LIGHTING In computer graphics, a set of methods for computing illumination at each rendered pixel of an image generally producing more realistic images than vertex lighting, which only calculates illumination at each vertex of a 3D model and then interpolates the resulting values to calculate the per-pixel color values.

PERSISTENCE OF VISION The tendency of the human eye and visual cortex to continue seeing or registering an image for a split second after a view has changed. This explains, in part, the ability of a rapidly projected series of still frames in movies to give the illusion of smooth motion. The length of time an image persists determines the minimum frame refresh rate.

Read more about this:
Giambruno, Mark, *3D Graphics and Animation*
O'Rourke, Michael, *Principles of Three-Dimensional Computer Animation*

PERSPECTIVE An effect of the distance of the camera from the subject when viewed against a structured background. When the camera is positioned close to a subject, a wide field of view is required to capture the whole scene; and, conversely, a narrower

field of view is required when the camera is located at a greater distance from the subject.

Changing perspective, moving the camera closer or farther from the subject, creates specific visual effects. Moving the camera closer produces a greater sense of depth between the subject and background, and makes the subject's motion appear to be faster. Opposite effects are produced by moving the camera farther from the subject.

Perspective is not changed by zooming in or out, which changes the apparent size of objects in a scene but not angular relationships, which are the principal depth cues of perspective.

PERSPECTIVE PROJECTION A method to produce a realistic two-dimensional image of a three-dimensional scene. The study of perspective projection goes back to the fifteenth century artists Leon Battista Alberti, Albrecht Dürer, and, of course, Leonardo da Vinci. They laid the aesthetic and empirical foundations for its subsequent analytical development.

Read more about this:
Giambruno, Mark, *3D Graphics and Animation*
Mortenson, M. E., *Geometric Transformations*
————, *Mathematics for Computer Graphics Applications*
Watt, A. and M. Watt, *Advanced Animation and Rendering Techniques*

PHONG SHADING MODEL A surface-shading technique that eliminates the faceted appearance of flat shading. It improves upon the Gouraud shading technique by adding an extra step in the rendering process: it interpolates additional surface normals between the vertices of each polygon. Although this makes it slower than the Gouraud method, it produces more realistic colors and highlights and eliminates the appearance of edges. It is especially good for plastics, metals, and glass. Phong shading is sometimes called *normal-vector interpolation shading*. Bui Tuong-Phong developed the Phong shading method in 1975.

Read more about this:
Giambruno, Mark, *3D Graphics and Animation*
O'Rourke, Michael, *Principles of Three-Dimensional Computer Animation*
Watt, A. and M. Watt, *Advanced Animation and Rendering Techniques*

PHOSPHORESCENCE Diffuse visible light emitted from a surface a short time after absorbing incident electromagnetic radiation (visible light or other frequencies). Under certain conditions it can be seen in the wake of a ship at sea or in the break of a wave on an ocean beach, and in many other natural or manmade phenomena.

PHOTOMETRIC RENDERING A rendering process using data describing real light sources; most often used in architectural renderings and industrial design studies to indicate how the final physical product will appear.

PHOTON MAPPING A technique for rendering the effects of indirect lighting. See also *radiosity*.

PHOTOPIC VISION Vision under levels of illumination high enough to activate the eye's cone cells, for example in daylight. Cone cells are responsible for color vision, but do poorly in dim light or darkness, in which case the eye's rod cells are active.

PHOTOREALISM A style of painting that resembles photography in its meticulous attention to realistic detail; the process of creating computer images that closely resemble photographs. See also **RENDERING**.

PHYSICS ENGINE A set of algorithms that simulates physics effects in animation, using variables such as mass, velocity, friction, and wind resistance.

PICTURE PLANE The mathematical plane on which a 2D image of a 3D model is projected.

PICTURE PLANE COORDINATE SYSTEM A 2D coordinate system for locating points on the picture plane; also called the *projection plane*.

Read more about this:
Mortenson, M. E., *Mathematics for Computer Graphics Applications*

PIECEWISE FLAT SURFACE A surface approximated by polygons.

Read more about this:
Mortenson, Michael E., *3D Modeling, Animation, and Rendering*
_____, *Geometric Modeling*
_____, *Mathematics for Computer Graphics Applications*

PIGMENT A colored substance, usually a pulverized solid, mixed with an otherwise translucent colorless medium to add color, which is that part of the spectrum of the incident light that has been reflected and not absorbed by it.

PINCUSHION DISTORTION An increase in image magnification with distance from the focal point or optical axis of a camera or projector, usually radially symmetric. See also **BARREL DISTORTION** and **DISTORTION**.

PIVOT POINT A user-defined center of rotation for an object, which may be chosen to conveniently coincide with the origin of the object's local coordinate system.

PIXEL A picture element; the smallest definable and addressable unit of graphics data on a computer graphics monitor; a physical limitation of the screen design and construction. Typically used in the specification and description of graphics processors and display monitors. Each pixel consists of three active color elements: a red one, a green one, and a blue one, whose intensities are varied to produce millions of colors in a 24-bit color monitor.

Read more about this:
Giambruno, Mark, *3D Graphics and Animation*
O'Rourke, Michael, *Principles of Three-Dimensional Computer Animation*

PIXELATION A coarse image produced when the resolution is too low, an effect caused by displaying a bitmap or a section of a bitmap at such a large size that individual pixels, small single-colored square display elements that comprise the bitmap, are visible to the eye. A picture that this has happened to is said to be *pixelated*.

PIXEL DIMENSIONS The number of pixels defining the height and width of a bitmap image. The computer graphic display size of an image depends on its pixel dimensions and the size and settings of the monitor. The file size of an image is proportional to the product of its pixel dimensions. See also **DISPLAY RESOLUTION** and **DOTS PER INCH**.

PIXEL IMAGE A computer graphics monitor image based on the pixel. There are several formats for saving, storing, and communicating pixel images: GIF, JPEG, and PNG, for example. See also **VECTOR GRAPHICS IMAGE**.

PIXEL SHADER A type of shader program often executed on a graphics-processing unit, typically used to perform complex per-pixel lighting effects.

PLANE A two-dimensional geometric object which may be defined as the locus of points equidistant between two given points in three-dimensional space; the flat face of a polyhedron (not a curved surface); or a construction element defining some geometric modeling or CAD construction limit.

Read more about this:
Mortenson, Michael E., *3D Modeling, Animation, and Rendering*
_____, *Mathematics for Computer Graphics Applications*

PLANT MODEL GENERATOR A specialized 3D modeling application used to produce models of plants.

Read more about this:
O'Rourke, Michael, *Principles of Three-Dimensional Computer Animation*

PLASTIC DEFORMATION Permanent shape change caused by stretching, compressing, bending, twisting or in some other way deforming an object beyond its elastic limit, for example, as a result of a collision. An object may exhibit a combination of plastic and elastic deformations when colliding with another object. Accounting for plastic deformations in the animation of a collision between objects enhances the realism of the scene.

Read more about this:
Mortenson, Michael E., *3D Modeling, Animation, and Rendering*

PNG A pixel-based image format used on the Web, using 36-bit color with alpha channel support and lossless data compression.

PNG-8 An 8-bit color format, using lossless data compression. See also **PNG**.

PNG-24 A 24-bit color format, using lossless data compression. See also **PNG**.

POINT The simplest of the three most elementary geometric objects: points, lines, and planes. A point cannot be defined in terms of anything simpler, except as a set of numbers giving a location in some coordinate space. Points are the basic building blocks for all other geometric objects, and elementary geometry demonstrates how many figures are defined as a locus of points with certain constraining characteristics. For example, in a plane, a circle is the locus of points equidistant from a given point, and a straight line is the locus of points equidistant from two given points. More complex curves, surfaces, and solids are also defined this way, by using equations to define the special conditions producing a locus of points.

Read more about this:
Mortenson, M. E., *3D Modeling, Animation, and Rendering*
_____, *Mathematics for Computer Graphics Applications*

POINT CLASSIFICATION The act of determining if a point is inside, outside, or on the boundary of a 3D solid. This important problem arises in constructive solid geometry when two or more primitives are combined to produce a more complex solid. Although it is routinely solved by the modeling software, it nonetheless demands a large amount of computing resources.

Read more about this:
Mortenson, M. E., *Geometric Modeling*
_____, *Mathematics for Computer Graphics Applications*

POINT CLOUD A three-dimensional distribution of points representing measured or computed (from theoretical models) values of some physical property; used in scientific visualization.

POINT LIGHT A light source illuminating a computer graphics scene that radiates light in all directions from a single point, and therefore shadows cast by objects it illuminates are hard edged, approximating the effect of a bare light bulb hanging from a cord. Note that light sources in the real world have extended shapes and finite volumes; because they are extended in 3D space they do not cast hard-edged shadows (see *penumbra* and *umbra*). The effect of any extended light source, if it is sufficiently distant relative to its own size, may be approximated by a point light source. Control parameters for a point light include its location, intensity, color, and decay rate.

Read more about this:
Birn, Jeremy, [digital] *Lighting & Rendering*
Giambruno, Mark, *3D Graphics and Animation*
O'Rourke, Michael, *Principles of Three-Dimensional Computer Animation*

POINT-OF-VIEW SHOT (POV SHOT) Positioning and aiming the camera to record the scene as seen by a character or subject in it, also known as a *subjective camera*. See also *camera angle*.

Read more about this:
Birn, Jeremy, [digital] *Lighting & Rendering*
Giambruno, Mark, *3D Graphics and Animation*
O'Rourke, Michael, *Principles of Three-Dimensional Computer Animation*

POLARIZED LIGHT Electromagnetic radiation having different properties in different directions perpendicular to its line of propagation. Special lens filters on a camera can make use of this difference, for example, to eliminate glare.

The waves of polarized light vibrate predominantly in one plane. The waves of unpolarized light vibrate in planes oriented randomly and are uniformly distributed with respect to the line of propagation. A polarizing filter allows only waves vibrating in a particular plane to be transmitted through it, the effect of which reduces the intensity or brightness of the transmitted light.

All sunlight is polarized to some extent as it passes through the atmosphere. The maximum polarization usually occurs over the sky in a direction perpendicular to the direction of the sun's rays. Sunlight is also polarized when it is reflected in water, because light vibrating in a horizontal plane is more efficiently absorbed by the reflecting surface than light that is vibrating vertically, so the reflected light has a higher proportion of light that is vibrating vertically.

Read more about this:
Naylor, John, *Out of the Blue*

POLARIZING FILTER A special glass that only allows light waves vibrating in a certain direction to pass through it; a filter that reduces reflections from non-metallic surfaces such as glass or water by blocking light waves that are vibrating at selected angles to the filter.

POLYGON A closed planar surface defined by its vertices and edges. A triangle is the simplest kind of polygon. There are many other kinds of polygons. One of the most important distinctions is that between convex and concave polygons. The familiar equal-sided, equal-angled regular polygons are concave, and the stellar and self-intersecting polygons are concave.

If the vertices all lie in the same plane, then the polygon is a *plane polygon*; otherwise it is a *skew polygon*. The polygonization of a surface is almost always used to produce triangular polygons, because the three vertex points are guaranteed to lie in a plane. Polygons whose edges are curve segments can be constructed on curved surfaces.

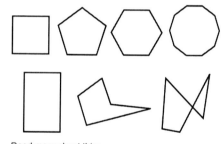

Read more about this:
Coexeter, H. S. M., *Regular Polytopes*
Mortenson, Michael E., *3D Modeling, Animation, and Rendering*
_____, *Mathematics for Computer Graphics Applications*
Watt, A. and M. Watt, *Advanced Animation and Rendering Techniques*

POLYGONAL APPROXIMATION A 3D modeling technique that uses a large number of small polygons to approximate a curved surface. The approximation improves as the size of the polygons decrease. This, of course, increases the number of polygons required and demands greater computational and rendering resources, which translates into slower display time and greater data storage requirements (factors that may be critical in real-time animation or in game interaction). Such surfaces appear faceted when rendered unless special shading techniques are applied (that is, Gouraud shading, Phong shading). See also **POLYGONIZATION**.

Read more about this:
O'Rourke, Michael, *Principles of Three-Dimensional Computer Animation*
Mortenson, Michael E., *3D Modeling, Animation, and Rendering*

POLYGONAL MODEL One of the basic 3D model-building methods, where surfaces are defined or approximated by a polygon mesh.

Read more about this:
Giambruno, Mark, *3D Graphics and Animation*
Mortenson, Michael E., *3D Modeling, Animation, and Rendering*
O'Rourke, Michael, *Principles of Three-Dimensional Computer Animation*

POLYGON COUNT The number of polygons used to approximate a surface, and usually taken as composed of triangles.

POLYGON EXPANSION A method that retains the shape of a surface while increasing the number of polygons representing it; the opposite of polygon reduction.

POLYGON MESH A grid-like assembly of polygons covering a model's surface.

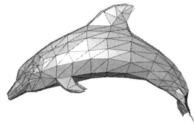

Wikipedia, chrschn (2007)

Read more about this:
Mortenson, Michael E., *3D Modeling, Animation, and Rendering*

POLYGON REDUCTION Reducing or limiting the number of polygons used to approximate a surface, either automatically invoked computational methods or user-specified constraints. One way to do this is to specify a limiting dihedral angle between adjacent polygons. This angle is an indicator of their relative difference in orientation. Two adjacent polygons with a dihedral angle sufficiently close to 180° may be treated as a single polygon without drastically changing the shape of the surface. See also **POLYGON CULLIN**g and **POLYGON THINNING**

POLYGON RENDERING A process that renders a surface that is represented as a set of polygons. See also **POLYGON SUBDIVISION**.

POLYGON RESOLUTION Determined by the number of polygons used to represent a given surface. More polygons mean a higher resolution image and a more accurate and smoother-looking surface.

POLYGON ROUNDING A surface smoothing technique that adds polygons to a polygonal model where the curvature is greatest, having the effect of rounding or smoothing the appearance of the surface.

POLYGON SUBDIVISION A procedure to approximate a curved surface with a network of polygons; the smaller the polygons, the closer the approximation to the true surface. However, more polygons require more time to be rendered. See also **POLYGONAL MODEL** and **POLYGONIZATION**.

POLYGON THINNING See **POLYGON CULLING** and **POLYGON REDUCTION**.

POLYGONIZATION Covering a surface with a polygon mesh, which then can be easily rendered and displayed.

POLYHEDRAL SYMMETRY All regular and semiregular polyhedra are highly symmetrical. For example, the cube has many axes of rotational symmetry. There is a family of three, one with an axis passing through the center of each pair of opposite faces; a family of four, each member being one of the four body diagonals; and a family of six axes of rotational symmetry, each member being one of the six lines passing through the centers of opposite pairs of edges.

Understanding and using these and other forms of polyhedral symmetry may lead to interesting modeling effects as well as to more efficient modeling of symmetrical elements of solid objects.

Read more about this:
Mortenson, M. E., *Geometric Transformations*

POLYHEDRON A three-dimensional object whose bounding surface is a finite, connected set of plane polygons, arranged so that every edge of each polygon also belongs to just one other polygon. The polygonal faces form a closed surface, dividing space into two regions: the interior space of the polyhedron and the exterior space, or outside. A cube is a familiar example of a polyhedron. The number of faces determines the name of a regular polyhedron.

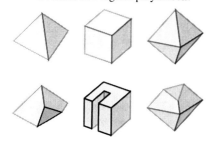

POLYLINE An open string of connected line segments. A closed string of line segments in a plane forms a polygon.

Read more about this:
Giambruno, Mark, *3D Graphics and Animation*

PORTRAIT VIEW A vertically oriented image.

POSE PLANNING Developing key poses by placing a figure in critical or extreme positions of planned motions. This is the first step in defining keyframes, inverse kinematics and inbetweening for an animation sequence.

POSITIVE SPACE That part of a frame containing the main subject and foreground objects. *Negative space* is the background or space surrounding the foreground objects. See also *framing*.

POSTERIZATION Becomes evident when a region of an image with a continuous gradation of tone is replaced with several regions of fewer tones, resulting in an abrupt change from one tone to another, an effect somewhat similar to that of a simple graphic poster. See **BANDING**.

POV See **POINT-OF-VIEW SHOT**.

PREVIEW A preliminary, simplified, rendering of a scene produced to verify the design objectives.

PREVISUALIZATION Preliminary planning and design of an animation project, including animatics and storyboard frames.

PRIMARY COLORS A small set of colors, such as red, green, blue, and yellow, which can be mixed to produce other colors. See also **COLOR MODEL** and **SECONDARY COLORS**.

Read more about this:
Demers, Owen, [digital] *Texture & Painting*

PRIMITIVE A simple solid shape, such as a cube or sphere. Most constructive solid geometry modeling systems provide just a few standard primitive shapes of a unit size, whose position, and orientation are initially set within the primitive's local coordinate system. The designer chooses appropriate primitives, then sizes, positions, and combines them to form complex shapes.

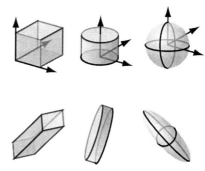

Specifying the values for a small set of variables controls a primitive's size, shape, position, and orientation. For example, rectangular solids, or blocks, are almost always available in a constructive solid geometry (CSG) system. A modeler specifies length, width, height, location, and orientation within a world coordinate system to produce a particular instance of a block. In some modeling systems, the initial untransformed primitive is presented, having unit dimensions and is conveniently positioned and aligned in its local coordinate system. For example, a primitive sphere would have a radius of one with its center at the origin of its local coordinate system; the modeler specifies a new center and radius to create the desired specific instance of a sphere in the world coordinate system or scene.

Some CSG primitives can be constructed as a Boolean combination of a small set of other primitives. For example, a properly sized and positioned cylinder primitive subtracted from a rectangular block primitive produces an inside fillet primitive. Furthermore, the block and cylinder primitives alone have the same descriptive power as a set of primitives consisting of a block or cube, cylinder, wedge, inside fillet, cylindrical segment, and tetrahedron, albeit with some extra effort.

Each primitive, in turn, is represented in a CSG modeling system as the intersection of half-spaces. For example, the appropriate intersection of six planar half-spaces creates a primitive cube, and the intersection of a cylindrical half-space and two planar half-spaces creates a cylindrical solid primitive. This level of the mathematical definition of the primitives is usually not accessible to the modeler.

Read more about this:
Giambruno, Mark, *3D Graphics and Animation*
Mortenson, M. E., *3D Modeling, Animation, and Rendering*
_____, *Mathematics for Computer Graphics Applications*

PRINCIPAL AXES The x-, y-, and z-axes in a 3D coordinate system.

PRINCIPAL PLANES A 3D rectangular coordinate system has three principle planes: the plane containing the x and y axes, the plane containing the y and z axes, and the plane containing the x and z-axes. They are also identified as the $z = 0$ plane, the $x = 0$, and the $y = 0$ plane, respectively.

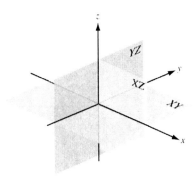

PRINTER RESOLUTION The number of ink dots per inch (dpi) produced by a printer.

PROCEDURAL ANIMATION Controlling the shape and animation of a model with an algorithm and supporting mathematical models to simulate natural force behavior; for example, the shape and motion of a wave approaching a beach, then cresting and breaking.

Read more about this:
O'Rourke, Michael, *Principles of Three-Dimensional Computer Animation*
Watt, A. and M. Watt, *Advanced Animation and Rendering Techniques*

PROCEDURAL MAPPING A mathematical process for creating 2D texture images that uses special-purpose applications to produce new images. This is an alternative to selecting a predefined image from a library of bitmapped images. See also **PROCEDURAL TEXTURE**.

Read more about this:
O'Rourke, Michael, *Principles of Three-Dimensional Computer Animation*

PROCEDURAL MODEL A model database in which the modeling process is stored; used in constructive solid geometry (CSG).

Read more about this:
Watt, A. and M. Watt, *Advanced Animation and Rendering Techniques*

PROCEDURAL TEXTURE A texture, such as wood or marble, whose image is mathematically defined rather than scanned, and which is scale and resolution independent; an algorithm for creating a texture.

Read more about this:
Giambruno, Mark, *3D Graphics and Animation*

PROCESS COLOR A combination of the four standard CMYK printing process ink colors.

PROFILE The shape-defining curve used to produce a lathing.

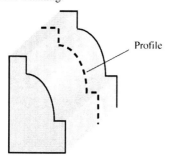

Profile

PROJECTION MAPPING A special surface mapping technique that projects an image onto objects in a scene, much like a slide projector projects an image onto a flat screen, or people or objects standing between it and the screen.

Read more about this:
Giambruno, Mark, *3D Graphics and Animation*
O'Rourke, Michael, *Principles of Three-Dimensional Computer Animation*

PROJECTION TRANSFORMATION A technique that produces a two-dimensional image of a 3D model on a specified plane. Orthographic and perspective projections are used extensively in 3D modeling and rendering.

A projective transformation preserves points, straight lines, intersections, the degree of a curve, and some other geometric properties. The properties not preserved by these transformations include parallels, angles, and the distance between points. Projection transformations are important for many reasons, not the least of which is that they produce two-dimensional images of three-dimensional objects.

The shadows cast by objects of various shapes are observable examples of these transformations. The shapes of shadows change when the position of the light source changes or when the object rotates. Although straight edges remain straight, angles are distorted where the shadows of angles are greater or less than the corresponding angles on the object itself, and parallel edges appear to converge.

Read more about this:
Mortenson, Michael E., *Geometric Transformations for 3D Modeling*

PROJECTIVE GEOMETRY The study of geometric properties that are invariant under projective transformations, which include perspective projections.

Read more about this:
Mortenson, Michael E., *Geometric Transformations for 3D Modeling*

PROJECTOR LIGHT See **PROJECTION MAPPING**.

PULL-BACK DOLLY Moving the camera back to reveal characters or objects not previously in the scene.

PULL-FOCUS SHOT A shot that shifts the optical focus of a camera from one object to another. For example, using manual control of a film or video camera, focus on a foreground object (a violinist) for about five seconds, then slowly change the focus until the full orchestra in the background comes into focus.; also called *rack-focus shot*.

PURKINJE EFFECT Red objects appear darker than blue or green objects under low levels of illumination, whereas the reverse is the case under normal lighting conditions. This is a physiological effect of the difference in light sensitivity of the rods and cones of the retina. Rods are sensitive to brightness and are not good at distinguishing between different colors. Cones are most sensitive to color and brightness, particularly to bright greens. Furthermore, rods are somewhat sensitive to the blue-green range of the spectrum. This combination of properties of the human visual system produces the Purkinje effect as light dims with the setting sun, for example. See also **COLOR VISION**.

Read more about this:
Naylor, John, *Out of the Blue*

Q

QUADRATIC A second-degree polynomial equation.

QUADRIC The three-dimensional analog of a conic (circle, ellipse, parabola, or hyperbola), a second-degree polynomial equation in x, y, and z.

QUARTIC A fourth-degree polynomial equation.

QUATERNION A mathematical object used to control and compute rotation transformations; a quadruple of real numbers, containing a scalar part and a vector part.

Read more about this:
Mortenson, Michael E., *Mathematics for Computer Graphics Applications*
Watt, A. and M. Watt, *Advanced Animation and Rendering Techniques*

R

RACK-FOCUS SHOT A shot technique changing a camera's focal distance during shooting to bring various subjects into and out of focus. The camera's position does not change. The intention of this shot is to shift the attention of the viewer. See also **CAMERA MOVES** and **PULLED-FOCUS SHOT**.

Read more about this:
Birn, Jeremy, [digital] *Lighting & Rendering*

RADIAL GRADIENT A continuous variation of fill color or shading outward in all directions from a given point. See also **GRADIENT**.

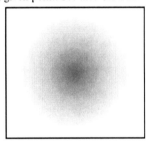

RADIOSITY A view-independent rendering method used to simulate light propagation in a scene and to determine how direct and ambient light illuminate a matte surface; also, the illumination of objects in a scene that takes into account both direct light sources and diffuse light reflected off all other objects. The computation of radiosity values depends upon only the spatial relationships between objects and objects and light sources in a scene, so it is independent of the location of the camera or viewer.

Rendering that includes radiosity effects produces near-photographic realism, surpassing even ray tracing. Radiosity is most effectively used for softly or diffusely-lit scenes, in an architectural walk-through, for example. However, the radiosity method is not accurate for scenes containing objects

that produce specular reflections, and it requires an order-of-magnitude more processing time than ray tracing.

Read more about this:
Birn, Jeremy, [digital] *Lighting & Rendering*
Giambruno, Mark, *3D Graphics and Animation*
Mortenson, Michael E. *3D Modeling, Animation, and Rendering*
O'Rourke, Michael, *Principles of Three-Dimensional Computer Animation*
Watt, A. and M. Watt, *Advanced Animation and Rendering Techniques*

RAGDOLL PHYSICS Describes an animated character's collapse, much like that of a toy ragdoll, often into comically improbable positions. Ragdoll physics is a type of physics engine, a collection of algorithms for computer graphics animation, used as a replacement for traditional static death animations.

Read more about this:
Mortenson, Michael E., *3D Modeling, Animation, and Rendering*

RAIN MODEL See *particle systems*.

RAINBOW An arc of prismatic colors appearing in the sky opposite the sun, produced by the refraction and reflection of sunlight in drops of rain. Rainbows may also appear in the spray of a waterfall in sunlight or in the mist of a fountain of water.

To see a rainbow certain conditions must be present: the sun must be shining at the same time that it is raining, the sun must directly light the rain, and the viewer must be between the sun and the rain. The chances of seeing a rainbow are increased if the viewer is within a mile or so of the rain, if the rain extends over a large enough area of the sky, and if the sun is near the horizon. A rainbow is not visible if the sun is more than 42° above the horizon. The closer the sun is to the horizon the fuller the rainbow will appear. Because rain showers are more likely to form in the late afternoon, this is usually the best time to see a rainbow.

The order of colors in the arc of the primary rainbow is fixed: violet and green hues appear on the inside of the arc, yellows and oranges the middle range, and reds the outer rim. The outer edge of the rainbow is more sharply defined than the inner edge. Under the right conditions, a secondary bow will form outside the primary bow. The secondary bow is less bright and its colors are in reverse order with respect to the primary. The presence of all of these effects in a model and scene rendering contribute to a realistic rainbow. See also **FOG BOWS** and **SPRAY BOWS**.

Read more about this:
Naylor, John, *Out of the Blue*
Watt, A. and M. Watt, *Advanced Animation and Rendering Techniques*

RAPID PROTOTYPING A manufacturing technique that constructs a 3D part by building up one thin cross-sectional layer after another, requiring much less time then older conventional methods. The time required to construct even complex parts is measured in hours instead of days or weeks. The first commercial process was introduced in 1987, by 3D Systems, Inc. The early technology was not refined enough to create good quality production parts, and the choice of materials from which to make them was limited. So these parts were used as prototypes, for study and analysis

Now many commercial rapid prototyping systems are available, and more are under development in research laboratories. Their accuracy has improved significantly, and the choice of materials has expanded to the extent that the term prototype is somewhat misleading; the parts now produced by these systems are used for proof-of-concept and functional testing, and to derive tools for pre-production testing.

Although rapid prototyping is possible using more conventional methods such as NC (numerically controlled) milling and hand carving, the term is normally reserved for the new technologies that build parts by adding material instead of removing it. The most important types of rapid prototyping methods include stereolithography, solid ground curing, selective laser sintering, and laminated object manufacturing.

RASTER A matrix of pixels covering the entire display screen or some subset of it; a set of horizontal raster lines composed of individual pixels; for example, the interlaced (interlacing) scanlines (scanline rendering) of a video display.

RASTER GRAPHICS See above and **BITMAP IMAGE**.

RASTERIZATION A technique that determines which pixels a polygon projects onto in screen coordinates; any process by which vector information can be converted into a raster format.

Read more about this:
Watt, A. and M. Watt, *Advanced Animation and Rendering Techniques*

RAY A segment of a straight line having a fixed point at one end and extending to infinity at the other, the basic geometric element used in a ray tracer.

RAY CASTING A rendering method similar to, but computationally simpler than, ray tracing, a hidden-surface removal method in which a ray is sent out from the view point or eye position and its intersections with various objects in a scene are computed. The intersection point at the least distance belongs to the visible surface.

Read more about this:
Mortenson, Michael E., *3D Modeling, Animation, and Rendering*
O'Rourke, Michael, *Principles of Three-Dimensional Computer Animation*
Watt, A. and M. Watt, *Advanced Animation and Rendering Techniques*

RAY-TRACE DEPTH The number of reflections between surfaces that a ray path is followed and computed; a rendering parameter that controls how many reflections are traced before computing which color and brightness to assign to a point on a surface. The more reflections that are calculated for a light ray, the more realistic is the final rendering. See also **RAY TRACING**.

Read more about this:
Birn, Jeremy, [digital] *Lighting & Rendering*
Mortenson, Michael E., *3D Modeling, Animation, and Rendering*

RAY TRACING A viewpoint-dependent rendering method that computes the visibility and illumination of objects and other elements in a scene by casting a hypothetical ray from the viewer's eye or virtual camera through each pixel of the computer display to determine the color, brightness, and other factors affecting the state of that pixel.

Ray tracing tracks light through successive reflections. Each ray is traced backwards through its interactions with objects in a scene until it exits the scene or reaches its source. The computation can be quite complex because secondary and tertiary reflections and refractions through translucent objects produce multiple branches, each of which must be traced and taken into account.

Ray tracing is more complex and requires more computational resources than ray casting. Under the right lighting conditions with few or no specular reflections, radiosity methods produce even more realistic images, but require about an order-of-magnitude more processing time than ray tracing. Ray tracing is most effective in scenes with shiny objects, producing specular reflections, whereas radiosity methods work best for matte surfaces and scenes that are diffusely lit. See also **RAY TRACING, STOCHASTIC**.

Read more about this:
Birn, Jeremy, [digital] *Lighting & Rendering*
Giambruno, Mark, *3D Graphics and Animation*
Mortenson, Michael E., *3D Modeling, Animation, and Rendering*
O'Rourke, Michael, *Principles of Three-Dimensional Computer Animation*
Watt, A. and M. Watt, *Advanced Animation and Rendering Techniques*

RAY TRACING, INTERACTIVE A rendering application that allows the user to interact with the ray tracing process, with the intent of speeding it up and resolving ambiguities.

RAY TRACING, STOCHASTIC An advanced ray tracing technique which assumes that rays hitting a surface are reflected randomly in different directions, with a probability distribution depending on the nature of the surface and other elements of the scene.

RAYLEIGH SCATTERING Selective scattering that occurs only when light encounters particles that are much smaller than the wavelength of the incident light. A typical molecule of gas is over a thousand times smaller than the wavelength of visible light, which is why selective scattering occurs within the atmosphere.

Visible light from that part of the spectrum with the shortest wavelength is scattered ten times more than that with the longest wave-

length. This means that scattered sunlight is mostly from the blue end of the spectrum, thus making the sky appear blue.

REACTION SHOT Captures a character's response to an event, usually a close-up. See also **SHOT** and **SHOT SIZE**.

RECTANGLE A four-sided polygon, with opposite sides of equal length and interior angles all right angles.

REFERENCE BALL Also called **LIGHT PROBE**.

REFLECT A geometric transformation for producing the mirror image of an object. Given a geometric shape and a reflection axis or plane, the mirror (or reflected) image of the shape is developed by simple constructions and equally simple mathematics. 3D modeling systems do both jobs. Reflection across a plane in space reverses the orientation of a shape; for example, a right hand becomes a left hand. Any number of shapes, both natural and manufactured, occurs in mirror-image pairs. Besides our right and left hands, there are the wings of airplanes and threads of a bolt. Many mineral crystals have both right- and left-hand (or mirror-image) forms. See also **REFLECTION TRANSFORMATION**.

Read more about this:
Mortenson, Michael E., *Geometric Transformations for 3D Modeling*

REFLECTION The redirection of light rays after striking a surface. An object that is not luminous itself is visible because its surface reflects light from other sources into the viewer's eyes or into the lens of a camera. Well-known laws of physics determine how light is reflected off a surface. Hard shiny surfaces reflect light differently from rough ones.

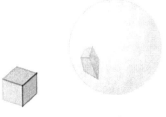

Two kinds of reflections must be accounted for: diffuse reflection and specular reflection. The surfaces of most objects produce a combination of both. Not all incident light is reflected. Some may be absorbed and converted into heat; some passes through an object if it is translucent.

Visible light, for example, is composed of a variety of superimposed wavelengths. How a surface absorbs and reflects this light depends on both the wavelengths present in the light and the physical properties of the surface. In 3D graphics, surface roughness is often modeled as part of the light and rendering computations. Reflection effects also depend on the angle of the incident light. Some otherwise diffusely reflective surfaces appear almost shiny under low angles of incidence and for certain wavelengths of light, while appearing dull at high angles of incidence.

The Phong-Gouraud reflection and shading method, sometimes called the *Phong reflection model*, is adequate for most applications. Although Phong computations require surface normal geometry, light sources are assumed to be point sources located at infinity (as is the camera or viewer), and their energy distribution is ignored. Diffuse and specular effects are treated as local components, where the size and shape of the specular reflection component are determined empirically and its color is assumed to be that of the light source. Finally, ambient light is treated as uniform throughout the model space.

Rendering more realistic reflections requires abandoning the Phong-Gouraud approximations and empirical approach for a more rigorous method based on the physics of light, which includes using electromagnetic wave theory and micro-modeling of surface roughness to more accurately predict the specular distribution geometry. Sophisticated modeling and rendering programs also account for the transmission of light through transparent and semi-opaque objects.

Multiple reflections are second-order effects in the presence of multiple reflecting surfaces, and are usually accounted for during rendering scenes of predominantly manmade objects rather than in natural scenes. The accurate rendering of multiple reflections enhances the reality of a scene.

Another kind of reflection is the reflection transformation, which has nothing to do with light reflection but with symmetry. See also **REFLECTION TRANSFORMATION**.

Read more about this:
Demers, Owen, [digital] *Texture & Painting*
Mortenson, Michael E., *3D Modeling, Animation, and Rendering*
Watt, A. and M. Watt, *Advanced Animation and Rendering Techniques*

REFLECTION MAPPING See **GLOBAL REFLECTION MODEL**.

REFLECTION MODEL An algorithm used to determine how light illuminates and reflects off an object, based on a set of assumptions about the behavior of light and the character of the object's reflecting surface. The oldest and simplest reflection model, familiar to the ancient Greeks, states that the angle of reflection is equal to the angle of incidence, where the angle is measured with respect to a perpendicular to the reflecting surface. This model works well for mirror-like surfaces.

Lambert's Law is another reflection model, which assumes that light reflects equally in all directions, independent of the incident direction. This law is a good approximation of the behavior of matte surfaces. A more recent and sophisticated reflection model uses a bi-directional reflectance distribution function (BRDF), which allows control of the distribution of light intensity of both the incoming and reflected light rays. See **BI-DIRECTIONAL REFLECTANCE DISTRIBUTION FUNCTION**.

Read more about this:
Watt, A. and M. Watt, *Advanced Animation and Rendering Techniques*

REFLECTION PASS Rendering separately the reflections of objects or the surrounding environment, often showing reflections from other layers or passes.

REFLECTION TRANSFORMATION For reflection in a plane, given a point P and a line L, the reflection of A across L generates A', called the *image point* of A. The line segment AA' is perpendicular to L and is bisected by it. See the figure that follows.

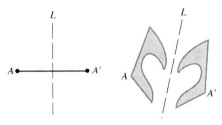

Read more about this:
Mortenson, Michael E., *Geometric Transformations for 3D Modeling*

REFLECTIVITY A surface property measured by how much incident light is reflected compared to that transmitted or absorbed. A mirror-like surface has a high reflectivity; a dark cloth has a low reflectivity. The left-most sphere is the most highly reflective. See also **DIFFUSENESS**, **TRANSMISSION**, and **ABSORPTION**.

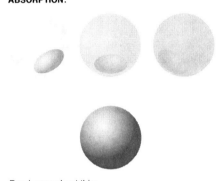

Read more about this:
Demers, Owen, [digital] *Texture & Painting*
O'Rourke, Michael, *Principles of Three-Dimensional Computer Animation*
Watt, A. and M. Watt, *Advanced Animation and Rendering Techniques*

REFLECTOR In photography and cinematography, an improvised or specialized reflective surface used to redirect light towards a given subject or scene.

REFRACTION The bending of light waves that occurs when these waves move across the boundary between two different light-transmitting materials or media. This effect is easily demonstrated by placing a spoon into a clear glass of water and observing that the handle appears to bend where it enters the water.

When light passes from one medium into another its speed changes. It slows down when entering a denser medium and speeds up when it enters a less dense medium. Light travels fastest in a vacuum. Because light waves remain parallel and their frequency remains constant, to adjust to the change in speed the wavelength must change. This produces a change in the direction of propagation on entering a new medium.

There is a mathematical relationship between the angle of incidence and the angle of refraction, but it is not as straightforward as that for reflection An index of refraction can be determined for any pair of media, and it turns out to be equal to the ratio of the speeds of the waves in each media. From this ratio it is possible to compute how much a beam of light is bent toward or away from the normal to the interface surface between the two media.

Read more about this:
Giambruno, Mark, *3D Graphics and Animation*
Naylor, John, *Out of the Blue*
O'Rourke, Michael, *Principles of Three-Dimensional Computer Animation*
Watt, A. and M. Watt, *Advanced Animation and Rendering Techniques*

REFRACTION MAPPING A view-dependent mapping technique, an approximation of ray tracing, which approximates the refraction of the environment through a transparent medium. As is true of chrome reflection mapping, the approximation works when the transmitting medium is turbulent or the interface surfaces are not perfectly smooth, which means that the reflection itself does not have to be perfectly rendered.

Read more about this:
Watt, A. and M. Watt, *Advanced Animation and Rendering Techniques*

REFRACTIVITY INDEX See **INDEX OF REFRACTION**.

REFRAMING The often imperceptible (intentionally so) camera movements that keep a moving subject in the frame.

REFRESH RATE The frequency with which an image is redrawn on a computer graphics monitor, measured in cycles per second (hertz); also called the *vertical scan rate* or *vertical frequency*. The higher the refresh rate, the less the image appears to flicker.

Read more about this:
Giambruno, Mark, *3D Graphics and Animation*

REGISTER To put in proper alignment or correspondence the separate but superimposed layers and masks of a scene or colors in printing.

REGULAR POLYHEDRA A convex polyhedron is a regular polyhedron if the following conditions are true:

1. All face polygons are regular.

2. All face polygons are congruent.

3. All vertices are identical.

4. All dihedral angles are equal.

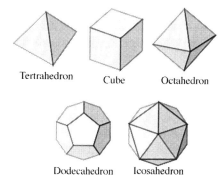

Tertrahedron   Cube   Octahedron

Dodecahedron   Icosahedron

The cube is a good example. All its faces are identical and all its edges are of equal length. In three-dimensional space only five regular polyhedra can be constructed (also called the five *Platonic solids*): the tetrahedron, hexahedron (cube), octahedron, dodecahedron, and icosahedron.

Read more about this:
Mortenson, M. E., *Mathematics for Computer Graphics Applications*

REGULARIZED BOOLEAN OPERATOR A technique that eliminates lower-dimension elements from a three-dimensional Boolean operation.

Read more about this:
Mortenson, Michael E., *Geometric Modeling*
_____, *Mathematics for Computer Graphics Applications*

RENDERING Image synthesis that transforms digital or other electronic information into a picture; the operations of computer graphics program that produce the displayed image of a 3D model or scene; an image produced from a group of 3D objects, light sources, and a viewpoint. With input from a graphics designer, a rendering program computes visibility, shading and shadows, reflections, color effects, highlights atmospherics, textures and many other factors affecting the final image. The image might be as simple as a wireframe rendering of an object, or as complex as a fully animated virtual reality scene, with multiple and variable light sources, color, shadows, reflections, textures, and more. Rendering is done in a sequence of passes

Rendering operations are usually performed on polygonal surfaces, where the effects of vertex and edge discontinuities are minimized by a shading technique (i.e., Phong or Gouraud shading). Reflection and shading values over the polygonal faces are computed by interpolating vertex geometry. Curved surfaces are subdivided and converted into a set of polygons in a computational process called *polygonization*. Each polygon is first transformed into the world coordinate system from its local coordinate and then into the view coordinate system. Visibility computations eliminate polygons that face away from the camera or viewer in a process called *culling*. Those that remain are visible, and they are clipped relative to a 3D viewing volume and projected onto the viewing plane. Finally, shading, and reflection computations determine pixel color values used in the displayed image.

Read more about this:
Birn, Jeremy, [digital] *Lighting & Rendering*
Giambruno, Mark, *3D Graphics and Animation*
Mortenson, Michael E., *3D Modeling, Animation, and Rendering*
O'Rourke, Michael, *Principles of Three-Dimensional Computer Animation*
Watt, A. and M. Watt, *Advanced Animation and Rendering Techniques*

RENDERING EQUATION A mathematical expression that describes how the light reaching a viewer or virtual camera is affected by its source, its interaction with the surfaces of objects in the scene, and the embedding media through which it passes. Here is one form of this equation (from the wikipedia entry):

$$L_o(x,\omega,\lambda,t) = L_e(x,\omega,\lambda,t)$$
$$+ \int_\Omega f_r(x,\omega',\omega,\lambda,t) L_i(x,\omega',\lambda,t)(-\omega' \cdot \mathbf{n}) d\omega'$$

λ is a specific wavelength of light

t is time

$L_o(x,\omega,\lambda,t)$ is the total amount of light of wavelength λ directed outward along the direction ω at time t, from a position xi

$L_e(x,\omega,\lambda,t)$ is emitted light

$\int_\Omega f_r(x,\omega',\omega,\lambda,t) L_i(x,\omega',\lambda,t)(-\omega' \cdot \mathbf{n}) d\omega'$ is the integral over a hemisphere of inward directions

$f_r(x,\omega',\omega,\lambda,t)$ is the bidirectional reflectance distribution function (BRDF), i.e., the proportion of light reflected from ω' to ω at position x, time t, and at wavelength λ

$L_i(x,\omega',\lambda,t)$

$-\omega' \cdot \mathbf{n}$ is the attenuation of inward light due to the incident angle

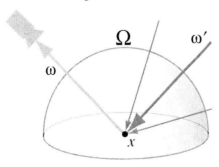

Read more about this:
Mortenson, Michael E., *3D Modeling, Animation, and Rendering*

RENDERING IN LAYERS Rendering some objects in a scene separately, combining the images later during compositing; for example, rendering an animation sequence as a separate layer from the background. See also **RENDERING IN PASSES**.

Read more about this:
Mortenson, Michael E., *3D Modeling, Animation, and Rendering*

RENDERING IN PASSES Rendering an attribute of a scene. Different attributes are rendered separately, in a process called *rendering in passes*, where the rendering order is important. The most common passes are beauty pass, highlight pass, reflection pass, shadow pass, lighting pass, effects pass, and depth maps.

The term *pass* is originally from the motion-control filmmaking technique, where a camera repeats a controlled sequence of motions through a scene under a variety of lighting, physical arrangements, film type, and camera settings. Finally, all the passes are optically merged and printed on a single filmstrip.

Read more about this:
Mortenson, Michael E., *3D Modeling, Animation, and Rendering*

RENDERING INTENT The specification of the method used to transform colors from one color space into another.

RESAMPLE UP Increase the overall pixel dimensions of an image. An interpolation scheme is applied to the original image's pixels to determine which colors to assign to the added pixels. See also **RESAMPLING** and **DOWNSAMPLE**.

RESAMPLING Changing the overall pixel dimensions of an image, which necessarily changes its display size. See also **DOWNSAMPLE** and **RESAMPLE UP**.

RESOLUTION The ability to distinguish between two adjacent and closely spaced images or light sources; the ability of a graphics monitor to display fine detail in a scene or object; the sharpness or clarity of an image; measured by total pixels, or the number of horizontal pixels by the number of vertical pixels of a graphics monitor (i.e., 1280×1024), or dots/inch (dpi): the higher the resolution, the finer the visible detail in the image.

Read more about this:
Giambruno, Mark, *3D Graphics and Animation*
O'Rourke, Michael, *Principles of Three-Dimensional Computer Animation*

RETROREFLECTION Light reflected off a surface in directions close to the incident direction.

REVERSE-ANGLE SHOT A shot taken from an angle opposite to that of the preceding shot. The reverse angle technique is employed in dialogue scenes to provide the editor with alternate facial shots of the actors speaking.

RGB COLOR MODEL Red, green, and blue: three primary colors in the additive (direct light) model. The brightness levels of red, green, and blue pixels on the screen of a computer graphics monitor are varied to create a full spectrum of displayable colors, usually under control of the rendering program. It is the color model used by computer monitors. In the RGB color model additive color mixing produces secondary colors where two primary colors overlap, and white where all three combine.

Shows best in color edition.

Read more about this:
Birn, Jeremy, [digital] *Lighting & Rendering*
Giambruno, Mark, *3D Graphics and Animation*
O'Rourke, Michael, *Principles of Three-Dimensional Computer Animation*

RIGGING In animation, creating the *skeleton* or *armature* that controls the motion of a character or object. An animator defines the links and joints, their constraints, and inter-relationships, whose motions are transmitted to the vertices of the polygonal mesh that skins the object. See also **INVERSE KINEMATICS** and **SKELETAL ANIMATIO***n* .

Read more about this:
Mortenson, Michael E., *3D Modeling, Animation, and Rendering*

RIGID-BODY MOTION The translation or rotation of an object without changing its size or shape. Translation and rotation are the only rigid-body transformations.

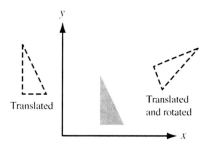

Translated

Translated and rotated

Read more about this:
Mortenson, Michael E., *Geometric Transformations for 3D Modeling*

RIGID-BODY TRANSFORMATION A transformation that does not produce changes in the size, shape, or topology of an object.

Read more about this:
Mortenson, Michael E., *Geometric Transformations for 3D Modeling*

RIM LIGHTS See **BACKLIGHT**.

ROLL To rotate the camera around its viewing axis, making the scene appear to spin about the center of focus. See also **BANK**.

ROLLING BALL Also known as *rolling ball blend*; a method for blending two adjacent surfaces. A sphere of a specified radius sweeps out a transition or blending surface as it rolls along tangent to and between the two surfaces.

ROOT NODE The highest node in a graph-based model, therefore having no parent node; also the fixed end in an inverse kinematic chain of links and joints. See also **END EFFECTOR** and **LEAF NODE**.

Read more about this:
Mortenson, M. E., *Mathematics for Computer Graphics Applications*

ROTATION A transformation that turns an object around a selected point in a plane or axis in space by a specified number of degrees clockwise or counterclockwise. One of the two rigid-body motions, the other being translation.

Rotation of a point in a plane always maintains a fixed distance from the pivot point (that is, the center of rotation) or in space, a fixed distance from an axis. Rotations in space may be about one of the principal coordinate axes or about some arbitrary axis.

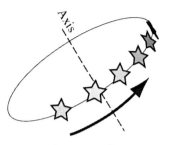

Every rotation about a coordinate system axis has a positive or negative sense assigned to it. A convention called the *right-hand rule* is used to determine this sense. Imagine grasping the axis of rotation with the fingers of your right hand with your thumb pointing in the positive sense of the axis itself. Then positive angles are measured in the same direction in which your fingers are curled around the axis. Rotations about an arbitrary line in space use the same rule but require that a positive sense be assigned to a direction on the line. If a vector defines the line, then the vector representation itself provides this direction.

A common approach to describing and controlling the orientation of an object is by a sequence of rotations about a local coordinate system rigidly attached to the object, and taking place within the global coordinate system. Usually this is done with Euler angles, an ordered set of three rotation angles in any one of several permitted sequences. An example of this is the roll, pitch, and yaw rotations common to naval and aeronautical reference frames. Rotation schemes based on a system of Euler angles may be subject to an unwanted loss of a degree of freedom, a condition called *gimbal lock* (not discussed here). Animation of complex rotations does not always lead to expected results, as different programs may interpolate rotations between keyframes in a variety of ways.

Initial position   Position 1   Position 2

In three-dimensional space, it turns out (no pun intended) that no matter how many

times an object is twisted and turned with respect to a reference position, it can always reach every possible new position with a single equivalent rotation. For example, visualize rotating the lettered block shown in the figure through $90°$ about an axis perpendicular to the center of face F, placing the block in position 1. Next, rotate it $180°$ about an axis perpendicular to face B, placing it in position 2. The block can be put into position 2 with a single rotation of $180°$ about an axis passing through the centers of opposite edges AB and CD.

Read more about this:
Giambruno, Mark, *3D Graphics and Animation*
Mortenson, Michael E., *Geometric Modeling*
_____, *Geometric Transformations for 3D Modeling*
_____, *Mathematics for Computer Graphics Applications*
O'Rourke, Michael, *Principles of Three-Dimensional Computer Animation*

ROTATIONAL SWEEP One way to generate a surface of revolution is by revolving a plane curve around an axis line in its plane. The plane curve is called the *profile curve*, and, in its various positions around the axis, it creates meridians. The circles created by each point on this curve are called *parallels*.

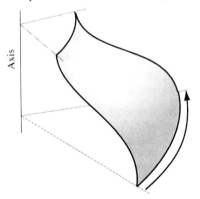

Read more about this:
Mortenson, Michael E., *3D Modeling, Animation, and Rendering*
_____, *Geometric Modeling*

ROTOSCOPING In computer graphics, to create an animated matte outlining the shape of an object at each frame of a sequence; a motion capture technique to create animation frames by tracing over a series of photographic or video still images displayed as temporary background images on a computer monitor. It is derived from techniques for hand-drawn cell animation using a series of still photographs of characters or objects in motion as templates.

Read more about this:
Birn, Jeremy, [digital] *Lighting & Rendering*
Giambruno, Mark, *3D Graphics and Animation*
O'Rourke, Michael, *Principles of Three-Dimensional Computer Animation*

RUBBER BAND BOX A temporary graphic selection or construction aid, under cursor or pointer control, used as a simplified representation of an object or geometric element being translated or rotated.

RUBBER BANDING See **RUBBER BAND BOX**.

RULED SURFACE A surface generated by a straight line whose end points move along separate curves. Every point on a ruled surface has at least one straight line passing through it that lies entirely in the surface.

Read more about this:
Mortenson, Michael E., *3D Modeling, Animation, and Rendering*
_____, *Geometric Modeling*

RULE OF THIRDS A rule-of-thumb for framing a scene, stating that a frame should be imagined to be divided into three equal parts both horizontally and vertically. The principal elements of a scene should be placed along or aligned with these divisions. This technique was used in composing the stunning image below.

Wikipedia, Moondigger (2006)

RULER An onscreen scale of length or distance, used as a drawing or modeling aid. See also **GRID**.

RUNNING SHOT A traveling shot that moves the camera to keep up with the motion of a subject or object.

S

SAMPLING RATE The interval (or rate) at which recorded measurements (samples) of an audio or visual source is made. The higher the rate, the more realistic the playback. A digital video signal has three components: Y (the brightness or luminance), R-Y (the color red minus brightness), and B-Y (blue minus brightness). During the recording process, each component is assigned a numeric sampling value.

SATURATION A measure of how much or how intense a color or hue appears to be; sometimes called *chroma*. A fully (100%) saturated red, for example, cannot be any redder. Lower saturations produce a watered-down effect. See also **HSB**.

0   100
Shows best in color edition.

Read more about this:
Demers, Owen, [digital] *Texture & Painting*
Giambruno, Mark, *3D Graphics and Animation*
O'Rourke, Michael, *Principles of Three-Dimensional Computer Animation*

SATURATION RENDERING INTENT A rendering intent that creates vivid color at the expense of accurate color.

SCALAR DISPLACEMENT MAPPING Deforms a surface by moving points in or out along the surface normals. See also **VECTOR DISPLACEMENT MAPPING**.

SCALE The ratio of the size of an object's graphic representation to the size of the actual object; the size of an object, or geometric element relative to some standard of measurement.

SCALING A transformation that changes the size or shape of an object. Uniform scaling changes an object's size without changing it shape. Nonuniform scaling changes the shape of an object by changing its dimensions along each coordinate axis by different amounts, changing a cube into a rectangular block, for example, or a sphere into an egg shape, while also changing its overall size.

Read more about this:
Mortenson, Michael E., *3D Modeling, Animation, and Rendering*
_____, *Geometric Transformations for 3D Modeling*
_____, *Mathematics for Computer Graphics Applications*

SCALING ANIMATION An editing method to control the timing of an animation sequence, speeding up or slowing down the action.

SCANLINE RENDERING A method used in non-ray tracing programs that renders the image of an object as a series of horizontal lines.

Read more about this:
Giambruno, Mark, *3D Graphics and Animation*
O'Rourke, Michael, *Principles of Three-Dimensional Computer Animation*

SCATTERING The random reflection, refraction, or diffraction of visible light or other electromagnetic radiation by particles, molecules, or atoms in the atmosphere, and redirecting the light in many directions. Scattering is also produced when photons of light are absorbed and reemitted with a different wavelength and in random directions.

Read more about this:
Naylor, John, *Out of the Blue*

SCENE All the elements of a three-dimensional setting intended to be captured on film or computer animation, including objects, light sources, bounding volumes and animation paths.

SCENE BACKGROUND Secondary objects in a scene, ranging from a simple monochrome background to something complex like an exquisitely rendered mountain or seascape. Scene background forms the setting for the principle objects or characters. In an animated sequence, the background objects may not be animated.

SCENE COMPOSITION The components and their arrangement in a computer graphic scene, including scene background and atmospherics, positioning objects, motion planning, lights (lighting effects, light placement, light animation), camera (direction, lines-of-sight or view points, line of action, consistent vertical, movement), and more.

Read more about this:
Giambruno, Mark, *3D Graphics and Animation*

SCIENTIFIC VISUALIZATION The application of computer graphics to calculate and present a visual interpretation of numerical data and physical phenomena that would ordinarily be visually inaccessible. Animation and volume rendering are the most important tools in producing a successful scientific visualization.

SCREEN COORDINATE SYSTEM The two-dimensional coordinate system of a computer graphics monitor onto which is projected the final image of a 3D object or scene. The coordinate system has horizontal and vertical limits, determined by the number of horizontal and vertical positions accessible to the electronics that generates the display. Two numbers serve to specify a location on this screen. The first number is the horizontal displacement from some reference point, and the second number is vertical displacement. These two numbers identify a discrete, uniquely addressable picture element, a pixel.

The complete rectangular array of pixels forms the physical basis of the screen coordinate system. Pixel coordinates (or *addresses*, as they are sometimes called) are always positive integers. The number of rows of pixels, *V*, defines the vertical dimension of a screen, and the number of pixels in each row, *H*, defines the horizontal dimension. *H* and *V* are not necessarily equal. There is a sequence of transformations from the infinite and continuous three-dimensional world coordinate system to the finite and discrete two-dimensional screen coordinate system. See also **WINDOW** and **VIEWPORT**.

Read more about this:
Mortenson, Michael E., *3D Modeling, Animation, and Rendering*
_____, *Mathematics for Computer Graphics Applications*

SCRIPT A plan detailing dialog, setting, and action of a live-action film or animation production.

SEAMLESS MODEL A single-mesh representation of an animated human or animal form. When a seamless model is rendered, there are no discontinuous surfaces or gaps at the joints. Extra detail is required in modeling the joint-covering surfaces, which must deform naturally and blend the surfaces on either side of the joint.

SECONDARY ACTION An action that results from another action, and that may itself become a primary action. Primary and secondary actions stand in direct relation as cause and effect, which effect may in turn become the primary cause of a subsequent effect. The animator/director becomes the final arbiter of emphasis.

SECONDARY COLORS Colors that are halfway between the primary colors on the color wheel; cyan, magenta, and yellow in the RGB color model.

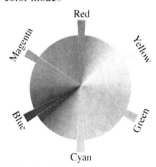

Shows best in color edition.
Read more about this:
Birn, Jeremy, [digital] *Lighting & Rendering*

SEGMENTED MODEL A multiple joint and link model of an animated human or animal form, simplified so that surface deformation and blending at the joints is ignored, making it possible to use simpler animation software. This approach works well when camera close-ups of the joints are not required or when joints are covered, as with the use of fur texturing for animals.

SELF-ILLUMINATION A lighting effect in which an object is lighted from within.

SELF-ILLUMINATION MAP A grayscale image that creates the visual effect that some portions of an object are lit from within.

SELF-SHADOWING A shadow an object or surface casts upon itself. a lighting effect, used in rendering images that enhances the illusion of reality.

The absence of self-shadowing produces a flat cartoon effect. In another sense, self-shadowing reduces the brightness of an object lying between the viewer and a light source because part or all of the object's surface that can be seen by the viewer is contained within the object's own shadow.

Read more about this:
Birn, Jeremy, [digital] *Lighting & Rendering*

SET THEORY A fundamental subdiscipline of mathematics, one of whose applications is in constructive solid geometry via Boolean operators combining primitive geometric solids to form more complex solids.

Read more about this:
Mortenson, M. E., *Geometric Modeling*
_____, *Mathematics for Computer Graphics Applications*

SHADE To add black to a color; the opposite of tint.

SHADER A set of surface characteristics and their values grouped together for ease of computing light and shading effects during rendering of a scene. Shaders allow blending together color, texture, and other surface characteristics to simulate and render almost any imaginable surface finish. Shaders, as modeling and rendering tools, are used to apply color, texture, and patterns to a surface.

Read more about this:
Birn, Jeremy, [digital] *Lighting & Rendering*
Mortenson, Michael E., *3D Modeling, Animation, and Rendering*
O'Rourke, Michael, *Principles of Three-Dimensional Computer Animation*
Watt, A. and M. Watt, *Advanced Animation and Rendering Techniques*

SHADING The effect of light reflecting off the surface of an object. Shading accounts for the effects of shape and texture, as well as the position of light sources with respect to the camera or viewer. Proper shading enhances the perception of depth and three-dimensionality of objects. The three principal techniques are flat shading, Gouraud shading, and Phong shading.

Read more about this:
Mortenson, Michael E., *3D Modeling, Animation, and Rendering*

SHADING MODEL An algorithm that determines how direct lighting interacts with a surface. The goal of all shading models is to determine the color at each point on a surface, given the local properties of the surface and the lighting environment.

SHADOW A lighting effect caused by an object that is between another object and a light source, where the object closest to the light intercepts all or part of the light falling on the more distant object's surface. A shadow is the absence of light in an otherwise directionally lighted environment. The most common problem is to compute the shadow cast by an object onto a ground plane or some other background. An extended (not point) light source causes an object to cast a dark central shadow, the umbra, bordered by a somewhat lighter region with soft edges, called the penumbra. The photo is from a Mars Rover taking a picture of its own shadow.

Shadow of Mars Rover, JPL, NASA

Properly rendered shadows increase a scene's realism and three dimensionality. Shadows provide important depth cues, reveal spatial relationships, indicate the position and nature of light sources, and add

hints about the degree of transparency of an object See also **TRANSPARENCY** and **SHADOWS**.

Computing shadows in a scene is time consuming. Two common ways to do this are by ray tracing and shadow depth mapping. Ray tracing computes the paths of light rays from the camera or eye back to their light source(s) as they are reflected and transmitted off and through objects along their paths, producing accurate and highly realistic shadows. A shadow depth map requires computing what the scene looks like from the point of view of each shadow-casting light source.

Read more about this:
Birn, Jeremy, [digital] *Lighting & Rendering*
Demers, Owen, [digital] *Texture & Painting*
Mortenson, Michael E., *3D Modeling, Animation, and Rendering*
Naylor, John, *Out of the Blue*
O'Rourke, Michael, *Principles of Three-Dimensional Computer Animation*
Watt, A. and M. Watt, *Advanced Animation and Rendering Techniques*

SHADOW DEPTH MAPPING Computation of shadows in a scene from the point of view of each light source.

SHADOW HIDING The shadow of an object at a viewer's antisolar point is not visible; the viewer sees only the illuminated surface. See also **SHADOW, ATTACHED SHADOW,** and **SELF-SHADOWING**.

SHADOW MAPPING A process rendering shadows of images by creating a grayscale texture map based on the lighting and objects in the scene.

SHADOW PASS A rendering that shows where shadows appear in a scene. See also **DOUBLED SHADOW** and **PASS**.

Read more about this:
Birn, Jeremy, [digital] *Lighting & Rendering*

SHADOWS FORMED BY CLOUDS Shadows of clouds in the atmosphere cast onto the ground. Atmospheric cloud shadows can be very dramatic, particularly at sunrise and sunset. These shadows form in the haze of airlight, and there is often enough contrast even on an otherwise bright clear day for them to be visible. Given the right conditions, even contrails will self-shadow, with the sunlit side bright and the other side

darker by contrast. A beautiful condition occurs when irregularly shaped clouds create
shadows that appear as dark and light bands
that fan out across the sky, an effect of perspective and airlight.

SHADOWS ON WATER Shadows may be seen
within turbid water but not on clear water.
Suspended particles in turbid water reflect
some light back toward the surface, but
those particles within a shadow are much
less illuminated, creating a contrast that allows a shadow to be seen.

Read more about this:
Naylor, John, *Out of the Blue*

SHADOWS UNDER TREES Elliptical patches
of sunlight are often apparent within the
leafy shadows. Some of the gaps between
leaves act like pinhole cameras, albeit im-
perfectly, each projecting a distorted image
of the sun onto the ground.

Read more about this:
Naylor, John, *Out of the Blue*

SHALLOW FOCUS A narrow *depth of field*.

SHEAR A shape transformation that proportionally distorts an object. A slippery deck
of cards provides a physical model of the
shear transformation. Place a deck of cards
on a table. Pushing down on the deck with
sufficient pressure to keep it in tact, while
pushing horizontally induces an overall deformation shown here. Assuming that the
bottom card is fixed, then each card moves
horizontally a distance directly proportional
to its vertical position in the deck. The top
card moves the farthest. It should be easy to
generalize this idea to sets of points in the
plane or in space that define a solid model.

Read more about this:
Mortenson, Michael E., *Geometric Modeling*
_____, *Geometric Transformations for 3D Mod-
eling*

SHEEN The brightness of a highlight seen at a
glancing angle. See also **GLOSS**.

SHEET METAL DESIGN A specialized application of mechanical CAD programs used to
implement the design and manufacture of
sheet metal parts, allowing a designer to
model such things as tabs, flanges, bends,
jogs, dimples, cut-outs, bend relief, and to
develop flat patterns. A flat pattern is cut
from sheet-metal stock and bent or stamped
into a final shape. See also **THIN-WALLED
SOLIDS**.

SHELLING A 3D modeling technique for creating thin-shelled objects or sheet-metal
parts using CAD/CAM.

SHININESS A qualitative expression of reflectivity. A shiny surface has a high reflectivity. In some renderers, shininess is a
measure of the size of the highlight region.

Read more about this:
Giambruno, Mark, *3D Graphics and Animation*
O'Rourke, Michael, *Principles of Three-Dimensional
Computer Animation*

SHININESS MAP A grayscale image that varies the reflectivity of a surface and introduces variations in its dullness or shininess.

SHOT To compose, frame, and capture an image on film or digitally. The term originated
in filmmaking and cinematography. Any
particular shot may be characterized by shot
size, staging to establish z-axis blocking,
camera angle, and framing. See also
ESTABLISHING SHOT, **REACTION SHOT**, and
SHOT/COUNTER-SHOT.

SHOT/COUNTER-SHOT Camera techniques
for framing the interaction of two characters
facing each other, as in a conversation: in a
two-shot the camera frames both characters,
usually in profile; in an over-the-shoulder
shot the camera shoots over the shoulder of
one of the characters to capture the face of
the other. See also **SHOT** and **SHOT SIZE**.

Read more about this:
Birn, Jeremy, [digital] *Lighting & Rendering*

SHOT SIZE Ranging from wide shot, medium
shot, medium close-up, and close-up, to extreme close-up, each of which describe the
size or proportion of a scene visible within a
frame.

SHUTTER ANGLE Adjustable opening angle in a camera's rotating shutter: the larger the angle, the longer the exposure time. Shutter angle and shutter speed are simulated in rendering programs to create special effects such as motion blur.

Read more about this:
Birn, Jeremy, [digital] *Lighting & Rendering*

SHUTTER SPEED A measure of how long a camera's shutter is open, exposing the film, and determining the frame rate. See also **SHUTTER ANGLE**.

Read more about this:
Birn, Jeremy, [digital] *Lighting & Rendering*

SILHOUETTE The visible outline of an object, represented by a closed curve that depends upon the viewpoint, also called the *occluding contour*.

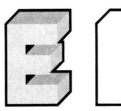

Read more about this:
Mortenson, Michael E., *3D Modeling, Animation, and Rendering*
_____, *Mathematics for Computer Graphics Applications*
Watt, A. and M. Watt, *Advanced Animation and Rendering Techniques*

SIMULATED RADIOSITY See **BOUNCE LIGHTS**.

SKATING In character animation, the undesirable effect in which the positions of characters feet appear to slide on the ground instead of remaining motionless. This effect is frequently the result of crudely executed forward kinematics or motion capture.

Read more about this:
Giambruno, Mark, *3D Graphics and Animation*

SKELETAL ANIMATION A technique in computer animation in which a character is represented in two parts: a surface representation used to draw the character (called the *skin*), and a hierarchical set of bones used for animation only (called the *skeleton*). See also **RIGGING**.

Read more about this:
Mortenson, Michael E., *3D Modeling, Animation, and Rendering*

SKELETON A linked internal structure associated with a model and used by animation and deformation applications to move or deform its bounding surface. A skeleton is not rendered. In 3D modeling of human and other animal motions, a carefully constructed skeleton and model surface produces realistic animation. The skeleton generally bears a close resemblance proportionally and mechanically to that of the animal being modeled.

Read more about this:
Mortenson, Michael E., *3D Modeling, Animation, and Rendering*
O'Rourke, Michael, *Principles of Three-Dimensional Computer Animation*

SKEW A global shape-changing transformation acting on a 3D object that has an effect similar to that of uniformly slipping cards in a deck past one another into the shape of a skewed rectangular block. See also **SHEAR**.

Read more about this:
Giambruno, Mark, *3D Graphics and Animation*
Mortenson, Michael E., *3D Modeling, Animation, and Rendering*
_____, *Geometric Transformations for 3D Modeling*

SKINNING Creates a surface over a sequence of control curves or cross sections. See also **LOFT SURFACE**.

Read more about this:
Giambruno, Mark, *3D Graphics and Animation*
Watt, A. and M. Watt, *Advanced Animation and Rendering Techniques*

SLOW CUTTING A film editing technique that uses shots of long duration. Depending on context, as a rule of thumb any shot lasting longer than about 15 seconds will seem slow to most viewers.

SMOKE MODEL See **PARTICLE SYSTEMS**.

SMOOTHING A process used by some printers to reduce the effect of aliasing, or the jagged staircase appearance of lines and curves by changing the size and horizontal alignment of the printed dots to make them look smoother.

SMPTE A time format given in minutes, seconds, and frames; for example, 43 17 03 is read 43 minutes, 17 seconds, and 3 frames; a standard established by the Society of Motion Picture and Television Engineers.

SNOW MODEL See **PARTICLE SYSTEMS**.

SOBEL FILTER An edge-detection application used on an alpha channel to support edge blending.

SOFT BODY An object that can deform during a collision. See also **ACTIVE BODY** and **SOFT OBJECT ANIMATION**.

SOFT FOCUS The deliberate blurring of all or part of a scene.

SOFT LIGHT Light that appears to wrap around objects, casting shadows with soft edges. The softness of the light depends on the distance and size and shape of the source.

SOFT OBJECT ANIMATION The use of shape deformations of an object to highlight natural force behavior, such as compressing or squashing colliding shapes, or creating personality and character of expression. The modeling procedures must include a way for the animator to control the nature of the deformations of the underlying geometric model, as well as the rates of change of various components of the deformations.

Deformation techniques can be unique and specific to the geometric model, whether it is based on a polygonal representation, parametric, B-spline, Bézier, or on some other form. Global and free form deformations are examples. Differential scaling produces these deformations, using a different scale factor for each of the three principle or local axes. Twisting, tapering, warping, and melting are typical distortions of the model; all produced by distorting an embedded coordinate frame or lattice. The animator of soft-object deformations is concerned with two main tasks: first, to specify the set of transformations that accomplish the desired shape changes; and second, to establish control curves for the rates of change of the deformations.

Read more about this:
Mortenson, Michael E., *3D Modeling, Animation, and Rendering*
Watt, A. and M. Watt, *Advanced Animation and Rendering Techniques*

SOFT SHADOW Produced by a light source that has physical extension, not a point light source; a shadow without hard edges. See also: **AREA LIGHT** and **PENUMBRA**.

SOLID MODEL A three-dimensional model, represented mathematically in a way that makes it possible to distinguish between inside, outside, and surface points, and in special cases, interior properties; a model produced by constructive solid geometry techniques or other 3D method such as extrusions, sweeps, and turnings (or lathings). Surface modeling offers an almost unlimited range of shapes, but does not easily account for interior properties.

Read more about this:
Giambruno, Mark, *3D Graphics and Animation*
Mortenson, Michael E., *3D Modeling, Animation, and Rendering*
_____, *Geometric Modeling*
_____, *Mathematics for Computer Graphics Applications*
O'Rourke, Michael, *Principles of Three-Dimensional Computer Animation*

SOLID TEXTURE MAPPING See **VOLUMETRIC TEXTURE**.

SOLO ACTOR A single animated character or object in a scene. See also **ACTOR**.

SPACE SUBDIVISION See **BOUNDING VOLUME HIERARCHY (BVH)**.

SPATIAL ANALYSIS A procedure to determine geometric properties and relationships, including length and distance, area, volume, nearest/farthest, and inside/outside relationships.

Read more about this:
Mortenson, Michael E., *Geometric Modeling*
_____, *Mathematics for Computer Graphics Applications*

SPATIAL RELATIONSHIPS Visual and quantitative information indicating the relative positions, sizes, order, and general arrangement of two or more objects. See also **GEOMETRIC RELATIONSHIPS**.

Read more about this:
Mortenson, Michael E., *Geometric Modeling*
_____, *Mathematics for Computer Graphics Applications*

SPECIAL EFFECTS (SPFX) Techniques used in film and television to create effects that cannot be done by normal methods, such as walking through walls, invisibility, traveling at the speed of light, leaping over tall buildings, historical or futuristic backgrounds or settings, prehistoric plants and animals, etc.

SPECIAL EFFECTS ANIMATION See **SPECIAL EFFECTS**.

SPECTRA The plural of *spectrum*.

SPECTRUM A band or range of colors ordered according to wavelength.

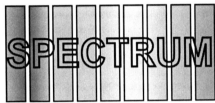

Shows best in color edition.

Read more about this:
Mortenson, Michael E., *3D Modeling, Animation, and Rendering*

SPECULAR BLOOM Also called *diffuse glow*, *bloom*, and *flare*. This effect can be simulated in computer graphics rendering.

SPECULAR COLOR The color of reflected highlights that appear on the surface of an object. The reflectivity and color of the surface, the color of lights, and atmospherics affect specular color. Specular color is usually assigned to a shade of white or gray, but any color may be used to achieve special effects.

Read more about this:
Giambruno, Mark, *3D Graphics and Animation*

SPECULAR HIGHLIGHT Bright reflections of light seen on shiny surfaces, usually reflections of the light sources themselves.

Read more about this:
Giambruno, Mark, *3D Graphics and Animation*

SPECULARITY The color and intensity of the object's reflection highlights, controlled by a variety of rendering parameters.

Read more about this:
Birn, Jeremy, [digital] *Lighting & Rendering*
Giambruno, Mark, *3D Graphics and Animation*
O'Rourke, Michael, *Principles of Three-Dimensional Computer Animation*

SPECULAR REFLECTION The mirror-like reflection of incident light off a shiny surface. A light ray striking a point on a shiny surface is not diffusely reflected (spread out more or less equally in all directions) but is concentrated in the mirror direction, where the angle of incidence of the light ray equals the angle of its reflection. If the camera or viewer is positioned along this line, then a bright reflection is apparent. From positions off this line, less light energy is detected, depending on the BRDF. Various forms of specular reflection are shown in the image.

Pawel Kotowski, Warsaw Polytechnic (no date)6

Read more about this:
Birn, Jeremy, [digital] *Lighting & Rendering*
Watt, A. and M. Watt, *Advanced Animation and Rendering Techniques*

SPECULAR SURFACE A surface that reflects a light ray in a single direction from any given point on it, where the angle of the reflected ray with respect to the surface normal at the point is equal to the angle between the normal and the incident ray. The normal and incident and reflected rays lie in the same plane.

Read more about this:
Watt, A. and M. Watt, *Advanced Animation and Rendering Techniques*

SPHERE A geometric primitive in constructive solid geometry. The illustration that follows shows a spherical primitive of unit radius and embedded in its local coordinate system.

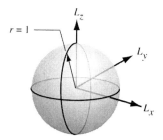

Read more about this:
O'Rourke, Michael, *Principles of Three-Dimensional Computer Animation*

SPHERE OF ATTRACTION A tool for reshaping a polygonal mesh model, displayed as a sphere whose size can be specified and which can be moved into position to capture and drag a set of vertices, changing the shape of the object.

SPHERICAL AREA LIGHT An area light simulating light radiating in all directions from a spherical shape, often used to replace a point light source to produce softer shadows and more diffuse lighting. See also **FLAT AREA LIGH***t*, **GEOMETRIC AREA LIGHT**, and **LINEAR LIGHTS**.

Read more about this:
Birn, Jeremy, [digital] *Lighting & Rendering*

SPHERICAL COORDINATE SYSTEM A three-dimensional coordinate system in which points are located by their radial distance from the origin and by two angular measurements from two independent reference planes or axes.

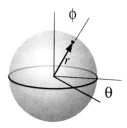

SPHERICAL PROJECTION MAPPING A multi-directional technique for mapping an image or texture onto the surface of an object. A suitably-sized spherical mapping tool is positioned around the object and an image on its surface is inwardly projected onto the object's surface.

Read more about this:
Mortenson, Michael E., *Geometric Transformations for 3D Modeling*
O'Rourke, Michael, *Principles of Three-Dimensional Computer Animation*

SPLINE A curve that closely approximates the shape of a strip of material that is gently bent; originally a draftsman's tool for drawing curves that represented the shapes taken by wooden and metal members of a ship's hull structure bent over fixed points or frames and, later, representing similar shapes in auto bodies and aircraft structures. A spline is the shape taken by bending material objects, like a beam that minimizes the elastic energy (or internal strain energy) stored in it. Mathematically, it is the smoothest curve that passes through a set of fixed points. In 3D modeling it is a curve defined by control points, often supplemented by interactive methods to modify tangents to the curve at these points and to adjust a local weighting factor. Bézier, B-spline, and NURBS are commonly used types of splines. Splines are frequently used to drive the pace of animated elements in a scene.

Read more about this:
Giambruno, Mark, *3D Graphics and Animation*
Mortenson, Michael E., *Geometric Modeling*
O'Rourke, Michael, *Principles of Three-Dimensional Computer Animation*
Watt, A. and M. Watt, *Advanced Animation and Rendering Techniques*

SPLINE-DRIVEN ANIMATION The motions of animated objects specified by cubic splines.

Read more about this:
Watt, A. and M. Watt, *Advanced Animation and Rendering Techniques*

SPLINE INTERPOLATION Computing an intermediate value of some property between bounding values; frequently used in animation to define the location of an accelerating object.

SPLIT COMPLEMENTARY COLOR The colors adjacent to a complementary color on a color wheel.

SPLIT SCREEN On a graphics display monitor, a display that is divided into two or more areas, so that each area can display a different image.

SPOT COLOR A special premixed colored ink supplementing the standard CMYK process inks.

SPOTLIGHT A light source producing a directional, narrowly confined cone-shaped beam of light, radiating from a single point and directed onto a specific object or limited region of a scene. The parameters controlling a spotlight include its location, intensity, color, decay rate, direction, spread and drop-off. Spread is the angle of the cone of light. Drop-off controls the variation of light intensity within the cone, diminishing nearer the outer surface of the cone.

The spotlight itself is not necessarily shown as part of the rendered scene, even if it lies within it. Neither is the cone of light rendered unless atmospheric effects make it desirable to do so. Usually only the effects of the light on objects in the scene are incorporated in the rendering.

Read more about this:
Birn, Jeremy, [digital] *Lighting & Rendering*
Giambruno, Mark, *3D Graphics and Animation*
O'Rourke, Michael, *Principles of Three-Dimensional Computer Animation*

SPRAY BOW A rainbow that appears in the spray of a waterfall, fountain, or breaking wave on the seashore.

Read more about this:
Naylor, John, *Out of the Blue*

SPREAD A kind of *trapping* where a light area overlaps an adjacent or surrounding dark background. See also **CHOKE**.

SPRITE One of a set of independently created animated objects that are later combined to form a complete animation sequence; a graphical object that moves independently of its background; a sequence of low-resolution images mostly used in multime-

dia games, allowing fast frame refresh rates and real-time user control of the action within a complex 3D scene. Each sprite may respond with its own unique rules of behavior with respect to its interaction with other sprites in the sequence.

SQUASH A modified scaling transformation that deforms an object as though it had constant volume. Squashing an object makes it spread out around its edges perpendicular to the squashing forces. The figure shows the effect of a vertical force applied to a sphere.

Squashing deformations combined with stretching during the movement of an animated object that represents something living adds realism. For example, the muscles may swell or stretch when flexed. Only some inanimate objects like rocks and chairs remain rigid when they move. An object doesn't have to deform in order to squash and stretch. For instance, a hinged object appears to squash by folding into itself and stretches by extending out fully.

In 3D computer animation, a scaling transformation is used to produce the squash and stretch deformations. It is generally a good idea to use a volume-preserving scaling transformation because it looks more realistic. The direction of the stretching component should be along the path of action, so a rotational transformation may be necessary to properly align the object.

Read more about this:
Giambruno, Mark, *3D Graphics and Animation*
Mortenson, Michael E., *3D Modeling, Animation, and Rendering*
Watt, A. and M. Watt, *Advanced Animation and Rendering Techniques*

SQUISHY BOX See **LATTICE**.

SQUISHY SOLID A 3D solid that reacts to certain deformations as though it were squishy like a soft lump of modeling clay; similar to squash.

STAGING The placement of characters and objects in a scene and their relationship to the camera; presenting an idea so that it is unambiguous and the viewer is clear about the scene's intent.

STATE VECTOR In animation, the set of independent variables that describe the position and orientation at the joints of each link in an articulated structure.

Read more about this:
Watt, A. and M. Watt, *Advanced Animation and Rendering Techniques*

STATIC FRICTION A special friction effect in natural force behavior that prevents an object from sliding down an incline unless the angle of inclination is increased beyond a critical angle, which depends upon surface roughness.

Read more about this:
Mortenson, Michael E., *3D Modeling, Animation, and Rendering*
O'Rourke, Michael, *Principles of Three-Dimensional Computer Animation*

STEREOGRAPHIC PROJECTION A one-to-one correspondence between the points on a sphere and the complex plane; used to produce two images of an object or scene from two slightly different viewpoints, so that when viewed through special equipment they give the impression of three dimensionality and depth.

Read more about this:
Mortenson, Michael E., *Geometric Transformations for 3D Modeling*

STEREOLITHOGRAPHY (STL) A computer-aided process for rapidly making a physical model based on digital input (data in STL format) from a 3D CAD model, used extensively in rapid prototyping.

STEREOSCOPIC DISPLAY The illusion of three-dimensionality created by using binocular cues of depth, by presenting a slightly different view of a scene to each eye of the viewer.

STILL A rendering and print of one of the frames of a motion picture or animation sequence.

STITCH, STITCHING Joining two distinct surfaces along a common boundary to form a single surface.

STL The acronym for *stereolithography*.

STL FORMAT A standard data format used in the rapid-prototyping industry for input to stereolithography processes. The STL format is a triangulated-surface representation of a 3D CAD model.

STOP-MOTION ANIMATION An animation technique to make a physically manipulated object appear to move on its own. The object is moved in small increments between individually photographed frames, creating the illusion of movement when the series of frames is played as a continuous sequence. Clay figures are often used in stop motion for their ease of repositioning.

STORYBOARD A sequence of sketches and descriptive text outlining an animation scene, encompassing a sequence of frames describing key actions; used in preliminary design and preproduction phases.

Read more about this:
Demers, Owen, [digital] *Texture & Painting*
Giambruno, Mark, *3D Graphics and Animation*
O'Rourke, Michael, *Principles of Three-Dimensional Computer Animation*

STRAIGHT-AHEAD ANIMATION The action of the principal animated actor or object moving in a direct path toward a specific goal; also, the process of designing each keyframe in order, from first to last, in contrast to top-down animation.

STRETCH A modified scaling transformation, like squash, that treats an object as though it had a constant volume. Stretching an object makes it become thinner in the middle.

Read more about this:
Mortenson, Michael E., *3D Modeling, Animation, and Rendering*
_____, *Geometric Modeling*
Giambruno, Mark, *3D Graphics and Animation*

STROBING Discontinuous or jerky motion of an animated object in a scene, usually caused by a low frame rate relative to the speed of the object.

STRUCTURAL ANALYSIS Determining stresses, strains, and deformations of structures and mechanical parts when they are subjected to various loading conditions.

SUBDIVISION SURFACE A method of representing a smooth surface using a mesh or grid of polygons, usually triangles. Recursive techniques further subdivide the surface into smaller faces.

SUBJECT CAMERA See **POINT OF VIEW SHOT, POV**.

SUBSURFACE SCATTERING A phenomenon of light transport. Some incident light penetrates the surface of an object, undergoes a number of reflections, and then emerges at an angle different from that of the incident ray. A computer graphics rendering technique can simulate this effect, which is necessary to create realistic images of translucent materials such as marble or skin.

U. Hasselt, T. Haber and T. Merton (2006)

SUBTRACTIVE COLOR MODEL A reflected-light color model in which varying proportions of cyan, magenta, yellow, and black (CMYK) are mixed to produce other colors. See also **ADDITIVE COLOR MODEL**.

Read more about this:
Demers, Owen, [digital] *Texture & Painting*
Giambruno, Mark, *3D Graphics and Animation*

SUNRISE AND SUNSET Atmospheric conditions that produce dramatic effects when the sun (or moon) is near the horizon. Rays of sunlight are refracted more when they enter the atmosphere at an oblique angle, which is the case at twilight and dawn. The amount of refraction is inversely dependent on the wavelength of the light passing through a refracting medium. Red light is refracted somewhat less than blue light, which helps produce the red sunsets we see. Dust, moisture, aerosols, and other suspended particles and pollutants all contribute to the colors of a sunset. Temperature inversion and atmospheric refraction also produce changes in

the apparent shape of the sun or moon as they rise or set. See also **CLOUDS AT SUNSET**.

Photographer /date unknown. Shows best in color edition.

Read more about this:
Naylor, John, *Out of the Blue*

SUPER QUADRIC A family of geometric shapes defined by formulas resembling those of ellipsoids and other quadrics, except that the squaring operations are replaced by arbitrary powers.

SURFACE The boundary of a solid object; a 3D geometric element having only two dimensions. See also **PARAMETRIC SURFACE** and **SURFACE PATCH**.

Read more about this:
Mortenson, Michael E., *Geometric Modeling*

SURFACE ATTRIBUTE Properties such as color, reflectivity, and texture.

SURFACE DEFORMATION A limited shape-changing transformation of a model, operating on it's bounding surface. Bend, twist, taper, skew, squash, stretch, bump, dent, morph, and flex are examples of such surface deformations.

SURFACE MODELING A 3D modeling method used to describe an object's geometry by defining its bounding surfaces. This method is used when surface shape is critical, for example, to satisfy aerodynamic requirements or aesthetics. Surface modeling allows the design of completely free form shapes unconstrained by whatever finite list of primitive shapes may be available in a solid-modeling application.

Read more about this:
Mortenson, M. E., *3D Modeling, Animation, and Rendering*
_____, *Geometric Modeling*
O'Rourke, Michael, *Principles of Three-Dimensional Computer Animation*

SURFACE NORMAL See **NORMAL**.

SURFACE PATCH A curve-bounded segment of a surface, whose points are given by continuous, two-parameter, single-valued polynomials of the form $x = f(u,w)$,

$y = g(u,w)$, and $z = h(u,w)$, where u and w are the parametric variables and where $0 \leq u \leq 1$ and $0 \leq w \leq 1$. The patch boundaries are usually curves of constant parameter value.

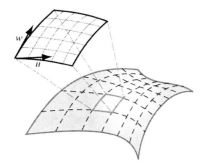

Read more about this:
Mortenson, Michael E., *Geometric Modeling*

SURFACE-TO-SURFACE CONSTRUCTIONS Methods for joining two surfaces, including joins, blends, fillets, offsets, and stitching.

SVG (SCALEABLE VECTOR GRAPHICS) a graphics file format used for web-page graphics. SVG images are mathematically defined, which means that the file format does not have to include the color of every pixel within the image, allowing a smaller file size and faster transmission over the internet. SVG files are resolution independent, allowing an image to be appropriately scaled to suit any display monitor. See also **VECTOR GRAPHICS**.

SWARMING Describes a behavior of an aggregate of animals of similar size and body orientation, generally moving en mass in the same direction. The term can be applied to fish, insects, birds, various microorganisms such as bacteria, and people.

SWEEP MODEL A generalized extrusion; a 3D model created by moving a closed curve or 2D cross section (constant or variable) along a sweep path. The orientation of the plane of the cross section is always perpendicular to the sweep path. A variation of the sweep process is used in specialized CAD/CAM applications to model ducts, pipes, and tubes.

Read more about this:
Giambruno, Mark, *3D Graphics and Animation*
Mortenson, Michael E., *3D Modeling, Animation, and Rendering*
_____, *Geometric Modeling*
_____, *Mathematics for Computer Graphics Applications*
O'Rourke, Michael, *Principles of Three-Dimensional Computer Animation*

SWEEP PATH A curve in 3D space defining the path along which a 2D cross section is moved to sweep out a solid; for example, some modelers include spiral paths and ways to generate toroidal shapes using closed paths.

Read more about this:
Giambruno, Mark, *3D Graphics and Animation*
Mortenson, Michael E., *3D Modeling, Animation, and Rendering*
_____, *Geometric Modeling*
_____, *Mathematics for Computer Graphics Applications*
O'Rourke, Michael, *Principles of Three-Dimensional Computer Animation*

SWEPT SOLID See **SWEEP MODEL**.

SWEPT SURFACE The surface created by moving a curve along some path. The curve may be constant or variable closed or open. See also **SWEEP MODEL**.

SWISH PAN A camera motion fast enough to completely blur a scene.

SYMMETRIC FEATURES Two or more features of a 3D model or CAD/CAM part, identical in size and shape or mirror images of one another, with a plane of symmetry separating them, or with rotational symmetry.

SYMMETRY A characteristic of certain geometric shapes (2D and 3D) that brings to
mind decorative patterns, tilings, and repetitive mirror images, with application in art,
engineering, science, and biology.

A figure or shape is symmetric if certain
motions or rearrangements of its parts leave
it unchanged as a whole. These motions or
rearrangements are called *symmetry transformations*. 3D modeling programs take advantage of the symmetry of some shapes by
allowing a designer to create only part of the
shape and then to reflect, translate, or rotate
it to create the other parts in their appropriate positions, thus completing the whole
model.

A figure is symmetric if it is congruent to itself in more than one way. For example, if a
square is rotated $90°$ about its center, no
difference exists between the original figure
and its rotated image. They coincide exactly. And if a horizontal line is drawn
through the center of a square, the top and
bottom halves are mirror images of one another; the square is, therefore, symmetrical
about this line. The other lines of symmetry
are obvious and easy to find. Here are lines
of symmetry for a hexagon:

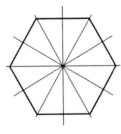

Read more about this:
Mortenson, Michael E., *Geometric Transformations
for 3D Modeling*
_____, *Mathematics for Computer Graphics
Applications*

SYMMETRY TRANSFORMATIONS Mathematically described motions or rearrangements of a geometric shape or its parts that
leave the shape unchanged, including rotation, reflection, and inversion. For any
symmetric figure, certain sets of points,
lines, or planes are fixed, or invariant, under
a symmetry transformation. They are easy to
identify in simple symmetric figure. For example, in two dimensions a hexagon is
symmetric under inversion through its cen-

ter point or under rotations that are integer
multiples of $60°$; also, it has six different
lines that are fixed under reflections. In
three dimensions, the cube has many lines
and planes of symmetry.

An equilateral triangle has six symmetries,
six different ways of transforming it that do
not change its overall appearance, orientation, or measurable properties. This means
that a symmetry transformation preserves
the distances between the vertices and the
angles between edges.

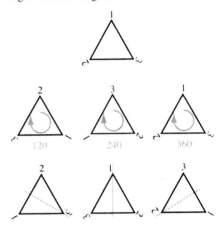

Rotating the equilateral triangle $0°$ or $360°$
does not change it. Mathematicians call this
the *identity transformation*. As simple and
seemingly superfluous as it appears, the
identity transformation is important in the
study of symmetry groups.

Rotating an equilateral triangle $120°$ about
its center either clockwise or counterclockwise leaves it unchanged.

Reflecting an equilateral triangle across
each of the three lines bisecting its vertex
angles also leaves it unchanged.

Inversion of an equilateral triangle through
its center is not a symmetry transformation.
The inversion produces an image equivalent
to that of a $180°$ rotation, which does not
have the same relative orientation as the
original.

Read more about this:
Mortenson, Michael E., *Geometric Transformations
for 3D Modeling*
_____,, *Mathematics for Computer Graphics
Applications*

T

TANGENT POINT A point on a curve or surface at which a straight line or plane is tangent; an interactive technique used by some modeling systems to alter the shape of curves; similar to control handle, direction line, and direction point.

TANGENT VECTOR A shape-control parameter of certain types of curves and surfaces, primarily Hermitian.

Read more about this:
Mortenson, Michael E., *Geometric Modeling*
O'Rourke, Michael, *Principles of Three-Dimensional Computer Animation*

TAPER A shape-changing transformation that tapers an object along a selected axis through it.

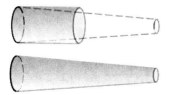

Read more about this:
Giambruno, Mark, *3D Graphics and Animation*
Mortenson, Michael E., *3D Modeling, Animation, and Rendering*
_____, *Geometric Transformations for 3D Modeling*
O'Rourke, Michael, *Principles of Three-Dimensional Computer Animation*

TARGET A displayed and controllable icon that indicates where a camera or light is pointed.

TCB CONTROLLER Tension-continuity-bias controller; procedure and parameters used to control the shape of spline curves used in keyframe inbetweening. See also **TCB WEIGHTING** and **TENSION**.

TCB WEIGHTING Adjusting tension, continuity, and bias to shape the spline curve(s) controlling the rate of inbetweening between keyframes. See also **TCB CONTROLLER** and **TENSION**.

TEETER A model deformation control used to rotate a cross section around the *x* or *y* axis perpendicular to the sweep path.

Read more about this:
Giambruno, Mark, *3D Graphics and Animation*

TEMPERATURE See **COLOR TEMPERATURE**.

TEMPLATE A pre-formatted basis for creating standard graphic elements or 3D objects.

TENSION In a TCB controller, the amount of curvature in the inbetweening development path before and after a keyframe.

TENSOR PRODUCT SURFACE See **BÉZIER** and **B-SPLINE SURFACES**.

TERMINATOR The line or zone of transition between full light and full shadow on the surface of an object; the boundary between day and night. In astronomy it is the boundary between the sunlit and dark sides of the moon.

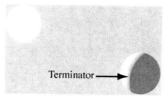

Terminator ⟶

Read more about this:
Naylor, John, *Out of the Blue*

TERRAIN MODEL A 3D representation of landscape or geographical features, generated by using a grayscale topographical map applying displacements to the surface of a model.

Read more about this:
Giambruno, Mark, *3D Graphics and Animation*

TESSELLATION The division of a surface into polygonal regions, not necessarily of uniform size and shape. The tessellation process is governed by mathematical or geometric rule. An example of a tessellation problem is: given a plane surface with a set of points on it, find the tessellation that represents the nearest neighbor boundaries for each point. See also **NEAREST NEIGHBOR SEARCH**.

Read more about this:
Grünbaum, B. and G. C. Shephard, *Tilings and Patterns*
Mortenson, Michael E., *Geometric Modeling*
_____, *Mathematics for Computer Graphics Applications*

TETRAHEDRON One of the five regular polyhedra. The regular tetrahedron has four
identical faces, each an equilateral triangle.
It has four vertices, six edges, and three
faces surround each vertex.

Read more about this:
Mortenson, Michael E., *Mathematics for Computer
Graphics Applications*

TEXEL Texture element; the basic unit of a
textured fill used to paint the surface of a 3D
object.

TEXTURE A general property of a surface;
roughness, either random or regular. The
texture of a surface may be natural like the
dimpled skin of an orange, or polished to a
very smooth finish like glass.

Read more about this:
Demers, Owen, [digital] *Texture & Painting*
Watt, A. and M. Watt, *Advanced Animation and
Rendering Techniques*

TEXTURE MAP A 2D image or pattern, created either for a specific model or part of a
standard set of such images, either scanned
or painted and applied to the surface of a 3D
object. It creates an appearance that isn't
possible by simply locally varying the surface's geometry. It may give the appearance
of texture (as cloth or coarse materials show
a texture) or it may simply map patterns
onto the surface. The 2D image may also be
used to produce a variety of color and transparency effects.

Read more about this:
Birn, Jeremy, [digital] *Lighting & Rendering*
Demers, Owen, [digital] *Texture & Painting*
Giambruno, Mark, *3D Graphics and Animation*
O'Rourke, Michael, *Principles of Three-Dimensional
Computer Animation*
Watt, A. and M. Watt, *Advanced Animation and
Rendering Techniques*

TEXTURE MAPPING A modeling and rendering procedure for applying a 2D pattern
onto the surface of a 3D object; a method
for pasting images onto arbitrary polygonal
objects, allowing a modeler to cover a surface with complex images or designs, with-

out having to build an equally complex surface model to portray characteristics like
bumps and dimples, or embossed or woven
patterns. The 3D models present before and
after effects of texture mapping.

Wikipedia, Anynobody (2008)

THEMATIC MONTAGE An editing technique
that combines shots for their symbolic relationships, rather than to achieve a realistic
effect.

THERMODYNAMIC ANALYSIS Determines
the effect of heat applied to an object, using
the object's surface geometry and certain
physical properties of its solid interior.
Thermodynamic analysis is performed on an
object whose surface is subjected to fric-
tional heating as it moves through some medium, usually the atmosphere; for example,
high-speed aircraft and spacecraft reentry
vehicles. The results of such analysis often
make use of scientific visualization.

THIN-WALLED SOLID A shell-like structure;
a specialized modeling application used to
design sheet metal parts.

THREE-POINT LIGHTING Three modes of
lighting a scene and objects in it: key light,
fill light, and backlight, usually used together. See **FILL LIGHT** and **LIGHT PLACEMENT.**

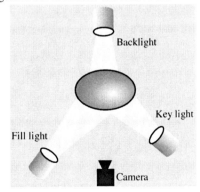

THROW The pattern or shape of light projected onto an object or surface; also called a *throw pattern*. In digital image making, a renderer creates a throw pattern using a texture map. In filmmaking, *gobos* and *cookies* create special throws.

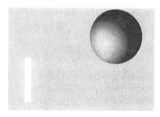

Read more about this:
Birn, Jeremy, [digital] *Lighting & Rendering*

TIFF The acronym for Tagged Image File Format.

Read more about this:
Giambruno, Mark, *3D Graphics and Animation*
O'Rourke, Michael, *Principles of Three-Dimensional Computer Animation*

TIGHT SHOT A shot where the principle subject or focus fills most of the frame.

TILING A set of polygonal shapes that are joined edge-to-edge, without gaps or overlaps, to cover a plane or other surface. There are only three so-called *regular tilings* of a plane. They are formed by equilateral triangles, squares, and hexagons. Each vertex of a regular tiling is surrounded identically with congruent faces. The regular pentagon cannot tile the plane without gaps or overlaps, because three pentagons at a single vertex leave a gap, and four must necessarily overlap.

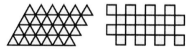

Read more about this:
Giambruno, Mark, *3D Graphics and Animation*
Grünbaum, B. and G. C. Shephard, *Tilings and Patterns*
Mortenson, Michael E., *Mathematics for Computer Graphics Applications*

TILT A camera motion executed by rotating the camera up or down around its horizontal axis without changing its location. Examples are following the action of a vertically moving object, like a rocket blasting off, or panning the vertical extent of a tall subject. See also **CAMERA MOVES** and **CAMERA TILT** .

Read more about this:
Mortenson, Michael E., *3D Modeling, Animation, and Rendering*

TIME-LAPSE ANIMATION Condensing a slow long-duration event into a shorter period of time; highlighting otherwise very slow motion or changes in a scene (e.g., the growth and development of a plant).

TIMELINE Animation execution schedule.

TIME STEP An increment in the time parameter affecting the rate of change of an animation element. A more natural and realistic motion or behavior is produced by small time steps. However, special artistic effects can be achieved by altering the rhythm of time steps within an animation sequence.

Read more about this:
O'Rourke, Michael, *Principles of Three-Dimensional Computer Animation*

TIMING Speed of an animated action. The speed of an action determines how a viewer will interpret the action. It suggests the weight and size of an object, and can carry emotional meaning.

TIMING CURVE A curve coordinated with a motion path to control the rate of an object's movement along the path. An object can be made to speed up or slow down or maintain a constant speed over various segments of the motion path. One way to accomplish this is to use parametric curves for both motion and timing and to coordinate their parametric variables.

TINT To add white to a color, the opposite of shade; a variation of a color or hue; a color diluted with white; the addition of a small amount of another color to an existing color.

TOLERANCE EFFECTS The effects of minor variations in size and shape of the separate moving parts of a mechanism on its function, or on the assembly of a multi-component object.

TONE Black and white added to a color to decrease its saturation; the prevailing effect of harmony of color and values in a rendering; to tone down is to make a color less intense in hue, less saturated; sometimes used to indicate value.

TONE MAPPING A technique used in image processing and computer graphics to map one set of colors to another set, often to approximate high dynamic range images in media with a more limited dynamic range. Print-outs, CRT or LCD monitors, and projectors all have a limited dynamic range that cannot reproduce the full range of light intensities present in natural scenes. Tone mapping resolves the problem of contrast reduction from the scene values (radiance) to the displayable range while preserving image details and color appearance.

TOOL ACCESS The free space required by tools and their motion envelopes for assembling a set of parts.

TOP-DOWN ANIMATION The process of first defining the major actions of an animation and then progressively filling in more detail until keyframes can be designed and developed. In contrast see also **STRAIGHT-AHEAD ANIMATION**.

TOPOLOGY The study of geometric properties of an object's shape that are unchanged when it is deformed according to some simple rules: Bending, twisting, and stretching are allowed, but cutting and gluing are not. The connectivity of the geometric elements of a model help to characterize its topology. For example, a polyhedron's topology is defined by specifying how the vertices are connected to form edges. See also **CONNECTIVITY MATRIX**.

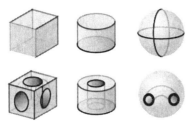

Read more about this:
Mortenson, Michael E., *Geometric Modeling*
_____, *Mathematics for Computer Graphics Applications*

TORUS A donut-shaped primitive in CSG.

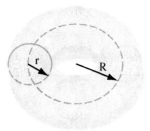

Read more about this:
Mortenson, Michael E., *Mathematics for Computer Graphics Applications*

TRACKING SHOT Also known as a *dolly shot* or *trucking shot* in which the camera is mounted on a wheeled platform that is pushed on rails while the picture is being taken; a camera motion in which the camera location and the aim point undergo identical translation movements; the motion of an object that follows or duplicates that of another object.

Read more about this:
Mortenson, Michael E., *3D Modeling, Animation, and Rendering*

TRANSFORMATION An operation that alters the size, shape, position, or orientation of a model, for example, translate, rotate, scale (uniform or differential, increasing or decreasing size), reflect, invert, bend, twist, skew, taper, and stretch.

Read more about this:
Giambruno, Mark, *3D Graphics and Animation*
Mortenson, Michael E., *3D Modeling, Animation, and Rendering*
_____, *Geometric Transformations for 3D Modeling*
_____, *Mathematics for Computer Graphics Applications*
O'Rourke, Michael, *Principles of Three-Dimensional Computer Animation*

TRANSFORMATION CONTROL In animation, the control and coordination of movement, shape changes, lighting, and atmospheric effects, using curves to determine rates of change.

TRANSLATE A modeling transformation that moves an object or geometric element without rotating it or changing its size or shape. Because of the last two characteristics, it is called a *rigid-body* motion or transformation.

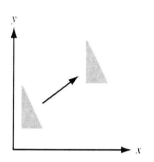

Read more about this:
Mortenson, Michael E., *Geometric Transformations for 3D Modeling*
_____, *Mathematics for Computer Graphics Applications*

TRANSLATIONAL SWEEP Defined by moving a planar curve or planar shape along a straight line normal to the plane of the curve, the former generating a surface and the latter a solid. A 3D modeler produces a less restrictive translation surface by sweeping one curve along another curve, where the generating curve remains parallel to itself if it is a plane curve.

Read more about this:
Giambruno, Mark, *3D Graphics and Animation*
Mortenson, Michael E., *3D Modeling, Animation, and Rendering*
_____, *Geometric Transformations for 3D Modeling*
_____, *Mathematics for Computer Graphics Applications*
O'Rourke, Michael, *Principles of Three-Dimensional Computer Animation*

TRANSLUCENT A light-transmitting property of a solid object, permitting light to pass through while diffusing it enough so that objects on the far side are not clearly visible. For example, frosted window glass is translucent, but not transparent.

TRANSMISSION The movement of light through a non-opaque object, with specular, diffuse, or mixed effects. See also **OPAQUE**.

TRANSMISSIVITY A measure of the ability of light to pass through an object, determined by the object's surface geometry and its internal optical properties.

TRANSPARENCY A quantitative measure of the amount of incident light that can pass through an object. The higher the percentage of light transmitted, the greater the transparency (the opposite of opacity). See also **OPAQUE**.

Read more about this:
Giambruno, Mark, *3D Graphics and Animation*
O'Rourke, Michael, *Principles of Three-Dimensional Computer Animation*

TRANSPARENCY AND SHADOWS Rendering shadows cast by transparent objects is much more difficult than rendering shadows cast by opaque objects. The physics involved is quite different. Absorption and dispersion are the principle phenomena involved in this effect.

Read more about this:
Naylor, John, *Out of the Blue*

TRANSPARENCY MAPPING Used to create areas of transparency in the surface of an object, where the shapes of the areas and degrees of transparency may vary.

Read more about this:
O'Rourke, Michael, *Principles of Three-Dimensional Computer Animation*

TRANSPARENT The physical property of an object that allows light to pass through it. You can see through a transparent object. You cannot see through an opaque object.

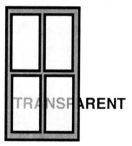

TRAPPING A process used in 2D multicolor rendering and printing of an image to adjust for colorless, or white, gaps that appear between slightly misaligned but adjacent objects or between an object and its background color. There are two kinds of trap: a spread, where a lighter colored area overlaps a dark background, and a choke where a light background overlaps a dark area.

TRAVELING MATTE A sequence of mattes or masks associated with a sequence of animation frames, used to superimpose animation or separately shot film or video onto the background media, creating special effects.

Read more about this:
O'Rourke, Michael, *Principles of Three-Dimensional Computer Animation*

TREE DATA STRUCTURE A data structure that resembles the hierarchical form of a tree, with nodes and branching relationships. A binary tree structure is used in constructive solid geometry.

Read more about this:
Mortenson, Michael E., *Mathematics for Computer Graphics Applications*

TRIANGULATION The subdivision of a surface into many small triangles; a preliminary rendering operation. Three non-collinear points are sufficient to define a triangle: with quadrilaterals and higher polygons, there is always the danger that the points chosen may not all lie on the same plane. For these reasons and others, nearly all mesh structures employ triangles.

Usually there is more than one way to divide a plane polygon into a set of triangles. The minimum number of triangles T, or the minimum triangulation, is given by $T = V - 2$. The figure shows two different ways to triangulate the given polygon. There are others.

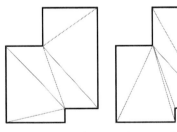

A parametric surface may be approximated by a set of triangular polygons by using the intersection points of an isoparametric mesh, as shown in the figure. Such a mesh can be locally refined to adjust to curvature or other geometric criteria available from the surface's mathematics.

TRIM A shape-changing modeling operation that cuts off or trims part of an object; used to modify a surface, creating a new surface. It differs from the Boolean difference operator in that it simply cuts a surface and does not add solid geometry.

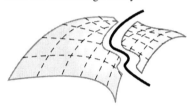

Read more about this:
Mortenson, Michael E., *Geometric Modeling*

TRIMLINE A method for blending two surfaces.

TRIMMED SURFACE A surface patch, or set of patches, whose boundaries are irregular as a result of design modeling actions and which do not necessarily conform to constant values of the underlying parametric variables.

Read more about this:
Mortenson, Michael E., *Geometric Modeling*

TRIMMING OBJECT The shape used to define the trim operator.

TRUCK A camera motion.

TUBES Highly constrained shapes used in CAD solid modeling. 3D modeling procedures to design tubes include tube sizing, routing, and bending; similar to ducts.

TURBULENCE The departure from a smooth flow of a liquid or gas as it moves across a surface. Below a critical speed, which depends on the properties of the liquid or gas and the properties of the surface over which it is flowing, the flow will be smooth or streamlined; however, as the flow rate increases beyond the critical speed, the once smooth-flowing liquid or gas breaks up into eddies and becomes turbulent.

TURBULENCE MODEL Representation of the appearance and effects of turbulence in gaseous or fluid media.

Read more about this:
Watt, A. and M. Watt, *Advanced Animation and Rendering Techniques*

TURNING A highly constrained shape used in solid modeling and created by rotating a cross section about an axis.

TWEENING See **INBETWEENING**.

TWIST A shape-changing transformation that twists an object about some axis, usually one passing through it.

TWO-SHOT See **SHOT/COUNTER-SHOT**.

TWO-UP VIEW Side-by-side display of two versions of a graphics rendering or sequence of animation frames. See also **FOUR-UP VIEW**.

U

UMBRA That part of the shadow of an object where the light source is completely cut off. A viewer within the umbra is unable to see the light source casting the shadow. See also **PENUMBRA**.

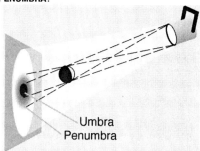

Umbra
Penumbra

Read more about this:
Watt, A. and M. Watt, *Advanced Animation and Rendering Techniques*

UNDEREXPOSURE The presence of only dark tones, with little or no contrast, caused by too little light in a scene and not enough light sources, or sources whose light intensity is too low. A histogram reveals an underexposed condition when all the highest frequency-of-occurrence tones are concentrated on the dark end of the graph.

Ways to correct an underexposed image include increasing the intensity of some of the light sources, adjusting global settings such as fog effects, chiaroscuro, and ambient light, increasing falloff distance before light intensity fades to zero, finding and minimizing accidental or unnecessary shadows, and making sure that reflective surfaces have something to reflect. See also **EXPOSURE** and **OVEREXPOSURE**.

Read more about this:
Birn, Jeremy, [digital] *Lighting & Rendering*

UNION OPERATOR A Boolean operator in constructive solid geometry (CSG), sometimes called *unite*. The union operator $\cup$ additively combines two shapes A and B to form a new shape C. If A is a distinct set of points and B is another distinct set of points, then $A \cup B = C$, where C contains all the points in A and B.

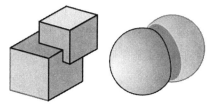

Read more about this:
Giambruno, Mark, *3D Graphics and Animation*
Mortenson, Michael E., *Geometric Modeling*
_____, *Mathematics for Computer Graphics Application*

UV COORDINATES The parametric reference grid for a surface, where the parametric coordinates are u and v.

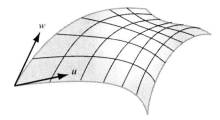

UV MAPPING Transforms a texture map onto the surface of a 3D object, usually with an embedded associated u, v coordinate system. See **UV COORDINATES**.

V

VALUE The degree of lightness or darkness of a color, where light or pale colors are high value, and dark colors are low value. Adding white to a pure color raises its value and creates a tint of that color. Adding black to a pure color lowers its value and creates a shade of that color. See also **HUE, SATURATION,** and **BRIGHTNESS (HSB)**.

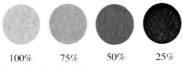

| 100% | 75% | 50% | 25% |

Shows best in color edition.

VARIATIONAL GEOMETRY A procedure that defines a model when given key dimensions and other geometric constraints. This procedure determines the final 3D shape by solving a set of simultaneous equations derived from the input dimensions and constraints. Using variational geometry it is easy to make changes and adjustments to the shape of some feature of an object or among related parts of a mechanical assembly.

VECTOR Perhaps the single most important mathematical device used in 3D modeling and animation is the vector. It has the properties of magnitude and direction, represented pictorially by a line segment with an arrowhead. In the figure, the vector **p** locates one corner of a rectangular solid.

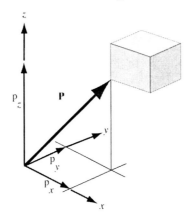

In 3D modeling a vector is given a geometric interpretation, for example, position or displacement. Vector methods offer a distinct advantage over traditional analytic geometry by minimizing computational de-

pendence on a specific coordinate system until the later stages of solving a problem. Vector algebra and calculus are effective tools for creating and manipulating certain kinds of models.

Read more about this:
Mortenson, Michael E., *3D Modeling, Animation, and Rendering*
_____, *Geometric Modeling*
_____ *Mathematics for Computer Graphics Applications*

VECTOR DISPLACEMENT MAPPING Deforms a surface by moving points in or out along vectors defined at each point. See also **SCALAR DISPLACEMENT MAPPING**.

VECTOR GRAPHICS Digital images that have mathematical constructs associated with the shapes and representation within the images. The image is created and saved as a sequence of vector statements, each representing a quantity and direction.

VECTOR GRAPHICS IMAGE A mathematically defined image and storage format for illustration and modeling, allowing images to be scaled and transformed without loss of image quality. A vector graphics image is independent of the limitations of the bitmap or pixel image format. See also **OBJECT-ORIENTED GRAPHICS** and **SVG**.

VELOCITY CURVE In animation, a 2D spline curve relating distance traveled to elapsed time for an animated object's movement, used in inbetweening.

VERTEX The point at the intersection of two edges of a polygon or at the convergence point of multiple intersecting edges of a polyhedron.

VERTEX, EDGE, FACE (V, E, F) The geometric elements of a polyhedron.

VERTEX SHADER A graphics processing function used to add special effects to objects in a 3D environment.

VERTEX SKINNING A modeling process that creates polygons to fill the visual gaps that may appear when an object is bent or otherwise deformed.

VERTICAL FOG An atmospheric effect blurring the image of an object in the y-direction. See also **FOG**, **FOG PRIMITIVE**, and **LAYERED FOG**.

Read more about this:
O'Rourke, Michael, *Principles of Three-Dimensional Computer Animation*

VERTICES The plural of vertex.

VIEW AXIS A line drawn between the eye or camera and the aim point.

VIEW COORDINATE SYSTEM A display coordinate system oriented relative to the camera or viewer (also called the *camera* or *eye coordinate system*). It is usually a left-handed system, with the positive x-axis pointing to the right, the positive y-axis pointing upwards, and the positive z-axis pointing away from the camera and into the view. The camera can be located anywhere in the world coordinate system, aimed in any direction, and given a reference "up" direction, thus determining the geometric relationship between the world and view coordinate systems.

Read more about this:
Giambruno, Mark, *3D Graphics and Animation*
Mortenson, Michael E., *Mathematics for Computer Graphics Applications*

VIEW PLANE A plane positioned in front of the eye or viewpoint. A rendered picture is the projection of the scene onto the view plane.

VIEWPOINT The point in a scene toward which the virtual camera or viewer is looking. See also **AIM POINT**.

Read more about this:
Giambruno, Mark, *3D Graphics and Animation*
Watt, A. and M. Watt, *Advanced Animation and Rendering Techniques*

VIEWPOINT MOVEMENT One of several ways to control the camera or viewing direction. Viewpoint movement through the 3D modeling workspace usually requires some form of user-controlled path, speed, and orientation. Exploratory movement may be a virtual walk-through of an architectural design. Targeted movement is used to move in for a close-up view of a detail of an engineering design. Specified-coordinate movement applies to movement of the viewpoint to a precise location and orientation within the workspace. Specified-trajectory movement is movement of the viewpoint along a user-designed position and orientation trajectory, such as a virtual camera position.

VIEWPORT A frame outlining or delimiting the part of a scene that is displayed.

Read more about this:
Giambruno, Mark, *3D Graphics and Animation*
Mortenson, M. E., *Mathematics for Computer Graphics Applications*

VIEW VOLUME The limits of the rendering space. Objects within or partially within the view volume are rendered; those outside it are not. The view volume is usually the frustum of a pyramid, defined by its six bounding planes. These planes are the clipping planes: the near and far clipping planes and the four clipping planes forming the sides of the frustum.

Read more about this:
Watt, A. and M. Watt, *Advanced Animation and Rendering Techniques*

VIGNETTING In film, the reduction of an image's brightness or saturation at the periphery compared to the image center. This effect can be accidental or intentional, optically produced or digitally rendered. It can be used to produce an atmospheric effect on a scene.

VIRTUAL CAMERA Represents the viewer's eye or recording camera within a computer graphics scene; not a real camera, but a convenient abstraction. (Note that the word *camera* is used instead of *virtual camera*, where its meaning is understood in context.) The camera location and aiming direction determine what part of the model space is displayed. It is the substitute for the viewer, representing where the viewer is standing and where the viewer is looking. The camera records the frame or image that is to be rendered as a still, or the sequence of images that are to be rendered as a live-action movie or animation. A virtual camera is usually available in different types with characteristics simulating those of real cameras, and can be positioned, oriented, and configured in a variety of ways.

Read more about this:
O'Rourke, Michael, *Principles of Three-Dimensional Computer Animation*

VIRTUAL REALITY (VR) A digital and graphical representation of the real world or an imagined artificial world within which a user can experience and interact with elements of that world through special interactive devices, including sight, sound, and touch. See also **VIRTUAL WORLD** and **HAPTIC INTERFACE DEVICE**.

Read more about this:
Giambruno, Mark, *3D Graphics and Animation*

VIRTUAL TRACKBALL An interactive modeling tool used to do free-form rotations of objects in 3D space. A transparent sphere, the virtual trackball, is displayed superimposed on or near the object to be rotated. Rotation takes place around the center of the sphere, so it must be translated to the appropriate point in space that is to be the center of the rotation. The mouse pointer is brought into "contact" with the sphere and then used to drag the surface of the sphere around its center in a direction that produces the desired rotation.

VIRTUAL WORLD A 3D model with stereo vision and haptic interface devices to enhance the realism of the model.

VISIBILITY The degree of transparency or opaqueness of atmospheric effects; the effect of the physical arrangement and spatial order of objects in a scene with respect to the camera or viewer.

VISIBILITY MAPPING See **CLIP MAPPING**.

VISUAL ACUITY The ability of the eye to resolve details. The eye of a person with perfect vision is able to resolve objects that have an angular diameter of at least one minute of arc, which means that under ideal seeing conditions he or she should be able to distinguish a 1 cm diameter circle from a 1 cm square at a distance of 34 meters. Visual acuity is also affected by the contrast between an object and its background. Modeling and rendering techniques use these effects to reduce the amount of detail that must be rendered to display distant or very small objects in a scene.

VISUAL RANGE The farthest distance at which an object can be unambiguously identified.

VISUALIZATION The graphical interpretation of engineering or scientific data and phenomena in forms that exploit the visual and cognitive skills of the human brain to detect patterns and draw inferences. Sometimes referred to as *scientific visualization*, the use of animation and volume rendering in computer graphics modeling, particularly of phenomena requiring many time-dependent variables to describe, is now an important research and analysis tool.

Read more about this:
Watt, A. and M. Watt, *Advanced Animation and Rendering Techniques*

VOLUME RENDERING See **VOLUMETRIC RENDERING**.

VOLUMETRIC ANALYSIS Analysis of multidimensional data, usually in conjunction with scientific visualization tools.

VOLUMETRIC FOG An atmospheric effect used to obscure the images of objects within a geometrically confined beam of light; may include shadows and random fog density.

VOLUMETRIC LIGHT A 3D light source whose geometry can be changed and that simulates the behavior of natural light in an atmosphere, like a spotlight penetrating a mist.

Read more about this:
Giambruno, Mark, *3D Graphics and Animation*

VOLUMETRIC MAPPING See **VOLUMETRIC TEXTURE**.

VOLUMETRIC MODEL A solid model that incorporates information about the state and distribution of interior properties, such as texture and density.

VOLUMETRIC PRIMITIVE A 3D modeling primitive whose volume can be adjusted to suit special circumstances. See also **VOLUMETRIC LIGHT**.

VOLUMETRIC RENDERING A method used to visualize three (or more)-dimensional phenomena, perhaps time dependent, by rendering images of plane sections or translucent solids to make interior details visible.

Read more about this:
Watt, A. and M. Watt, *Advanced Animation and Rendering Techniques*

VOLUMETRIC TEXTURE Uses a volumetric or three-dimensional patterned space, such as wood grain or marble, in which an object is embedded to give it the appearance of a textured interior.

Read more about this:
Watt, A. and M. Watt, *Advanced Animation and Rendering Techniques*

VOXEL A volume element, representing a value on a regular grid in three-dimensional space, used in modeling and rendering.

VR Acronym for *virtual reality*.

VRML FILES Acronym for *Virtual Reality Markup Language* files.

W

WALLPAPER GROUP A collection of 2D symmetric patterns on a plane surface, containing two nonparallel translations. There are only 17 kinds of these patterns in the wallpaper group. (Note that the term *group* refers to a special kind of set.) All two-dimensional repetitive patterns in wallpaper, textiles, brickwork, or the arrangement of atoms in a plane of a crystal are variations on one of these 17 patterns. Thirteen of them include some kind of rotational symmetry, and four do not. Each wallpaper pattern is uniquely identified by its translation and rotation symmetries.

Read more about this:
Mortenson, Michael E., *Geometric Transformations for 3D Modeling*

WASH Modify a color by changing both hue and saturation.

WATER AND WAVE MODELS Specialized 3D modeling applications for representing of water behavior, such as waves, currents, eddies, ripples, and turbulence. Natural bodies of water are seldom perfectly still. Wind-generated waves may crest and break upon approaching a shoreline. Waves reflect off obstacles, bend (diffraction) around obstructions, and change speed and direction to align with the shore (refraction). These phenomena may be represented and animated by using physics-based modeling techniques and natural force behavior.

The interaction between light and water involves careful model setup and complex rendering computations. Modeling and animation criteria determine the air and water interface and the reflection and refraction effects. Caustics are usually involved, too; for example, the shifting interplay of light and shadow on a ship's hull or on the bottom and sides of a swimming pool is determined by these phenomena.

Read more about this:
Watt, A. and M. Watt, *Advanced Animation and Rendering Techniques*

WAVE THEORY Mathematics and physics describing the propagation of light (electromagnetic radiation) through space or a transmitting medium, based on Maxwell's wave equations; wave theory does not describe color effects of selective absorption, which is a quantum mechanical effect.

WAVELENGTH The distance, measured along the direction of propagation of a wave, between successive peaks or, equivalently, between two successive points in the wave that are in the same phase of oscillation. The wavelength of a light ray is the reciprocal of its frequency multiplied by the speed of light.

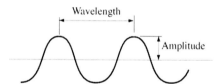

The wavelength of an ocean wave is simply the distance from one crest to the next. The distance over which the wind is blowing and bottom topography determine wavelength and wave height. Waves generated by storms in different parts of the ocean may meet and pass through one another, creating distinct interference patterns. And when they have passed beyond the area of their intersection, each resumes its previous waveform.

WEATHERING A surface characteristic indicating long-term exposure to atmospheric or environmental factors causing progressive changes in the appearance of a surface.

WEDGE A common geometric primitive solid in constructive solid geometry (CSG) systems. An instance of a wedge is defined by specifying its length, width, and height.

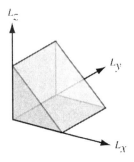

WEIGHT A variable parameter in curve design and shaping; a physical property of a solid object depending upon its mass and the effects of gravity.

Read more about this:
Giambruno, Mark, *3D Graphics and Animation*

WELD See **FUSE**.

WHITE BALANCE See **COLOR BALANCE**.

WHITE LIGHT Light composed of a mix of many frequencies broadly spread over the visible portion of the electromagnetic spectrum. Very little light is absorbed by a white surface, and all the visible wavelengths are reflected equally. White paint is white because it contains titanium oxide particles in suspension. These particles are almost perfect reflectors, absorbing very little of the incident light energy. When visible light strikes white paint it encounters the suspended titanium particles that scatter it many times before it finally exits the emulsion. The more the light is scattered, the more randomized the directions of the exiting light rays, and the more matte appearing is the surface.

WHITE POINT The brightest highlight in a rendering.

WIDE SCREEN A film image with an aspect ratio greater than the ordinary 35mm frame.

WIDE SHOT A shot framing most, if not all, of a scene; for example, a shot of the entire court of a tennis game in progress. A wide shot helps establish a character in a specific location. See also **SHOT SIZE**.

WINDOW A limited 2D view into 3D model space; a rectangular boundary that encloses that part of the 2D picture-plane image to be displayed. The image in the window is then mapped onto another bounded area called the viewport, in the display-screen coordinate system. Multiple windows may be used simultaneously in a single display, showing a model from more than one viewpoint, as an aid to constructing and visualizing it.

Read more about this:
Mortenson, Michael E., *Mathematics for Computer Graphics Applications*

WIPE A transition between two animation sequences in which a sequence or image slides across the screen revealing the next sequence as it passes over it. Wipes can be performed horizontally, vertically, diagonally, or with a circular window.

Read more about this:
O'Rourke, Michael, *Principles of Three-Dimensional Computer Animation*

WIREFRAME MODEL A specialized 3D model of an object consisting only of edges and vertices; used as an efficient way to swiftly and temporarily display the basic outlines of an otherwise solid model.

Read more about this:
Giambruno, Mark, *3D Graphics and Animation*
Mortenson, M. E., *Geometric Modeling*
O'Rourke, Michael, *Principles of Three-Dimensional Computer Animation*
Watt, A. and M. Watt, *Advanced Animation and Rendering Techniques*

WORKING BOX See **WORK SPACE**.

WORKING PLANE See **CONSTRUCTION PLANE**.

WORKSPACE A local coordinate system placed anywhere within a scene's world coordinate system in which objects, lights, and cameras can be created and positioned. Sometimes called the *working box* or *workbox*, it is usually displayed in perspective projection and shows the three intersecting principle planes as reference grids. See also **ACTIVE PLANE**.

WORLD COORDINATES SYSTEM The principal coordinate system of a 3D workspace,
which is independent of viewpoint and display. Also known as the *global coordinate
system* or the *scene universe*. Individual objects are each defined in their own local coordinate systems. Objects are assembled and
positioned in a scene. It is the coordinate
system of the scene that is the world coordinate system. Light sources and the viewer or
cameras are positioned in this system, and
animation moves the objects within it.

Read more about this:
Giambruno, Mark, *3D Graphics and Animation*
Mortenson, Michael E., *Mathematics for Computer
Graphics Applications*
Watt, A. and M. Watt, *Advanced Animation and
Rendering Techniques*

WRAPPING An effect of texture mapping. An
image can be repeated all around the surface
of an object. This is usually controlled by
interactive procedures.

Read more about this:
Giambruno, Mark, *3D Graphics and Animation*
O'Rourke, Michael, *Principles of Three-Dimensional
Computer Animation*

X

Y

Z

Z-AXIS BLOCKING Staging a scene with several subjects, each a different distance from
the camera; for example, framing a pride of
lions drinking at a water hole and then focusing on a lion approaching the camera.
See also **SHOT** and **SHOT SIZE**.

Z-BUFFERING A rendering technique that re-
serves a block of computer memory that or-
ganizes and stores the distance from the eye
or camera to a surface along a ray through
each pixel.

Read more about this:
Watt, A. and M. Watt, *Advanced Animation and
Rendering Techniques*

Z-DEPTH The *z* coordinate in the view coordinate system; a pass that computes and
stores the distance from the camera to the
subject for each pixel in a scene; also called
depth map and *depth pass*. This data is used
to adjust pixels in an image to better simulate the effect of depth.

Z-DEPTH FOG An atmospheric effect, muting
color and blurring the image of an object,
where the effect increases with distance in
the *z*-direction; also called *horizontal fog*.

Read more about this:
O'Rourke, Michael, *Principles of Three-Dimensional
Computer Animation*

ZOOM A camera lens adjustment used to
magnify the image, focusing on details in a
scene; also called *zooms*. Zoom-in and
zoom-out are considered photographic effects and are not the same as moving the
camera closer to or farther away from the
subject, which changes perspective. Zoom-
in, producing a narrower field of view for a
close-up of a subject, may result in a distorted perspective that may not be desirable.
Zoom-out widens the field of view, showing
more of a scene. The camera remains in a
fixed location. See also **HITCHCOCK ZOOM**.

Read more about this:
O'Rourke, Michael, *Principles of Three-Dimensional
Computer Animation*

CPSIA information can be obtained at www.ICGtesting.com
Printed in the USA
LVOW111433210912

299797LV00005B/5/P